Lang

Introduction to the Law of Double Taxation Conventions

Introduction to the Law of Double Taxation Conventions

Michael Lang

3rd edition

IBFD

Linde international

Zitiervorschlag: *Lang*, Introduction to the Law of Double Taxation Conventions[3] (2021) p.

Bibliografische Information der Deutschen Nationalbibliothek

Die Deutsche Nationalbibliothek verzeichnet diese Publikation in der Deutschen Nationalbibliografie; detaillierte bibliografische Daten sind im Internet über http://dnb.d-nb.de abrufbar.

Hinweis: Aus Gründen der leichteren Lesbarkeit wird auf eine geschlechtsspezifische Differenzierung verzichtet. Entsprechende Begriffe gelten im Sinne der Gleichbehandlung für alle Geschlechter.

ISBN 978-3-7143-0367-4 (Print, Linde)
ISBN 978-90-8722-684-8 (Print, IBFD)
ISBN 978-3-7094-0862-9 (E-Book-PDF, Linde)
ISBN 978-90-8722-686-2 (E-Book-PDF, IBFD)
ISBN 978-3-7094-0863-6 (E-Book-ePub, Linde)
ISBN 978-90-8722-685-5 (E-Book-ePub, IBFD)

1210 Wien, Scheydgasse 24, Tel.: 01/24 630
www.lindeverlag.at

Druck: Hans Jentzsch & Co GmbH
1210 Wien, Scheydgasse 31
Dieses Buch wurde in Österreich hergestellt.

Gedruckt nach der Richtlinie des Österreichischen Umweltzeichens „Druckerzeugnisse", Druckerei Hans Jentzsch & Co GmbH, UW-Nr. 790

PRINTED IN AUSTRIA

Preface

The first edition of this book was published in June 2010, the second in September 2013. Since then, legislation, case law and academic discussion have developed further.

Accordingly, since the last version, this book takes into account the developments and recommendations from the OECD/G20 Base Erosion and Profit Shifting (BEPS) Project, changes of the new UN Model and OECD Model that have taken place in its more recent versions published in 2017, modifications on the application of some existing tax treaties according to Action 15 BEPS Project "The Multilateral Convention to Implement Tax Treaty Related Measures to Prevent Base Erosion and Profit Shifting" (MLI), and the most recent judgments delivered by courts all over the world.

I would like to thank the entire team of the Institute for Austrian and International Tax Law that has considerably supported me over several months in the course of this project. Especially, research and teaching associates Cristóbal Pérez Jarpa, Xiangdan Luo, Jean-Philippe van West, Christina Dimitropoulou, Ioana-Felicia Rosca, Gabriela Capristano Cardoso, Martin Klokar, Florian Fiala, Raphael Holzinger, Svitlana Buriak, Andreas Ullmann, Annika Streicher, Claire Peng, Shimeng Lan, Clement Migai, Angelina Papulova, and Karol Dzwinski have worked intensively towards the publication of this book. I would like to thank them with all my heart for their excellent commitment and efforts as well as for their numerous critical remarks that have substantially enriched the contents of this book. Moreover, I am grateful to the publishing houses Linde (Vienna) and IBFD (Amsterdam), who have taken over this publication project. I am happy about this cooperation, which will ensure that the book will be available globally.

Vienna, November 2020 *Michael Lang*

Preface to the first edition

For many years now I have been holding lectures on the law of double taxation conventions. In the course of my teaching activities I have also developed relevant course materials. In 1997, these materials were compiled in a small book, which I first published in German. In 2002, the second edition of this book was released. From its conception, the book was aimed to provide both students and practitioners with the basic issues of the system and the application of double taxation conventions.

Originally published in German, the book now serves as a basis for this volume. It has been fundamentally edited and modified. Not only were the developments in international tax law that have occurred during the past 8 years incorporated but the contents of the book were also globalized: The book will be useful for all students and practitioners who are dealing with questions of double taxation conventions – irrespective of their national background. The book therefore does not consider one jurisdiction in particular but rather takes examples from a wide range of different countries and their jurisdictions. I hope that in this way it can be of help and use for students and practitioners from all around the world.

I would like to thank the entire team of the Institute for Austrian and International Tax Law that has considerably supported me over several months in the course of this project. Especially, the research and teaching associates Veronika Daurer and Oliver-Christoph Günther and the research associates Francesco Avella and Shauna Pitman have worked intensively towards the publication of this book. I would like to thank them with all my heart for their excellent engagement and efforts as well as for their numerous critical remarks which have substantially enriched the contents of the book. Moreover, I am grateful to the publishing houses Linde (Vienna) and IBFD (Amsterdam), who have taken over this publication project. I am happy about this cooperation, which will ensure that the book will be globally available.

Vienna, June 2010 *Michael Lang*

Table of Contents

List of abbreviations

AB	*Aktiebolaget* (Swedish public limited company)
AG	*Aktiengesellschaft* (Austrian/German public limited company)
AOA	Authorized OECD approach
ASA	*Archiv für Schweizerisches Abgabenrecht* (Swiss periodical)
AStG	*Außensteuergesetz* (German International Transaction Tax Act, contains inter alia the German CFC legislation)
AWD	*Außenwirtschaftsdienst des Betriebsberaters* (German periodical)
BAO	*Bundesabgabenordnung* (Austrian Federal Tax Code)
BB	*Der Betriebsberater* (German periodical)
BEPS	Base Erosion and Profit Shifting
BFH	*Bundesfinanzhof* (German Federal Tax Court)
BFIT	Bulletin for International Taxation (IBFD journal)
BMF	*Bundesministerium für Finanzen* (German/Austrian Federal Ministry of Finance)
BNB	*Belissingen in Belastingzaken-Nederlandse Belastingsrechtspraak* (Netherlands Taxation Reports)
BStBl	*Bundessteuerblatt* (German Federal Tax law Gazette)
BTR	British Tax Review (British periodical)
BV	*Besloten Vennootschap* (Dutch limited liability company)
CGT	Capital gains tax
CP	Cost plus
CTC	Canadian Tax Cases
CUP	Comparable uncontrolled price
DB	*Der Betrieb* (German periodical)
DBA	*Doppelbesteuerungsabkommen* (German for double taxation convention)
DStZ	*Deutsche Steuerzeitung* (German periodical)
DTC(s)	Double taxation convention(s)
EC	European Community
EEC	European Economic Community
EFG	*Entscheidungen der Finanzgerichte* (collection of German court decisions)
ET	European Taxation (IBFD journal)

EU	European Union
FJ	*Finanzjournal* (Austrian periodical)
FS	Festschrift
G-20	Group of Twenty
GAAR	General anti-avoidance rule
IBFD	International Bureau of Fiscal Documentation
IEHC	Irish High Court decisions
SEK	Swedish krona
IFOWS	International Food and Wine Shows (Indian trade fair)
Introd.	Introduction (in Vogel, DTC)
InvFG	*Investmentfondsgesetz* (Austrian law applicable to investment funds)
IRS	Internal Revenue Service (United States)
IStR	*Internationales Steuerrecht* (German periodical)
IT	Information technology
ITA	Income Tax Act
ITLR	International Tax Law Reports (UK periodical)
ITR	Indian Tax Reports
Ltd.	Limited liability company
MAP	Mutual agreement procedure
MLI	Multilateral Instrument
m.no.	Marginal number
NC	Nordic Convention
NV	*Naamloze Vennootschap* (Dutch public limited company)
OECD	Organisation for Economic Co-operation and Development
OECD Model	OECD Model Tax Convention on Income and on Capital
OEEC	Organisation for European Economic Co-operation
OJ	Official Journal (European Community)
ÖStZ	*Österreichische Steuerzeitung* (Austrian periodical)
PE	Permanent establishment
RIW	*Recht der Internationalen Wirtschaft* (German periodical)
RP	Resale price
RStBl	*Reichssteuerblatt* (Tax gazette of the German Reich)
SA	*Société anonyme* (French public limited company)

STC	Simon's Tax Cases (UK)
StuW	*Steuer und Wirtschaft* (German periodical)
SWI	*Steuer und Wirtschaft International* (Austrian periodical)
TPGs	Transfer Pricing Guidelines (OECD)
TTCL	Tax Treaty Case Law (IBFD database)
UCITS	Undertakings for collective investment in transferable securities
UN Model	UN Model Tax Convention on Income and on Capital
USD	US dollar
VAT	Value added tax
VCLT	Vienna Convention on the Law of Treaties

Literature cited in the text

Avery Jones et al., The interpretation of tax treaties with particular reference to Article 3(2) of the OECD-Model, *BTR* 1984, 14 et seq.

Avery Jones et al., Treaty Conflicts in Categorizing Income as Business Profits Caused by Differences in Approach between Common Law and Civil Law, *BFIT* 2003, 237 et seq.

Avery Jones, Credit and Exemption under Tax Treaties in Cases of Differing Income Characterization, *ET* 1996, 118 et seq.

Avery Jones, Tax Treaties: The perspective of common law countries, in Maisto (ed.), *Courts and Tax Treaty Law*, 31 et seq. (cited as: Avery Jones, in Maisto (ed.), *Courts*).

Avery Jones, The Effect of Changes in the OECD Commentaries after a treaty is Concluded, *BFIT* 2002, 102 et seq (cited as: Avery Jones, *BFIT* 2002).

Avi-Yonah/Tittle, The New United States Model Income Tax Convention, *BFIT* 2007, 224 et seq.

Baker, *Double taxation conventions* (loose-leaf status: Oct. 2008), London: Sweet & Maxwell (cited as: Baker, *DTC*).

Baker/Bobbett, *Tax Polymath: A Life in International Taxation – Essays in Honour of John F. Avery Jones*, Amsterdam: IBFD Jan. 2011 (cited as: Lang, in Baker/ Bobbett, *Tax Polymath*).

Bauer/Schuch, Die Überlegungen des OECD-Steuerausschusses zur Lösung von Qualifikationskonflikten, in Gassner/Lang/Lechner (eds.), *Personengesellschaften im Recht der Doppelbesteuerungsabkommen* (2000) Vienna: Linde, 27 et seq. (cited as: Bauer/Schuch, in Gassner/Lang/Lechner (eds.), *Personengesellschaften*).

Coulombe, Besteuerung von Zahlungen an Nichtansässige für selbständige Arbeit, Generalbericht, CDFI LXVIIb 1982, 64.

Csoklich/Günther, Visiting Academics in Double Tax Treaties, in *Intertax* 2011, 578 et seq.

De Bont, Tax Treaty Interpretation in the Netherlands, in: Lang (ed.), *Tax Treaty Interpretation* (2001) Vienna: Linde, 246 et seq. (cited as: De Bont, in Lang (ed.), *Interpretation*).

De Broe, Belgium's tax treaty policy and the Draft Belgian Model Convention, in *BFIT* 2008, 322 et seq (cited as: De Broe, *BFIT* 2008).

Debatin, Replik auf Vogel, *DB* 1986, 510 et seq.

Debatin, System und Auslegung der Doppelbesteuerungsabkommen, *DB* 1985 Beilage 23.

Déry/Ward, National Report Canada, in IFA (ed.), *Interpretation of Double Taxation Conventions*, CDFI LXXVIII a (1993) Rotterdam: IFA, 259 et seq. (cited as: Déry/Ward, in IFA (ed.), *Interpretation*).

Djanani/Hartmann, Der Progressionsvorbehalt im Nichtansässigkeitsstaat und bei subjektiven Qualifikationskonflikten, *IStR* 2000, 321 et seq.

Dunahoo/Sprague, 2008 OECD Model: Changes to the Commentary on Article 5 Regarding the Treatment of Services: More Choices, Less Clarity, *BFIT* 2009, 191 et seq.

Engelen, *Interpretation of Tax Treaties under International Law* (2004) Amsterdam: IBFD (cited as: Engelen, *Interpretation*).

Gassner/Lang, Double Non-Taxation of a Belgian Tax Law Professor Lecturing in Vienna, in: Vanistendael (ed.), *Liber amicorum honouring Luc Hinnekens* (2002) Brussels: Bruylant Bruxelles, 219 et seq. (cited as: Gassner/Lang, in Vanistendael (ed.), *Liber amicorum Hinnekens*).

Gassner/Lang, Treaty Shopping, in: Gassner /Lang /Lechner (eds.), *Aktuelle Entwicklungen im internationalen Steuerrecht* (1994) Vienna: Linde, 43 et seq. (cited as: Gassner/Lang, in Gassner/Lang/Lechner (eds.), *Entwicklungen*).

Hofbauer, Tax Treaty Interpretation in Austria, in Lang (ed.), *Tax Treaty Interpretation* (2001) Vienna: Linde, 13 et seq. (cited as: Hofbauer, in Lang (ed.), *Interpretation*).

Huemer, *Die unbeschränkte Steuerpflicht natürlicher Personen* (1996) Vienna: Linde (cited as: Huemer, *Steuerpflicht*).

Jirousek, Der Fall Saint-Gobain im Lichte der österreichischen DBA-Anwendungspraxis, *ÖStZ* 1999, 604 et seq.

Kippenberg, Anmerkung zu BFH-Urteil, 19.12.2001, I R 63/00, *IStR* 2002, 243 et seq.

Kolb, Überblick über die Teilrevision 2000 des OECD-Musterabkommens, *ASA* 2001, 860 et seq.

Kosters, The United Nations Model Tax Convention and Its Recent Developments, *Asia-Pacific Tax Bulletin* 2004, 4 et seq.

Lang, Auslegung von Doppelbesteuerungsabkommen und authentische Vertragssprachen, *IStR* 2011, 403 et seq. (cited as: Lang, *IStR* 2011).

Lang, Die Anwendung des Multilateralen Instruments (MLI) "Alongside Existing Tax Treaties", *SWI* 2017, 624 et seq. (cited as: Lang, *SWI* 2017).

Lang, *The Application of the OECD Model Tax Convention to Partnerships* (2000) Vienna: Linde (cited as: Lang, *Partnerships*).

Lang, The procedural conditions for the implementation of tax treaty obligations under domestic law, *Intertax* 2007, 146 et seq (cited as: Lang, *Intertax* 2007).

Lang/Zieseritsch, Der Begriff der unselbständigen Arbeit nach Art 15 OECD-MA, in Gassner/Lang/Lechner/Schuch/Staringer (eds.), Arbeitnehmer im Recht der Doppelbesteuerungsabkommen (2003), 31 et seq.

Lang, Die Bedeutung von Verständigungsvereinbarungen nach Art. 3 Abs 2 OECD-Musterabkommen 2017: in Ismer et al, Territorialitat uns Personalitat Festschrift fur Moris Lehner Zum 70 Geburtstag, Otto Schmidt 2019, 209 ff. (cited as: *Lang, Otto Schmidt 2019*).

Loukota, Die Bedeutung der Änderungen des OECD-Musterabkommens für Österreich, *SWI* 1995, 450 et seq.

Matsubara, Japan: International Tax Aspects of the Tokumei Kumiai, Asia Pacific *Tax Bulletin*, Jan/Feb 2004, 76 et seq (cited as: Matsubara, *Asia Pacific Tax Bulletin* 2004).

Michelsen, Tax Treaty Interpretation in Denmark, in: Lang (ed.), *Tax Treaty Interpretation* (2001), Vienna: Linde, 63 et seq. (cited as: Michelsen, in: Lang (ed.), *Interpretation*).

Mössner, Anmerkung zu BFH, 19.12.2001, I R 63/00, *IStR*2002, 242.

Ritter, Steuerbeziehungen mit der Dritten Welt, *DStZ/A* 1979, 419 et seq.

Rust, Other Income (Article 21 OECD Model Convention), in Lang/Pistone/Schuch/Staringer (eds.), *Source versus Residence* (2008), New Delhi: Taxmann Publications, 359 et seq. (cited as: Rust, in Lang/Pistone/Schuch/Staringer (eds.), *Source versus Residence*).

Sasseville, Court Decisions and the Commentary to the OECD Model Convention, in Maisto (ed.), *Courts and Tax Treaty Law* (2007) Amsterdam: IBFD, 189 et seq. (cited as: Sasseville, in Maisto (ed.), *Courts*).

Smit, Classification of Income Under a Tax Treaty – Application of the Vienna Convention on Treaty Law, *ET* 1992, 57 et seq.

Szczepański, The Dual System of OECD Model Tax Conventions from the Evolutionary Perspective, *Intertax* 2018, 766 et seq. (cited as: Szczepański, *Intertax* 2018).

Vann, Liable to tax and company residence, in Maisto (ed.), *Residence of Companies under Tax Treaties and EC Law* (2009) Amsterdam: IBFD, 197 et seq. (cited as: Vann, in Maisto (ed.), *Residence of Companies*).

Vogel, Das oberste österreichische Steuergericht erklärt Verluste bei DBA Freistellung für abzugsfähig, *IStR* 2002, 91 et seq (cited as: Vogel, *IStR* 2002).

Vogel/Lehner, *Doppelbesteuerungsabkommen*[6] (2015) Munich: C.H. Beck (cited as: Vogel, *DBA*).

Vogel, *Klaus Vogel on Double Taxation Conventions*[4] (2015) Kluwer Law International (cited as: Vogel, *DTC*).

Vogel, Probleme der Auslegung von Doppelbesteuerungsabkommen, *SWI* 2000, 103 et seq (cited as: Vogel, *SWI* 2000).

Vogel, Steuerumgehung nach innerstaatlichem Recht und nach Abkommensrecht, *StuW* 1985, 369 et seq.

Vogel, The Influence of the OECD Commentaries on Treaty Interpretation, *BFIT* 2000, 612 et seq (cited as: Vogel, *BFIT* 2000).

Vogel, Zu einigen Fragen des Internationalen Steuerrechts, *DB* 1986, 507 et seq.

Vogel/Prokisch, General Report, in IFA (ed.), *Interpretation of Double Taxation Conventions*, CDFI LXXVIII a (1993) Rotterdam: IFA, 55 et seq. (cited as: Vogel/Prokisch, in IFA (ed.), *Interpretation*).

Ward, Is there an obligation in international law of OECD Member Countries to Follow the Commentaries on the Model?, in Douma/Engelen (eds.), *The legal status of the OECD Commentaries* (2008) Amsterdam: IBFD, 73 et seq. (cited as: Ward, in Douma/Engelen (eds.), *Legal status*).

Ward, Use of Foreign Court Decisions in Interpreting Tax Treaties, in Maisto (ed.), *Courts and Tax Treaty Law* (2007), Amsterdam: IBFD, 161 et seq. (cited as: Ward, in Maisto (ed.), *Courts*).

Wassermeyer, Der BFH und der Progressionsvorbehalt, *IStR* 2002, 289 et seq.

Wassermeyer, in: Debatin/Wassermeyer (eds.), *Doppelbesteuerung: Kommentar zu allen deutschen Doppelbesteuerungsabkommen*, Band I: Kommentierung des OECD-MA (looseleaf status: Dec. 2002) Munich: C.H. Beck (cited as: Wassermeyer, in Debatin/Wassermeyer, *Musterabkommen*).

Wattel/Marres, The Legal Status of the OECD Commentary and Static or Ambulatory Interpretation of Tax Treaties, *ET* 2003, 222 et seq (cited as: Wattel/Marres, *ET* 2003).

Wurm, Treaty Shopping in the 1992 OECD Model Convention, *Intertax* 1992, 658 et seq.

Zimmer, Tax Treaty Interpretation in Norway, in: Lang (ed.), *Tax Treaty Interpretation* (2001) Vienna: Linde, 261 et seq. (cited as: Zimmer, in Lang (ed.), *Interpretation*).

Zorn, Verwertung von Auslandsverlusten bei DBA mit Befreiungsmethode, *SWI* 2001, 456 et seq (cited as: Zorn, *SWI* 2001).

List of court cases

1. The problem of double taxation

1.1. Basics of international law

States can levy taxes by virtue of their sovereignty. Tax sovereignty, however, is not unlimited. Not all situations can be taxed. There must either be **a personal or an objective nexus**, or connection, **between the taxpayer and the state**. With respect to a personal connecting factor, it is sufficient that this exists with respect to the person concerned. Connecting factors for individuals frequently include domicile, residence or citizenship. For legal entities, the factors usually include the place of incorporation and the place of effective management. With regard to an objective connecting factor, it is sufficient that parts of the transaction or activity involve the taxing state or that the object of the action is somehow connected to the taxing state. 1

In international law practice, there are no significant limits on the tax sovereignty of states. In designing the domestic personal tax law, the national legislator can even tax situations when, for example, only a "**genuine link**" exists. It is only when neither the person nor the transaction has any connection with the taxing state that tax cannot be levied. 2

Example 3

According to the Indian legal tax system, tax is levied when a "genuine link" exists. Pursuant to Sec. 9(1)(i) of the Income Tax Act, tax is levied on all income earned outside India which accrues, whether directly or indirectly, through or from any business connection in India. This principle formed the basis for the opinion of the Indian Authority for Advance Rulings (AAR) that a commission paid to a non-resident agent may be taxable in India even if the services are rendered outside India. Those services consisted of pursuing and soliciting the particiation of foreign concerns, undertakings and government departments in the International Food and Wine Show (IFOWS) in India. Although the activity of the agent was carried on abroad, the AAR observed that the agent's right to receive commissions arose in India when the foreign concerns, undertakings and government departments participated in the IFOWS. Therefore, the AAR considered that the agent's income accrued from a business connection in India (cf. IN, AAR 3 Jul. 2006, Rajiv Malhotra, AAR/671/2005).

1.2. Circumstances giving rise to double taxation

1.2.1. Taxation of worldwide income (full tax liability) in two states

Since international law places few limits on the tax sovereignty of states, the same event may be taxed in two or more states. Under many domestic tax law systems, a person's worldwide income is taxed if a close personal connection exists between the taxable person and that state (**universality principle**). This is called full tax liability. However, if the connection is weak or consists only of objective 4 factors, only the income earned in that state is taxed (**principle of territoriality**). This is called limited tax liability.

5 A taxable person can have close personal connections with two or more states. Under the tax laws of various states, for example, the person's domicile is a connecting factor. In others, residence and citizenship are connecting factors. Depending on the applicable laws, each of these criteria can lead to full tax liability. Therefore, it is not rare in practice, for the same person to be **subject to full tax liability in two or more states**. This can lead to the levying of taxes on worldwide income in two or more states.

6 **Example**

An individual who lives in Spain and whose centre of economic interests is in France is subject to full tax liability in both states. If there were no DTC between France and Spain, both countries would tax the person's entire worldwide income.

1.2.2. Full tax liability and limited tax liability

7 More frequently, persons are subject to full tax liability on the basis of their residence, citizenship, or any other criterion of a similar nature, in just one state and receive income from another state. In that other state, they are subject to limited tax liability. This limited tax liability applies only to the income earned in that other state. When the state of residence levies tax on worldwide income, the **income from the other state is taxed twice**. Thus, full tax liability in a state and limited tax liability in another can lead to double taxation.

8 **Example**

A person resident and domiciled in the United Kingdom and subject to full tax liability therein holds shares in a Swiss corporation. The person does not have a home or domicile in Switzerland. The person receives dividends from the Swiss shares. These dividends are taxed in the United Kingdom since the person is subject to tax there on his worldwide income. In Switzerland, limited tax liability exists. Consequently, the dividends are also taxed in Switzerland.

1.2.3. Limited tax liability in two states

9 Double taxation will usually not arise when a person is subject to limited tax liability in two states. Limited tax liability is based on the principle of territoriality. The two states will levy tax only on income arising in their respective territories. However, since the scope of the limited tax liability may not be the same in both states, double taxation may even arise **on the basis of limited tax liability**.

10 **Example**

A person lives in Italy and is subject to full tax liability therein. The person receives income from shares of a corporation that has its legal seat in Germany and its place of effective management in Belgium. The dividends received from these shares are subject to limited tax liability in Germany and in Belgium. The income would be taxed a third time in Italy on the basis of the person's full tax liability if the DTCs did not provide a remedy.

1.2.4. Economic double taxation

Thus far, the discussion has focused on double taxation arising from the taxation of the same person with respect to the same income in two or more states (juridical double taxation). However, it is also possible for the same income to be **taxed in the hands of different persons**. This situation is known as economic double taxation. 11

Example 12

The parent company of an unlimited company incorporated in the United Kingdom was a US corporation. The income of the UK unlimited company was taxable in the United Kingdom in the hands of the UK unlimited company itself. For US federal income tax purposes, the UK unlimited company was classified as a disregarded entity because it had a single shareholder, unlimited liability and had not made a "check-the-box" election. The income earned by the UK unlimited company was therefore considered to belong to the US parent corporation even if this income had not been distributed by the UK unlimited company. Thus, the income of the UK unlimited company was taxable in the United Kingdom and in the United States in the hands of the US parent corporation (cf. UK, SCITD 19 Nov. 2008, Bayfine UK Products v. Revenue and Customs Commissioners).

The problem of economic double taxation frequently arises in cases in which **affiliated or associated corporations,** with their legal seats in different states, enter into transactions with each other. Each residence state determines the taxable base for corporate income tax under its domestic corporate tax law. If the two companies enter into transactions with each other, the tax authorities of the two states could assign different values to those transactions (for a detailed description of transfer pricing issues, cf. m.no. 464 et seq.). Economic double taxation may then arise. 13

Example 14

A multinational group of companies has subsidiaries in China and Brazil. The Chinese company sells products to the Brazilian company for CNY 100,000. The Chinese tax authorities consider that the CNY 100,000 price is appropriate, whereas the Brazilian tax authorities are of the opinion that the appropriate price would be CNY 80,000. This may lead to economic double taxation.

1.3. Elimination of double taxation

1.3.1. Double taxation conventions

Cross-border economic relations would be considerably threatened if two or more states subjected the same income to taxation. Many states therefore enter into **bilateral international tax conventions** in order to eliminate double taxation. These agreements are called double taxation conventions (DTCs). They determine the extent to which each state may levy tax. 15

The number of DTCs is constantly growing. At present, **more than 3,000 DTCs** exist. For example, the Netherlands is party to over 90 DTCs, while Switzerland is party to over 80 DTCs and the United Kingdom has concluded more than 125 DTCs. 16

1.3.2. Unilateral measures

17 Notwithstanding the extensive DTC network, not all cross-border relations are covered by DTCs. However, many states enact **unilateral measures** to prevent international double taxation in cases that are not covered by DTCs. Unilateral measures to prevent international double taxation differ from country to country. Essentially, three types can be distinguished: the exemption of foreign-sourced income, the tax credit for foreign taxes paid on foreign-sourced income and the deduction from the taxable base of foreign taxes paid on foreign-sourced income. The United States, for example, unilaterally grants a tax credit for foreign taxes paid on foreign-source income.

18 The unilateral measures mentioned above are granted under approaches that also **vary from country to country**. Generally speaking, two approaches can be distinguished: in some countries (e.g. Germany), precise rules are set out in the law; in other countries (e.g. Austria), much leeway is left to the tax authorities. Unilateral relief from international double taxation is sometimes granted subject to reciprocity (e.g. Brazil).

19 In some countries, the unilateral measures' provisions only apply when a **DTC is not applicable**, either because no DTC is in place with the country where the income is derived from or because the personal (cf. m.no. 177 et seq.) or the substantive scope (cf. m.no. 220 et seq.) of the DTC is not fulfilled. In others, the unilateral measures' provisions also establish the details for the concrete **application of the methods** to relieve international double taxation provided for by DTCs. In the latter countries, therefore, the criteria set forth by the unilateral measures' provisions apply to determine the relief to be granted to a taxpayer under the applicable DTC.

2. State practice in the conclusion of DTCs

2.1. Conventions in international law

At the conclusion of a DTC, the two parties to the convention accept an **international law obligation**. They commit themselves to relinquishing, completely or partially, the imposition of taxes in specific situations. The convention is subject to the rules of public international law. 20

The contracting states are free to decide the manner in which they will give up taxing rights. For example, they may change domestic law so that only the transactions set out in the DTC regarding the imposition of taxes remain. Often, however, the conventions are **directly applicable** as domestic law. In this case, the DTC rules override the otherwise applicable domestic tax rules. 21

2.2. The importance of model conventions

Every DTC is negotiated separately. Nevertheless, many of the existing DTCs throughout the world resemble each other. This can be traced to the model tax conventions developed by international organizations. These **model tax conventions are** usually the starting point for bilateral negotiations. The parties to the convention only need to negotiate those points upon which they wish to deviate from the model tax convention. 22

The **work of the League of Nations** contributed to the development of standardized model tax conventions. In the years between World Wars I and II the League of Nations produced several model tax conventions which gained importance in the negotiations of bilateral tax conventions between states and left their mark on the later work of other international organizations. 23

The OEEC, and later the **OECD**, continued the work of the League of Nations. In 1963, 1977 and 1992, the OECD published model tax conventions in the area of taxes on income and on capital (cf. m.no. 29 et seq.). These agreements were further developed in 1994, 1995, 1997, 2000, 2002, 2005, 2008, 2010, 2014 and 2017. In 1966 and in 1982, model tax conventions in the area of inheritance taxes were published (cf. m.no. 533 et seq.). 24

The United Nations published an independent UN Model in 1980; revised and updated versions were subsequently published in 2001, 2011 and 2017. 25

In most respects, the **UN Model** follows the OECD Model and deviations exist only with respect to certain issues. Major differences can be found in Art. 5 (permanent establishment), Art. 7 (business profits), Art. 9 (associated enterprises), Art. 10 (dividends), Art. 11 (interest), Art. 12 (royalties), Art. 13 (capital gains) and Art. 21 (other income). Since the UN Model is based on the interests of developing countries, these differences mostly try to ensure that the source country retains certain taxing rights. 26

27 **Example**

The OECD Model provides that royalties are taxed exclusively in the state of the recipient's residence, to the exclusion of the source state (Art. 12 OECD Model, cf. m.no. 298 et seq.). According to the UN Model, royalties may also be taxed in the state in which they arise. The UN Model does not establish a tax rate for the source state but leaves this question open. The rate is to be established in bilateral negotiations. The UN Model's principle regarding source taxation for royalties considers the situation of the developing countries: know-how is provided primarily by entrepreneurs of developed countries to enterprises in developing countries. Only rarely does the opposite occur. Thus, developing countries want to retain the right to tax remuneration paid in return for know-how.

2.3. The importance of the OECD Model

28 The OECD Models have had considerable influence in international tax law. They influenced other model tax conventions and many states use the OECD Model as a basis for their **DTC negotiations**.

29 In the area of taxes on income and on capital, the first OECD Model Tax Convention was published, along with a Commentary, in 1963. Over the years the Commentary has become more and more detailed. It explains the rules extensively and provides numerous examples to better understand the provisions of the OECD Model. Both documents were developed by the OECD Committee on Fiscal Affairs. The OECD Council recommended to the Member countries to make use of the Model and the Commentary: The Council thereby recommended that Member countries should continue with their efforts to enter into bilateral tax conventions, that they should adopt the OECD Model as a basis for their negotiations and that they should continue to notify the Committee on Fiscal Affairs of their reservations on articles and observations on the Commentary. Non-Member countries are invited to express their divergent views in the positions to the OECD Model (cf. m.no. 33).

30 In **1977**, a revised OECD Model was published by the OECD Committee on Fiscal Affairs. This revision took practical experience with negotiating DTCs into account. In particular, the Commentary was considerably amended and expanded. Since then, the OECD often changes the Commentary even if the relevant provision of the OECD Model was not changed. The OECD revises its positions, sometimes they even deviate from a position they took before.

31 In **1992**, the OECD Model was again revised. The speed increased: between 1994 and 2014 there were ten amendments. Some of these were only of minor relevance. Most of the changes concerned the Commentary to the OECD Model.

32 The **2017** Update of the OECD Model was again of major relevance. It primarily comprises changes to the OECD Model that were developed through the OECD/G20 BEPS (Base Erosion and Profit Shifting) Project. The OECD tried to reduce tax planning opportunities at all levels. Tax treaties should not create opportunities

for non-taxation or reduced taxation through tax evasion or avoidance. Some of the changes were very general, such as mentioning that goal already in the preamble, others were very technical. The 2017 Update also included certain other changes to the OECD Model that had been discussed for some years and were not developed as part of the work on the treaty-related BEPS measures. Again, the Commentary was amended significantly.

2.4. Bilateral peculiarities

States that use the OECD Model as a basis for negotiations usually deviate from the model on some points. This is because most states cannot agree with all the rules of the OECD Model. Many OECD Member countries have entered reservations on specific rules of the OECD Model. The contracting states furthermore try to take into consideration their **own economic interests** as well as the **peculiarities of their law and social systems**. 33

Example 34

In the OECD Model, the PE concept is used to determine the right of a contracting state to tax the profits of an enterprise of the other contracting state. Sometimes, however, it is questionable whether certain activities constitute a PE in a contracting state. Therefore, considering the special problems in applying Art. 5 OECD Model to certain activities, Denmark reserved the right to insert in a special article relating to offshore hydrocarbon exploration and exploitation and related activities: The DTC between Denmark and Slovenia (concluded in 2001), for example, constitutes that such activities are deemed to be a PE.

Numerous states also use the OECD Model as a basis for their **own model tax conventions** and incorporate their own deviations. They use these deviating models during their bilateral negotiations. 35

Example 36

The United States is concerned about the improper use of a DTC. In order to prevent abuse, the United States attaches great importance to restrictions on the entitlement to the benefits of the DTC. Given this concern as well as other issues, the United States published its own Model Tax Convention in 1996 and issued, after an update in 2006, a new version of this model in 2016. The United States uses this model in its bilateral negotiations. Thus, many DTCs concluded by the United States contain many similarities (cf. Avi-Yonah/Tittle, BFIT 2007, 224).

Model tax conventions are also published by countries that generally agree with the OECD Model standards but want to make clear the policy principles followed by their own treaty negotiators. For example, in 2007, Belgium published its own Draft Standard Model Convention and related Protocol although, at that time, it had made only seven reservations on the OECD Model and two observations on the Commentary. The **Belgian Model** (further updated in 2010) officially sets forth the policy principles that the Belgian negotiators will follow in negotiating tax treaties and is presented as such to countries that want to enter into treaty 37 negotiations with Belgium (cf. De Broe, *BFIT* 2008, 322 et seq.; the 2010 version no longer totally reflects Belgium's current tax treaty policy).

2.5. Bringing the Tax Treaties in Line with the OECD Model

38 Countries revise their bilateral tax treaties from time to time. Often, they take the opportunity to adapt their treaty to changes of the OECD Model. However, most governments have limited resources to negotiate new and renegotiate existing DTCs. It therefore often takes many years until updates of the OECD Model find their way in the bilateral DTCs. It is not rare that existing tax treaties reflect old versions of the OECD Model.

39 Since the OECD saw an urgency to implement the new and modified provisions developed under the BEPS Project in the DTCs, the "Multilateral Instrument" (MLI) was developed under the auspices of the OECD. The MLI is a multilateral convention, which swiftly modifies the application of existing bilateral tax treaties without the need to renegotiate each such treaty individually. It does not replace the existing tax treaties, but rather changes their content (cf. Lang, *SWI* 2017, 625).

40 In principle, the provisions of the MLI are optional. If a country wishes not to apply a certain provision, it can simply opt out of its application. However, the negotiating parties (a group of more than 100 jurisdictions) agreed to set a number of mandatory rules, the so-called minimum standards, which each country wishing to use the MLI has to implement. Part of these minimum standards are measures primarily to counter treaty abuse and to a lesser extent also to improve dispute resolution mechanisms while providing flexibility to accommodate specific tax treaty policies.

41 In order for a tax treaty to be modified by the MLI, it is necessary for both signatory states to a certain tax treaty to have signed the MLI and listed the relevant treaty in its MLI position under Art. 2. Only when both signatory states have notified the same treaty, their notifications match and the MLI will be able to modify the underlying bilateral tax treaty.

42 Besides the minimum standards representing the mandatory part of the MLI, all other provisions are optional. States may choose from the provisions and apply only those they wish to modify their treaties with. Through this flexible mechanism, states are able to consider their individual tax policy approaches and only choose the provisions that make sense for their treaty network. As mentioned above, if a state wishes not to apply a certain provision, it is required to formulate a reservation and thereby opt out of the relevant provision. An exception of this general mechanism can be found in Part VI of the MLI: in order to apply the part about the arbitration provisions, a state must choose to specifically opt in.

43 The MLI was finalized in November 2016 and a first signing ceremony was held in Paris on 6 June 2017. A total of 76 jurisdictions signed the MLI in this first ceremony. In the meantime, the MLI covers almost 100 jurisdictions.

3. The effects of DTCs

3.1. The allocation of taxing rights

In DTCs the two contracting states commit themselves to relinquishing or restricting their taxing rights. This should result in the elimination of double taxation. According to some DTC rules, certain income or capital can be taxed only in one of the two contracting states. Other income or capital can be taxed by both states proportionately: the right to tax for the source state, however, is usually limited to a certain percentage. Via the application of the so-called method articles, the state of residence has to avoid double taxation (**exemption method**, cf. m.no. 412 et seq and **credit method**, cf. m.no. 430 et seq.). 44

Example 45

Under Art. 12(1) OECD Model, royalties can only be taxed in the state of residence. The source state is precluded from taxing. Dividends can, however, be taxed by the source state (Art. 10(2) OECD Model). Depending on the percentage of participation and the beneficial owner, the source state may tax dividends at 5 or 15% of the gross amount. The state of residence will also tax but will credit the taxes paid in the source state.

In tax literature, it is frequently said that DTCs **allocate jurisdiction to tax**. This terminology has been criticized (cf. Vogel, *DTC* Introd., m.no. 50). States have original jurisdiction to tax and this is in accordance with international law. If this premise is accepted, it does not make any difference, in my view, whether the effects of a DTC are described as division, allocation or distribution of taxing rights, or whether one prefers, instead of the term "taxing rights", one of the following terms: tax sources, tax claims or taxable objects. 46

In DTCs the contracting states bind themselves not to raise any taxes with respect to taxing rights that are given to the other contracting state under the tax convention. The DTC rule applies even if one of the contracting states to which the right has been given does not impose taxes. In this respect, the application of the DTC can lead to **double non-taxation**. 47

Example 48

An individual resident in Munich has immovable property in Italy. The individual sells those assets long after their acquisition and realizes a gain. Under German tax law, the individual would be liable to tax in Germany. Under the DTC, however, Germany is bound to exempt this gain from tax. Italy may tax such profits under the DTC but is limited by its domestic law to taxing within the speculation period. Under Italian domestic law, therefore, the gain on the sale is exempt from tax. As a result, the gain from the sale is taxed neither in Germany nor in Italy.

3.2. The limiting effects of DTCs

In DTCs the contracting states mutually agree to limit their taxing rights. Thus, DTCs affect the legal systems of both contracting states. In both states, domestic tax law is **restricted**. 49

50 Vogel compares the way how a DTC applies to a "**stencil**" (cf. Vogel, *DTC* Introd., m.no. 58): the treaty acts like a stencil that is placed over the pattern of domestic law and covers over certain parts. In some areas, the pattern covers the domestic tax liabilities. In these cases, the imposition of taxes is restricted or eliminated. In the areas in which the pattern has holes, the domestic tax liability remains.

51 In tax literature, it has been said that DTCs **cannot generate tax liability**; however, there is no legal basis for this statement. There is no international law rule preventing tax liabilities from being increased because of a DTC. In practice, however, DTCs serve as a limitation on tax liabilities. This does not mean though that the application of a DTC could not worsen the position of the taxable person.

52 From the limiting effects of DTCs it can be understood that the exemptions granted by DTCs only affect positive income. DTCs would therefore not prevent foreign-source **losses** from offsetting the taxpayer's taxable base in the residence state. This conclusion has been drawn by the courts of several countries (e.g. Austria, Belgium, Finland, the Netherlands and Switzerland). According to the courts of other countries (e.g. Germany), however, DTCs have effects on positive and negative income. Thus, the DTC would prevent foreign-source losses from being taken into account in determining the taxpayer's taxable base in the residence state (for a comparative summary, cf. Vogel, *DTC* Art. 23, m.no. 50 et seq.).

3.3. The relationship to domestic law

3.3.1. Implementation of DTCs into domestic law

53 DTCs are treaties under international public law. It is up to the contracting states to decide how they are implemented into domestic law. Usually, this is a **constitutional issue**. According to constitutional provisions, DTCs might either have the same status as domestic provisions or they are superior to domestic provisions or their status might be below domestic provisions.

54 The contracting states oblige themselves to **implement the substance** of the provisions of a DTC. It is up to them whether they prefer to have the DTCs as such applicable or whether they introduce domestic provisions for that purpose.

3.3.2. Priority of DTC law

55 Irrespective of their status in domestic law, the content of the rules of a DTC often contradicts with domestic rules. According to most scholars, DTC rules are **special rules** in relation to domestic tax rules. However, the priority of DTC law is based on their intention to reduce or abolish domestic tax liabilities.

56 **Example**

A construction company resident in Bangladesh is hired to build an office in India and requires 4 months for the construction. Under the Bangladesh–India DTC, the income from this project cannot be taxed by India; Art. 7 of the DTC provides that income of a company resident in Bangladesh can only be taxed in Bangladesh. An exception exists if the Bangladesh company carries on business in India through a PE (Art. 7(1) of the Bangladesh–India DTC). Under Art. 5(2), however, a construction site constitutes a PE only if it lasts for more than 183 days. Therefore, there is no PE in India under the DTC. According to Indian domestic law, income received in India or arising in India is taxable under Sec. 4 of the Indian ITA. Since the DTC is the more specific law, India will apply the DTC and not the domestic rules. The imposition of tax by India would constitute an infringement of international law.

3.3.3. Priority of domestic law

As a rule, a treaty prevails over domestic law, even if the domestic provisions are 57
enacted after the conclusion of the treaty. The lex posterior rule usually does not play a role. However, if a domestic provision is designated to prevail over a treaty rule, the result must be regarded as a "**treaty override**". To the extent that a national legal system does not provide any constitutional law protection against international law violations by the legislator, this has to be accepted under national law. Although a "treaty override" leads to a breach of international law, not much can be done on an international level, besides terminating or suspending the treaty.

Example 58

Individuals resident in Germany were partners in a limited partnership in Belgium. Under the Belgium–Germany DTC, the income earned by the individuals was exempt from tax in Germany because the exemption method applies to exempt income derived from the capital invested in a Belgian limited partnership. Instead, however, the individuals were subject to tax in Germany and were given a credit for tax paid to Belgium. German domestic law (the Außensteuergesetz) provided that when income derived from the capital invested in a foreign partnership is subject to a tax on profits of less than 30% in the source state, the credit method applies rather than the exemption method. The domestic law provision was introduced after the entry into force of the Belgium–Germany DTC and constitutes a treaty override (cf. ECJ, 6 Dec. 2007, Case C-298/05, Columbus Container Services BVBA & Co v. Finanzamt Bielefeld-Innenstadt).

3.3.4. What to consider first in practice: DTC or domestic law?

In practice, the question of the relationship between domestic law and treaty law 59
arises when cross-border situations have to be analysed. In determining whether the contracting state has any taxing rights, what should be **examined first**: domestic law or DTC? Should domestic law establish tax claims first or should the DTC be tested first to determine whether there is any right to tax under the DTC? This issue was extensively discussed in Germany (cf. Debatin, *DB* 1985 Beilage 23, 5 et seq.; Vogel, *DB* 1986, 508 et seq.; Debatin, *DB* 1986, 512 et seq.). The discussion has since ceased.

Vogel concisely summarizes the results of the discussion (Vogel, *DTC* Introd., 60
m.no. 58; emphasis added): "Only very little legal background is required to recognize that logically, **both methods of procedure are equivalent**. Illustratively expressed: the treaty acts like a stencil that is placed over the pattern of domestic law and covers certain parts. Whether the stencil or the pattern is examined first,

the same conclusion results, so the order of application can be decided pragmatically from case to case." (cf. m.no.50). The order is therefore not a matter of interpretation and does not have any impact on the content of individual treaty articles. Anyone applying the treaty must consider this issue in every particular case exclusively under practical criteria.

61 **Example**

In an Indian case, ITAT 30 Jun. 2008, Epcos AG v. Assistant Commissioner of Income Tax, a German company earned income from the provision of technical services to an Indian subsidiary. The German company paid taxes in India at a rate of 10%, relying on the applicability of Art. 12 of the Germany–India DTC ("Royalties and fees for technical services"). The Indian Tax Officers assessed the German company arguing that Art. 7 rather than Art. 12 of this treaty was applicable. The Indian Tax Officers argued that the German company had a PE in India and therefore the income in question should be taxed in India in accordance with Art. 7 of the Germany–India DTC. They therefore assessed tax at 20% instead of 10%. The Indian Tax Officers gave an interpretation of Indian domestic law by which the onus of proving the non-existence of a PE in India was upon the German company, supporting their argument by stating that domestic law is to be applied first and tax treaty law is to be applied thereafter. The ITAT stated that there is no "conceptual support or other material whatsoever for 'domestic law first' approach, though, in all fairness, there is literature to support the proposition that the debate regarding whether one should see the treaty first or domestic law first is a non-starter. Whichever path we follow, we reach the same destination anyway; whether or not cross- border income is taxable in the source state in the light of the domestic tax laws read with the applicable tax treaty, it would not make any difference, in the ultimate analysis, whether one examines the case on the touchstone of the scheme of the treaty first and domestic law later, or vice versa."

62 What has proven to be **useful** is the practice of first consulting domestic law to determine whether any liability for tax exists and then consulting the DTC to determine whether it provides any relief from this liability. If there is no liability for tax under domestic law, there is no need to consult the DTC since the DTC in practice does not create a liability to tax (cf. m.no. 51). The mere allocation of taxing rights to a contracting state does not create an independent basis for taxation. On the other hand, it can occasionally be useful to consult the DTC first to determine whether a contracting state has the right to tax at all, and, as a second step, to determine the manner in which the contracting state exercises this right. If, under the treaty, there is no right to tax, there is no need to consult domestic law.

63 **Example**

A resident of Canada wins a lottery in Austria. One begins with the domestic right to tax. Since Canadian domestic law does not tax lottery winnings, the winnings are not taxable in Canada. From the point of view of Canadian tax law, an examination of the DTC between Austria and Canada is therefore unnecessary. This is not altered by the fact that under Art. 21(1) of the DTC between Canada and Austria, Canada has the right to tax this income. Furthermore, the lottery winnings are neither taxed in Austria because they are not regarded as taxable income. The DTC does not provide an independent legal basis for taxing this income.

4. The interpretation of double taxation conventions

4.1. Principles of interpretation in international law

Interpretation is always about establishing the scope and meaning of a rule. It does not matter which area of law is concerned since there are no particular methodologies for special fields of law. Thus, in international law, one also uses **the grammatical, systematic, teleological and historical interpretation methods**. With the help of all interpretation methods, the meaning of DTC rules is to be derived exclusively from the convention. One interpretation method does not prevail over another. Which argument is the most convincing depends on the weight of the argument. 64

There is definitely no need for specific interpretation rules. There is even a controversial debate whether it is at all possible that specific interpretation rules can give guidance for the interpretation process. However, in international law interpretation principles have been codified in Art. 31 et seq. of the **Vienna Convention on the Law of Treaties** (VCLT). The VCLT itself is an international convention, which has the same rank as tax treaties. According to the prevailing opinion, the interpretation rules of the VCLT are part of international customary law, which does not have a higher rank than tax treaties either. Therefore, the relevance of these rules for tax treaty interpretation depends on whether they fit for tax treaties. Courts tend to rely on these rules when they interpret tax treaties, although for convincing reasons, which will be explained below, some courts put less emphasis on some of these rules. 65

Pursuant to **Art. 31(1)** VCLT, a treaty must be interpreted in good faith with the ordinary meaning to be given to the terms of the treaty in their context and in the light of its object and purpose. For the purpose of the interpretation of a treaty, Art. 31(2) VCLT provides that the context includes, "in addition to the text, including its preambles and annexes", any agreement made between the parties in connection with the treaty as well as any instrument which was made by one or more parties in connection with the conclusion of the treaty and accepted by the other parties as an instrument related to the treaty. Art. 31(3) VCLT requires that together with the context, there shall be taken into account "any subsequent agreement between the parties regarding the interpretation of the treaty or the application of its provisions", "any subsequent practice in the application of the treaty which establishes the agreement of the parties regarding its interpretation", and "any relevant rules of international law applicable in the relations between the parties". A special meaning is to be given to a term, pursuant to Art. 31(4) VCLT, "if it is established that the parties so intended". Recourse may be made to supplementary means of interpretation, according to Art. 32 VCLT, including the 66 preparatory work of the treaty and the circumstances of its conclusion, in order to confirm the meaning resulting from the application of Art. 31 VCLT, or when the application of Art. 31 VCLT leaves the meaning ambiguous or obscure or leads to a result which is manifestly absurd or unreasonable.

67 It is sometimes argued that Art. 31(3)(a) VCLT provides grounds for peculiarities in the interpretation of international law. **Art. 31(3)(a)** VCLT provides that "any subsequent agreement between the parties regarding the interpretation of the treaty or the application of its provisions" shall be taken into account when interpreting a convention. However, in my opinion, this rule does not provide grounds for peculiarities in the interpretation of international law. Art. 31(3)(a) VCLT cannot be interpreted as an authorization for changing the content of the treaty. The VCLT distinguishes between the interpretation on the one hand and the amendment and modifications of a convention on the other hand. Art. 31 VCLT is a part of the rules of interpretation, which limits the scope of Art. 31(3)(a) VCLT. This suggests that it is not possible for administrative bodies to change DTCs by means of a new interpretation. In addition, when distinguishing between the interpretation of conventions and amendments to conventions, one must differentiate between different types of international law conventions. In principle, there is a difference between conventions that are only binding on states and those that, once implemented, give rise to rights for persons. Provided that the legal systems of the contracting states are founded upon the rule of law, it is difficult to argue that conventions that create rights for persons are capable of further dynamic development. In particular, the purpose of DTCs is to restrict existing tax claims. They cannot, therefore, be interpreted in a way that will modify this restriction. According to this view, therefore, tax authorities have no leeway for developing the law in a way that would add to or change the meaning of a provision of a DTC. In the interpretation of a convention, one must assume that the negotiators did not intend to violate basic constitutional principles of the legal systems of the two contracting states. Tax authorities have no greater leeway, in the interpretation of a DTC, to develop the law through a later agreement than they do in the interpretation of domestic law. Therefore, the interpretation principles contained in Art. 31(3)(a) VCLT do not deviate from the principles of interpretation of other areas of law.

68 **Example**

The taxpayer was a resident of France and worked in Germany for a German company. Under the France–Germany DTC, if the taxpayer is a frontier worker, he should be exempted from tax in Germany. Under Art. 13(5) (Income from employment) of the DTC, the frontier worker must generally return home every day in order for the state of residence to have the right to impose income tax. The French and German tax authorities had agreed, in a mutual agreement procedure pursuant to Art. 25(3) (Mutual agreement procedure) of the DTC, that a taxpayer would not lose his status as a frontier worker if he did not return home the same day or worked outside the border zone on

45 or fewer days in a full calendar year. This mutual agreement had been duly published. In the tax years under review, on a considerable number of days, the taxpayer did not return home the same day, or worked in Germany outside the border zone, or in third countries. The taxpayer relied on the mutual agreement and claimed an exemption from income tax in Germany. The German Federal Tax Court (BFH), however, ruled that Art. 13(5) of the DTC requires a frontier worker to return home every day. Consequently, the status of frontier worker is lost if the employee does not return home on one or more nights for reasons related to the exercise of the employment. The mutual agreement between the competent authorities could not alter the provisions of the treaty. Therefore, the taxpayer could not rely on the mutual agreement (GE, BFH 10 Dec. 2001, I B 94/01; cf. also GE, BFH 11 Nov. 2009, I R 84/08).

The same considerations apply with respect to **Art. 31(3)(b)** VCLT. According to this rule, "any subsequent practice in the application of the treaty which establishes the agreement of the parties regarding its interpretation" is to be taken into account in the interpretation. The "agreement" referred to in Art. 31(3) VCLT is not the one existing at the time of the conclusion of the DTC. According to prevailing opinion, a new understanding of the convention can be taken into account – provided it has found its way into later practice. Consequently, later administrative practice between the two contracting states can have an impact on the interpretation of the DTC. However, this does not confer an unlimited right for the development of the law by administrative interpretation. International law acknowledges that the interpretation of the convention by means of later practice is limited. With tax conventions that create rights for persons, the interpretation of the convention through subsequent practice of the administrative authorities can only be of **minor importance**. An accurate interpretation of Art. 31(3)(b) VCLT is therefore that the development of the law through subsequent practice of the administrative authorities of the two contracting states is as limited as it is in the interpretation of other provisions. 69

Example 70

An individual resident in Germany is an authorized signatory (Prokurist) of a Swiss company. For this purpose, he sometimes works in Switzerland but most of the time in Germany. Under Art. 15(4) of the Germany-Switzerland DTC, the income derived from his function may be taxed in Switzerland – where the company is resident. Double taxation is avoided by the exemption method, "provided the employment is exercised in Switzerland" (Art. 24(1)(1)(d) of the Germany-Switzerland DTC). The German Federal Tax Court had to interpret the term "exercised in Switzerland" and for this purpose, the court referred to how the provision had been interpreted since it first came into effect. It was argued that already in earlier tax treaties concluded by the countries the treaty partners considered the activity of an authorized signatory as being exercised where the company was resident. This view has not been changed in subsequent conventions or protocols and has been confirmed in prevailing case law. Even though the wording of the provision could lead to a different understanding, the court held that subsequent practice in the meaning of Art. 31(3)(b) VCLT is an even stronger indication as to how the provision has to be interpreted (cf. GE, BFH 25 Oct. 2006, I R 81/04).

4.2. The use of principles of interpretation stemming from international law with respect to DTCs

4.2.1. Autonomy of DTC law

71 DTCs, as international law conventions, have an impact not only on the domestic tax law of one contracting state but also on the laws of at least two states. DTC provisions aim to shape the legal order of the contracting states in a way that the respective taxing rights are assigned to one of the contracting states or to both contracting states proportionately. In order to guarantee an exact meaning, the DTC must therefore be viewed separately from domestic legal systems and the meaning of the DTC provision must be determined without reference to any domestic law. Accordingly, **DTC law** must be regarded as **autonomous** with respect to domestic law. Domestic law and treaty law can only be interpreted within their own contexts.

72 **Example**

In many countries, domestic law contains a definition of "permanent establishment". When a DTC patterned after the OECD Model uses the term "permanent establishment", it cannot be understood in terms of the domestic law but rather in accordance with the DTC. In DTCs that follow the OECD Model, Art. 5 contains an autonomous definition of "permanent establishment". This definition is to be used for the interpretation of the concept in the DTC.

73 In interpreting a DTC "within its own context", it is necessary to determine the objectives of the respective DTC provisions and to take them into account. The main goal of DTCs is the **avoidance of double taxation**. However, the interpretation of the DTC provisions should not be based on this general purpose because DTCs do not avoid all cases of double taxation but only those within their scope. If, for example, a person is subject to limited tax liability in both contracting states, double taxation may remain despite a DTC (cf. m.no. 177). The same is true for cases in which a tax or a duty is not covered by Art. 2 of DTCs patterned after the OECD Model ("taxes covered") (cf. m.no. 220 et seq.). Nor can cases of double taxation, pursuant to which income is assigned to different taxable persons in the two contracting states, be typically resolved by means of a DTC (cf. m.no. 410). Since DTCs only avoid double taxation under the conditions established therein, the purpose of the avoidance of double taxation is of no assistance if the question is whether, in a certain situation, these conditions are met. The situation is similar in domestic law when it comes to the general objective of taxation, which is to raise revenues for the state. In determining whether tax may be levied in a certain situation, there is no point in taking this objective into account. Thus, the proposition that the purpose of a DTC is the avoidance of double taxation does not help in resolving individual DTC questions. Furthermore, in DTC law, it is not enough to refer to general principles. The object and purpose of every single provision needs to be understood.

According to the preamble to the OECD Model Convention, the purpose of DTCs is the avoidance of double taxation. For similar reasons as those mentioned above, this goal does not give much guidance either. Moreover, the preamble already makes clear that such a goal would be too general. Therefore, the phrase, which had been added to the goal of avoidance of double taxation is rather lengthy: "without creating opportunities for non-taxation or reduced taxation through tax avoidance or evasion (including through treaty-shopping arrangements aimed at obtaining reliefs provided in this Convention for the indirect benefit of residents of third States)". This phrase makes it already clear that there are situations where non-taxation is perfectly legitimate; for example, the exemption method (in detail cf. m.no. 412 et seq.) may lead to non-taxation, unless it is combined with a "subject-to-tax clause" (cf. m.no. 416). In this case, taxation is secured in at least one of the two states and double non-taxation is thereby avoided. Double non-taxation can otherwise be a legitimate result of the interpretation of the treaty if, for example, one of the two states may not tax due to the provisions of the treaty and the other state cannot exercise its taxing rights because there is no domestic legal right to tax. The principle of avoidance of double non-taxation is therefore not sustainable as a principle of general interpretation (differently Zorn, *SWI* 2001, 461). 74

Example 75

An individual resident in the United Arab Emirates held shares in a private Indian corporation, which she sold in 2000. The former Art. 13(3) India–United Arab Emirates DTC stated that capital gains on the alienation of shares are taxable only in the contracting state of which the alienator is a resident. Under the domestic tax law of the United Arab Emirates the capital gain is tax free. The Indian court decided that entering into a tax treaty, which may leave scope for double non-taxation is a conscious decision of the respective contracting state, but once such a tax treaty, as may leave scope for double non-taxation, is entered into, judicial forums have to interpret the provisions of the tax treaty as they exist. The capital gain of the individual resident in the United Arab Emirates was therefore neither taxed in the residence state nor in India (IN, ITA 29 Oct. 2009, No. 1876/Mum/2006, Meera Bhatia v. ITO).

4.2.2. The importance of domestic law

Domestic law is taken into account for the interpretation of a DTC when nothing more can be derived from the treaty itself. One must first, however, try to find a solution in the DTC by means of all methodological possibilities. All systematic, teleological and historical aspects must be considered. It is extremely rare that a solution cannot be found by taking these aspects into account. 76

Example 77

The term "employment" is an important term in the context of the OECD Model. It is used for example in Art. 15 OECD Model and is indirectly relevant for the scope of other allocation rules. The OECD Model does not contain a definition of employment.

However, in my view, this does not mean that each state is free to use its own domestic definition for treaty purposes. Studies have shown that there is a common understanding of that concept by most countries (see in detail Coulombe. CDFI, LXVIIb, 1982, 64) and that the OECD had this common understanding in mind when provisions such as Art. 15 OECD Model were drafted. Employment involves two parties: employer and employee. The understanding is that employment is exercised by an employee who is subjected to the authority and directions of the employer (to the extent to which instructions can be given). However, such employee does not bear any entrepreneurial risk for the results of the work (in detail Lang/Zieseritsch, in: Gassner/Lang/Lechner/Schuch/Staringer (eds.), Arbeitnehmer im Recht der Doppelbesteuerungsabkommen, 2003, 46 et seq.). This interpretation, which is exclusively obtained from the treaty, makes it possible to attribute the income to the same allocation rule in both states. If, however, the tax authority of one state rejects this interpretation and instead consults the respective domestic law provisions, the outcome can be that the income falls under Art. 15 OECD Model in one state and under another allocation rule in the other state. Double taxation or double non-taxation can therefore arise.

78 In certain cases, however, the autonomous interpretation of the DTC rules indicates that **domestic law** needs to be taken into account. In addition to their international law character, the special objective of DTCs must be considered during the interpretation process. DTCs aim at restricting the domestic taxing powers of the contracting states. This goal can only be reached if there is a close connection between the DTC provisions and the rules of domestic law. In order to be able to impose the restrictive legal consequence, the DTC must cover the domestic rule that is intended to be restricted. For this reason, there must be a connecting factor between domestic law and DTC law.

79 The **references to taxpayer and tax base** in the convention are linked to the domestic laws of the contracting states and must therefore be understood as a dynamic cross reference because the DTC provisions refer to the applicable law of the two contracting states. Thus, if the treaty mentions the term "person", this is to be understood with reference to the respective applicable legal provisions of the contracting states, which regulate the liability to pay taxes. The expressions "profit", "income" and "property" refer to the established law of the contracting states, which describes the factual part of the taxation situation. In the personal as well as in the substantial sense, the structure of the DTC requires a reference to domestic law.

80 **Example**

A Greek lawyer visits a client in Switzerland to provide legal advice but does not have an office in Switzerland. Pursuant to Art. 14(1) of the Greece–Switzerland DTC (Art. 14 of the former OECD Model), the income derived by the lawyer is taxable only in Greece unless the lawyer has a fixed base regularly available to him in Switzerland. Consequently, the income is taxable only in Greece. With respect to the concept of "income", Greek domestic law will determine the taxable base with regard to the factors to be taken into account in determining income.

Some individual DTC provisions contain an express **reference to domestic law**. Several provisions refer to the domestic law of one of the two states. The other contracting state must abide by the interpretation of the state to which the provision refers. 81

Example 82

Under Art. 6(2) OECD Model, the term "immovable property" shall, under several conditions, have the meaning which it has under the law of the contracting state in which the property in question is situated. Consequently, the interpretation of the situs state is decisive. The legal situation of the situs state is also decisive for the interpretation of the DTC in the residence state.

Some bilateral DTC provisions deviate from the wording of the OECD Model provisions as a consequence of the legal situation in one or both contracting states at the time of the conclusion of the treaty. This can arise in cases in which provisions of a DTC contain wording that is identical to that found in **domestic law at the time of conclusion of the treaty**. In this case, what must be determined is whether these conceptual parallels are merely accidental or whether the DTC negotiators intended to refer to the domestic law meaning. If this connection was intended, the meaning of the term in domestic law at that time prevails. Consequently, in these cases the reference to established law is static, i.e. the provision is to be given the meaning it had at the time of conclusion of the treaty. 83

Example 84

Several Japanese tax treaties contain special provisions for income from "tokumei kumiai", the Japanese silent partnership. If a treaty mentions this special type of silent partnership, the treaty term has to be understood under Japanese law. In case Japanese law changes in that respect, the meaning of the term at the time the specific treaty was concluded is relevant.

4.2.3. The importance of the OECD Model and its Commentary

The OECD Model and the Commentary of the OECD Committee on Fiscal Affairs are important for the interpretation of tax treaties. There are different positions which provisions of the VCLT are relevant in that respect, e.g. Art. 31(2), Art. 31(4) or Art. 32 VCLT. However, there is general agreement that the OECD Model and the Commentary which existed at the time the bilateral treaty was concluded may be taken into account. It can be argued that the parties so intended when they adopted the text of the OECD Model without changes. 85

The OECD Model and the Commentaries do not, however, have as much weight as the wording of the convention itself because they are not a part of the agreement. In addition to the OECD Model and the Commentary, other historical, teleological and systematic aspects, as well as the wording of the convention itself, have to be taken into account. Which arguments are more convincing depends on their weight. Art. 31 VCTL does not provide for a rule under which one interpretation method takes precedence over another. 86

87 **Example**

A company resident in the United Kingdom was engaged in the transportation of goods by international shipping and had, amongst others, an agent in India, who arranged cargo and shipping activities on ships of the UK company as well as on ships operated by third parties. Under Art. 9(1) of the India–UK DTC (Art. 8 OECD Model) "income of an enterprise of a Contracting State [UK] from the operation of ships in international traffic shall be taxable only in that State". Consequently, the UK company claimed that its activities were not taxable in India. The Indian tax authorities argued, however, that the income relating to the activities carried on by ships operated by third parties was not income from the "operation of ships". The UK company appealed. The phrase "operation of ships" was not defined in the India–UK DTC. The ITAT, therefore, relied upon the Commentary in force at the time of conclusion of the treaty because the wording of the DTC was similar to that of the OECD Model. The Tribunal referred to the OECD Commentary on Art. 8, holding that freight income was income from the operation of ships and exempt from tax in India (IN, ITAT 13 Aug. 2008, DDIT v. Balaji Shipping).

88 In the opinion of some tax authorities, the OECD Model and the Commentary of the OECD Committee on Fiscal Affairs should also be taken into account for the interpretation of DTCs that **do not follow the OECD Model**. In my view, there are no grounds for taking the OECD Model or the Commentary into account when interpreting DTCs, which do not follow the OECD Model. If the contracting states did not use the OECD Model as a guideline for their bilateral agreement, it cannot be assumed that they understood the provisions of the treaty in the same way as the OECD Model or the Commentary do.

89 **Example**

A German teacher worked at a school in Spain and received her salaries from German public funds. She rendered her services not to Germany but at least in Germany's public interest. The taxpayer argued that she was not taxable under Art. 18 of the Germany–Spain DTC (government services), because she did not render her services to the state and therefore was not liable to German income tax. In interpreting the respective provision, the German Federal Tax Court stated that since Art. 18 of the treaty does not exactly correspond to Art. 19 OECD Model, the OECD Commentary cannot be taken into account. Instead, the court interpreted the case exclusively on the basis of the wording of the Germany–Spain DTC (GE, BFH 13 Aug. 1997, I R 65/95).

90 Occasionally, domestic law existing at the time of conclusion of a DTC might be considered relevant for the interpretation of DTCs that **follow the OECD Model**. In my view, this practice is incorrect in so far as provisions are concerned that are taken from the OECD Model. If the DTC negotiators transferred a wording contained in the OECD Model to the bilateral DTC, it is to be assumed that they wanted this wording to have the same meaning as it has under the decisive provision of the OECD Model. Without any indication to the contrary, it cannot, therefore, be assumed that the understanding of the treaty is based on the domestic understanding of one of the two contracting states at the time of conclusion of the agreement.

Example 91

An individual resident in Austria was a manager of a Swiss company and owned 95% of the shares of that company. In 1974, the DTC between Austria and Switzerland came into force. At that time, Austrian tax law did not include a rule according to which a participation higher than 25% is decisive for the characterization of income of the shareholder-manager as independent personal services, as opposed to employment income. This rule was only later introduced in Austrian tax law. The Austrian Supreme Administrative Court (VwGH) took into account the domestic legal situation at the time of the conclusion of the DTC and concluded that income derived by the individual was covered by Art. 15 of the Austria–Switzerland DTC (cf. AT, VwGH 20 Sep. 2001, 2000/15/0116; for a similar conclusion cf. e.g. AT, VwGH 21 May 1997, 96/14/0084; for a different conclusion drawn earlier cf. AT, VwGH 31 Jul. 1996, 92/13/0172). This line of reasoning is not convincing. The Court should have interpreted the term "employment" in its treaty context.

Sometimes the wording of the DTCs varies because of language differences. These differences can cause conflicts in the interpretation of the specific provisions by the countries involved. 92

On the conclusion of a tax treaty, the contracting parties often agree on authentic languages. Frequently, the parties agree on using the respective national languages and a "neutral" third language, such as English or French. When it comes to interpreting a certain term of the treaty, one might then ask which language should be used. It can therefore be argued that if the contracting states' intention was to follow the OECD Model, the interpretation should also be in line with the original languages as used in the drafting of the Model (English and French). The respective national languages should only be given more importance if the contracting states wanted to deviate from the OECD Model (Lang, IStR 2011, 403). 93

Example 94

A Swiss resident and a Belgian resident received severance payments from German companies in respect of their past employment contracts. The German tax authorities were claiming the taxation rights on such payments since, under the OECD wording of Art. 15(1), "salaries, wages and other similar remuneration derived by a resident of a Contracting State in respect of an employment" could be taxed also by the source state. The German Federal Tax Court (BFH), instead, looked into the German wording of Art. 15(1) where only "salaries, wages and other similar remuneration derived by a resident of a Contracting State for an employment" could be taxed by the source state. The court established that the German wording of the article required a closer connection between the payment and the performance of the work and, therefore, it stated that Germany was not entitled to tax such severance payments (GE, BFH 2 Sep. 2009, I R 111/08; GE, BFH 2. Sep. 2009, I R 90/08). Had the court paid attention to the fact that the relevant phrase had been taken from the OECD Model, it should have also looked at the English and French versions of the OECD Model, irrespective of the authentic language of the treaty. The phrase "in respect of an employment" would then have required only a loose connection between the payment and the performance.

4.2.4. The importance of changes in the OECD Model and its Commentary

95 The OECD Model on income and on capital exists in **different versions**. The first version was published in 1963, the second in 1977 and the third in 1992. Since then, the OECD Model has been continuously revised (cf. m.no. 24). The same is true for the Commentary. Scholars discuss which version of the OECD Model and the Commentary should be used for the interpretation of DTCs.

96 The Introduction to the OECD Model states that existing DTCs should, as far as possible, be **interpreted in the spirit of the revised Commentary**. It specifies that amendments to the articles and resulting changes to the Commentary are not relevant to the interpretation or application of previously concluded DTCs where the provisions of those DTCs are different in substance. Where, however, changes or additions to the Commentary are not different in substance, they are normally applicable to the interpretation and application of DTCs concluded before their adoption because they reflect the consensus of the OECD Member countries as to the proper interpretation of existing provisions and their application to specific situations.

97 This approach has been convincingly criticized by some commentators, as these **later versions of the Commentary** have not been considered by the parliament who approved the DTC. Later versions of the Commentary are not "context" for the purpose of Art. 31(1) VCLT because only Commentaries that are made in connection with the conclusion of the treaty can be considered context. They cannot be considered "subsequent agreements" for the purposes of Art. 31(3) VCLT since that would require parliamentary approval. In order to be considered "subsequent practice" within the meaning of Art. 31(3) VCLT, evidence would be required to show that the Commentary reflected the actual subsequent practice of both contracting states; relying on the words of the OECD Commentary would not suffice for this purpose. Finally, later changes to the Commentary cannot be considered "special meaning" within the meaning of Art. 31(4) VCLT since the parties could not have intended an interpretation that did not exist at the time the DTC was concluded (cf. Vogel, *BFIT* 2000, 612; cf. also Wattel/Marres, *ET* 2003, 222).

98 It has, however, been pointed out that refusing to take later Commentaries into account can result in the Commentaries being frozen in time and therefore failing to adapt to changes in business or technology. If later Commentaries are not used, the result could be a **different interpretation** of identical wording in treaties entered into at different times. This goes against the goal of uniform interpretation of DTCs (cf. Avery Jones, *BFIT* 2002, 102; Baker, *DTC* Introd., E.15). However, one must not confuse the legal and factual environment: changes in business and technology have to be considered under the existing rules, and one has to examine under which rules a new situation fits best, according to the object and purpose of the rules. This would have to be done in any case, even in the absence of a Commentary. If the OECD Commentary suggests dealing with new factual developments,

this might be helpful, as articles by authors on these questions might be, but is in no way authoritative.

Moreover, adopting later Commentaries would interfere with the **competence of the legislative bodies**. A change in the Commentary can never overrule an existing DTC. If the interpretation of a DTC inevitably leads to a result that deviates from the Commentary, this interpretation will legally prevail (Wattel/Marres, *ET* 2003, 222). 99

For all these reasons, only the version of the OECD Model and the respective Commentary **existing at the time of conclusion of the corresponding DTC** can be considered for the interpretation of a DTC that follows the OECD Model, since the DTC negotiators could only have an understanding of the version of the Commentary existing at that point in time. It cannot, therefore, be assumed that they attached a meaning to a DTC provision which it only acquired in a later version of the Commentary (affirmative, Vogel, *SWI* 2000, 109; Wassermeyer, in Debatin/Wassermeyer *Musterabkommen* Vor Art. 1, m.no. 62; Ward, in Douma/Engelen (eds.), *Legal status*, 86). 100

Example 101

In CA, TCC 18 Aug. 2006, MIL Investments SA v. Her Majesty the Queen, the taxpayer was a company resident in the Cayman Islands that held shares in a Canadian corporation. The taxpayer was relocated to Luxembourg. He then sold the shares in the Canadian corporation and claimed an exemption under the Canada–Luxembourg DTC of 1990. The tax authorities denied the exemption under the general anti-avoidance rule (GAAR) of the Canadian Income Tax Act, which is, according to Canadian domestic law, applicable to DTCs. The Tax Court of Canada ruled that the GAAR did not apply since the transactions were not avoidance transactions. The tax authorities then argued that the DTC contained an inherent anti-abuse rule which applied in this case to deny the exemption. The tax authorities relied on the 2003 OECD Commentary in support of the argument that the DTC contained an inherent anti-abuse rule. The 1977 OECD Commentary on Art. 1 stated, however, that if contracting states wanted to have an anti-abuse provision in the DTC, such a provision should be included in the DTC. The Tax Court ruled that only the Commentary from 1977 was relevant for the interpretation of the 1990 DTC and agreed with the taxpayer that there was no inherent anti-abuse provision in the DTC. In other words, the court was of the opinion that statements found in the Commentary from 2003 had no effect on the interpretation of Canada's 1990 DTC with Luxembourg.

The fact that a particular version of the Commentary was altered or supplemented does not always mean, however, that a DTC, which was concluded before that version of the Commentary was published, has a **different content**. It is possible that that version confirms an opinion, which could be deduced from the version of the OECD Model existing at the conclusion of the relevant DTC, by means of historical, systematic or teleological arguments. In this case, the opinion represented in the later version of the Commentary can be used for the interpretation of DTCs concluded before that version was published. The reason for this is not 102 that the opinion was explicitly set out in the Commentary but that it could already be established by interpretation.

103 **Example**

Art. 17(2) OECD Model states that "Where income in respect of personal activities exercised by an entertainer or a sportsperson acting as such accrues not to the entertainer or sportsperson but to another person, that income may, notwithstanding the provisions of Article 15, be taxed in the Contracting State in which the activities of the entertainer or sportsperson are exercised". The wording of the article made it clear that its scope was not limited to cases of anti-abuse. Nevertheless, the OECD Commentary originally established that the purpose of the article was "to counteract certain tax avoidance devices". In the 2002 version of the OECD Commentary, such interpretation was abandoned and the sentence was deleted. The 2002 version of the Commentary now describes the content of the rule correctly.

104 This view that only the Commentary existing at the time of the conclusion of the DTC may be used in the interpretation of the latter (cf. m.no. 97 et seq.) does not mean that later versions of the Commentary are completely irrelevant. Undoubtedly, the members of the working parties and the OECD Committee on Fiscal Affairs are highly qualified experts. More recent versions of the Commentary are therefore of importance as **expert opinions**. They have the same relevance as other articles by experts and other scientific publications; they can influence the understanding of provisions in practice, if the arguments are convincing. Frequently, however, the Commentary only presents the result of a certain interpretation without reference to the main arguments that led to this result. Consequently, they often lack the persuasiveness necessary for influencing practice.

105 In some cases, however, a more recent version of the OECD Commentary can be helpful in the interpretation of an older DTC because that **version reflects practice** already previously common. The first OECD Model and Commentary from 1963 were not created overnight but followed existing bilateral treaty practice.

106 **Example**

In CA, FCA 19 Oct. 1998, Cudd Pressure Control Inc. v. Her Majesty the Queen, the issue was the independence of the PE under the 1942 Canada–US DTC. The court justified taking the later OECD Commentaries into account as follows: "The relevant commentaries on the OECD Convention were drafted after the 1942 Convention and therefore their relevance becomes somewhat suspect. In particular, they cannot be used to determine the intent of the drafters of the 1942 Convention. However, although the wording and arrangement of the provisions are significantly different in the two Conventions, the 1942 Convention follows the same general principles as the OECD Model. The OECD Commentaries, therefore, can provide some assistance in discerning the 'legal context' surrounding double taxation conventions at international law, and in particular in ascertaining when it is appropriate to allow a deduction for a notional expense." In this case, the court's proceedings, in my opinion, were feasible and well founded. The provisions of Art. 7 OECD Model were based on the work of Mitchell B. Carroll and it can therefore be assumed that the negotiators of the DTC in question were also influenced by these considerations (cf. also Vogel/Lehner, DTC Grundlagen m.no. 70).

When an amended version of the Commentaries of the OECD Committee on Fiscal Affairs provides an opinion regarding the interpretation of a provision of the OECD Model that cannot be derived from the former version of the OECD Model by means of general principles of interpretation, this change causes the **content of the existing DTCs to drift apart**. For the interpretation of a DTC, the version of the OECD Model and the Commentary available at the time of conclusion of the bilateral DTC must be used. This development is regrettable considering the fact that DTCs are gaining more and more importance. It would therefore be desirable for the OECD Committee on Fiscal Affairs to effect changes in the OECD Model and the Commentary at wider intervals after having intensely discussed the change. In practice, the frequent changes of the OECD Model and the Commentary of the OECD Committee on Fiscal Affairs lead to an increase in interpretation conflicts, since in some states, courts are quite inclined to at least partially follow more recent versions of the OECD Commentary when interpreting older DTCs (cf. for the discussion in Norway e.g. Zimmer, in Lang (ed.), *Interpretation*, 266). However, many of those applying the law are not always willing to follow the most recent version of the Commentaries without legal authority (cf. e.g. Michelsen, in Lang (ed.), *Interpretation*, 72, discussing a Danish court decision from 3 Feb. 2000). Provisions of the very same treaty are therefore more frequently understood differently. Altogether, the authority of the OECD Commentary has suffered considerably from the repeated changes. 107

4.2.5. The importance of OECD reports

The OECD Committee on Fiscal Affairs' Working Parties frequently work on controversial or insufficiently discussed DTC issues and write "**OECD reports**". After approval by the OECD Committee on Fiscal Affairs, these reports are usually published. They often provide reasons for changes to the OECD Model or the Commentary. 108

If the reports have been the reason for changes in the OECD Model or the Commentary, they are a useful reference **for understanding the changes**. They must be taken into account in the interpretation of those DTCs which follow the OECD Model or a particular Commentary that was changed on the basis of the OECD report. 109

The OECD reports can even be relevant for the interpretation of a DTC if they were available at the time of conclusion of a DTC that follows the OECD Model and if it can be assumed that the negotiators of the DTC were **aware of the opinion represented in the OECD report and shared it**. However, the assumption that the negotiators of the DTC followed the opinion represented in an OECD report is not as obvious as it is when it comes to the Commentary. Occasionally, however, the OECD Commentary refers to an OECD report. In these cases, it can be 110 assumed that if the negotiators followed the OECD Model and the Commentary, they also took into account the opinion set out in the report as represented in the Commentary.

111 **Later OECD reports**, however, are, like a later OECD Commentary (cf. m.no. 95 et seq.), not to be taken into account for the interpretation of older DTCs because it cannot be assumed that the negotiators of the DTC based their understanding of certain DTC provisions on opinions of a version of the Commentary that had not yet been developed at the time of the conclusion of the treaty. Well-founded opinions in the OECD Commentary are relevant, however, as expert opinions, in the same manner as opinions of other experts.

4.2.6. The importance of administrative practice

112 The tax administrations of two contracting states frequently seek agreement on the interpretation of DTC rules. They enter into "**mutual agreements**" with respect to a common interpretation of a certain treaty provision. The tax administrations occasionally expect that these mutual agreements, like the DTC provisions, will be binding on all parties. In practice, mutual agreements are therefore important. However, interpretative mutual agreements are legally **not binding** (cf. Vogel, *DTC* Art. 25, m.no. 107; Avery Jones, in Maisto (ed.), *Courts*, 78 et seq.; for a different view, cf. Ward, in Douma/Engelen (eds.), *Legal status*, 81).

113 **Example**

The Belgian Court of first instance, 7 January 2016, case 14/931/A, had to decide whether a pension paid by a Belgian public broadcasting service to a French resident having dual Belgian-French nationality in the period at stake had to be taxable in Belgium under Art. 10(3) of the treaty. A mutual agreement between Belgian and French competent authorities provided interpretation on how Art. 10(1) in connection with Art. 10(3) of the tax treaty had to apply. Nevertheless, the Court denied the relevance of the mutual agreement for the interpretation of the provisions since, according to the Court, the agreement added a new condition to Art. 10(3) and therefore went beyond merely interpreting them. In addition, the Court observed that the mutual agreement had not been approved by the Belgian parliament as required by the Belgian Constitution. Hence, the agreement could not be regarded as a valid binding international treaty.

4.2.7. The importance of other countries' court decisions

114 Courts, authors and tax authorities often consider foreign court decisions regarding treaty interpretation. Foreign court decisions can provide useful guidance with respect to **how other countries interpret and apply** a particular provision. Foreign court decisions are also often explicitly cited by a court interpreting the same provision. Furthermore, when national courts give important treaty interpretations, the OECD discusses them to determine whether the interpretations are correct with respect to the wording of the OECD Model (cf. Sasseville, in Maisto (ed.), *Courts*, 189).

Foreign court decisions, however, are **not formally binding** on a court. The weight to be given to them may vary for a number of reasons. If the decision was not rendered by the highest court of the foreign jurisdiction, it may be given less weight. If the decision was based on a later version of the OECD Commentary, care must be taken to ensure that the court does not inadvertently adopt a later Commentary and give it the same weight as the existing Commentary. Additionally, there is no assurance that the foreign court has decided the matter correctly or has given the provision a correct interpretation (Ward, in Maisto (ed.), *Courts*, 161). Summing up, the relevance of a foreign court decision depends on how convincing its reasoning is. **115**

Example **116**

The Supreme Administrative Court of Luxembourg had to decide whether an income of Luxembourg resident partners from their activities in a German partnership could be classified as business income under Art. 5 (Income from a commercial enterprise) of the Germany-Luxembourg Double Tax Treaty (1958). The treaty does not define the term "profits from a commercial enterprise". Therefore, according to Art. 2 of the treaty, the Court referred to its domestic law to interpret the term. From a Luxembourgish perspective, the enterprise had carried on a "deemed commercial activity". Therefore, the main issue was whether a deemed commercial activity is covered by the scope of Art. 5(1) of the treaty. In this respect, the Court referred to the German case law on the issue (Bundesfinanzhof of 28 April 2010, I R 81/09, BFHE 229, 252). The case referred stipulated that "deemed commercial income" was not covered by the definition of business profits under the Germany-US double tax treaty. The Court followed the approach of the German Court considering that the German and Luxembourg legislation on direct taxes has a common historical origin and parallelism of the fundamental concepts (The Supreme Administrative Court of Luxembourg of 8 February 2018, 39274C).

4.3. The importance of interpretation rules set out in DTCs

4.3.1. Art. 3(2) OECD Model

The OECD Model contains a **separate interpretation rule** in Art. 3(2), which reads as follows: "As regards the application of the Convention at any time by a Contracting State, any term not defined therein shall, unless the context otherwise requires or the competent authorities agree to a different meaning pursuant to the provisions of Article 25, have the meaning that it has at that time under the law of that State for the purposes of the taxes to which the Convention applies, any meaning under the applicable tax laws of that State prevailing over a meaning given to the term under other laws of that State." **117**

The content of Art. 3(2) OECD Model is highly controversial and has been discussed extensively in international tax literature (cf. Engelen, *Interpretation*, 474, with further references). One could claim that, pursuant to Art. 3(2), **domestic law is decisive**. This interpretation, however, overlooks the fact that according to the wording of Art. 3(2) OECD Model, the domestic law of the contracting states is decisive "unless the context otherwise requires". The concept of "context" there- **118** fore is determinant. Its meaning, like the meaning of Art. 3(2) OECD Model in its entirety, needs to be determined according to international law principles of interpretation. Consequently, if the object and purpose of a DTC, which are primarily decisive under Art. 31(1) VCLT, are taken into account, this leads to a broad understanding of the concept of "context" in Art. 3(2) OECD Model. DTCs can only fulfil their purpose, i.e. the allocation of taxing rights, if the tax authorities of both contracting states understand terms in the same way. Falling back to the domestic law of the respective contracting state would conflict with this purpose. Thus, the reference to domestic law contained in Art. 3(2) OECD Model should be understood as restrictively as possible and the concept of "context" in Art. 3(2) OECD Model should be interpreted widely. Namely, the concept of "context" should comprise all of the interpretation materials set out in Art. 31 et seq. VCLT. Historical arguments support this view. The reference to domestic law in Art. 3(2) OECD Model is therefore only important if the application of all possible interpretation methods does not lead to a satisfying solution. However, if all systematic, teleological and historical aspects are taken into account for the interpretation, this will be very rare.

119 **Example**

In 2013 the High Court of Andhra Pradesh, Hyderabad had to decide the case "Groupe Industrial Marcel Dassault and Sanofi Pasteur Holdings SA v. The Department of Revenue" on the interpretation of Art. 14(5) and (6) of the DTC between India and France (the said article is the equivalent of Art. 13(5) OECD Model). In the given case, the taxpayers sought an advance ruling from the tax authorities to confirm that any capital gains from the sale of their shareholding in the French holding company were not taxable in India under Art. 14 of the treaty. The Indian tax authorities made reference to Art. 3(2) of the treaty to contend that since the terms "alienation" and "participation" in Art. 14(5) of the DTC between India and France were not defined in the treaty, they had to be understood by reference to the meaning of the term "transfer" as defined in the Indian Income Tax Act. Based on that, the Indian tax authorities claimed, the gains from the transfer of the shares of the French holding company had to be taxable in India. The High Court of Andhra Pradesh, Hyderabad, however, rejected that proposition and pointed out that the treaty did not contain any textual, grammatical or syntactic ambiguity warranting an interpretive recourse to national law, meaning that recourse to Art. 3(2) would violate the principle of good faith interpretation. Eventually, the High Court of Andhra Pradesh, Hyderabad decided that the capital gains from the transfer of shares of the French holding company were not taxable in India under Art. 14(5) of the treaty.

120 A group of authors coordinated by Avery Jones advanced the view that the treaty is only applied in the source state and, consequently, the reference to domestic law of the "user state" contained in Art. 3(2) OECD Model leads to the situation that the residence state is bound by the qualification of the source state (Avery Jones et al., *BTR* 1984, 48 et seq.). The idea behind this approach is to ensure a common understanding of treaty terms in both states by referring to only one of the two states. This interpretation, however, has not been generally accepted

because the residence state not only "reads" but also applies the DTC. In order to be able to determine the legal consequences resulting from the method article, the residence state must also apply an allocation rule (cf. in detail and convincingly Vogel, *DTC* Art. 3, m.no. 67 et seq.).

For all these reasons the phrase "unless the context otherwise requires" bears a lot of weight. Under Art. 3(2) OECD Model the reference to domestic law only has relevance if it is not possible to arrive at conclusions from the treaty context. Since all the aspects mentioned in Art. 31 et seq. VCLT can be taken into account, it is highly unlikely that one has to go back to domestic law. Since 2017 Art. 3(2) OECD Model requires that in case the autonomous treaty interpretation does not lead anywhere, mutual agreements have to be taken into account before domestic law comes into play (see Lang, Otto Schmidt 2019). **121**

In my view, Art. 3(2) OECD Model merely emphasizes what is valid according to the interpretation principles of international law: a solution should first be sought on the basis of the systematic, objective and historical development of the treaty, and only when this fails can one refer to domestic law. Art. 3(2) OECD Model merely confirms that treaty provisions should be interpreted in the context of the treaty. The rule is therefore dispensable. If it were simply abolished, nothing would change. Given its controversial content, some writers have proposed either to fundamentally revise it or to remove it from the OECD Model (Vogel/Prokisch, in IFA (ed.), *Interpretation*, 84). **122**

Given the opinion represented here, it is not important whether the reference to domestic law is to be understood **dynamically or statically**. Since the 1995 update of the OECD Model, Art. 3(2) OECD Model explicitly states that the reference to domestic law is to be understood dynamically. This means that the legal situation existing at the time of the application of the DTC must be taken into account. However, prior to the change in 1995, systematic arguments did not support an understanding of the references to domestic law as a static reference. Thus, even before 1995, the prevailing opinion was not to refer to domestic law of the point in time of conclusion of the treaty. **123**

Example **124**

A Spanish resident company paid royalties to various US resident companies for the right to use computer software combined with the provision of technical assistance. Under the treaty signed in 1990 between Spain and the United States, royalties may be taxed in the source state. However, the maximum tax rate depends on the type of royalty. Under Art. 12(2) Spain–US DTC, royalties paid for the use of copyright of literary work may be taxed at source at a rate of 5%, royalties paid for the use of copyright of scientific work may be taxed at a rate of 8% and royalties paid in any other case may be taxed at a rate of 10%. The 1990 Spain–US DTC includes a provision patterned after Art. 3(2) OECD Model. In a decision rendered on 17 Apr. 2008 (ES, TEAC, 17 Apr. 2008, 3604/2006), the Spanish Tribunal Económico-Administrativo Central concluded that royalties for the right to use computer software combined with the provision of technical assistance do not correspond to royalties for the use of copyright of literary or scientific work and therefore may be taxed in Spain at a rate of 10%. The court based its decision on Art. 3(2) of the 1990 Spain–US DTC and made reference to the definition of royalty adopted in Spanish domestic law in 2002. Noticeably, the court accepted that the reference to domestic law under Art. 3(2) of a treaty concluded prior to the 1995 update of the OECD Model was dynamic.

4.3.2. The binding qualification of the source state according to Art. 23(1) OECD Model

125 The OECD made another attempt to ensure a common understanding of treaty terms. The OECD assumed, contrary to the position taken here, that states often have to use their own domestic law in order to interpret terms of their DTCs. However, these conflicts can be resolved if the residence state accepts the **qualification by the source state**. The new idea was to consider as a legal basis for this the DTC provisions patterned after Art. 23(1) OECD Model. This measure provides that the residence state shall either exempt the income or credit the foreign taxes paid on the income, where such income "may be taxed in the other Contracting State" in accordance with the provisions of the convention. This opinion was advanced by Déry/Ward (in IFA (ed.), *Interpretation*, 259 et seq.), then developed by the group of authors coordinated by Avery Jones (*ET* 1996, 125 et seq.) and by the OECD Partnership Report (1999) and eventually included in the OECD Commentary in 2000 (OECD Commentary on Art. 23, para. 32.1 et seq.).

126 **Opposing arguments** have been made in relation to this interpretation of Art. 23(1) OECD Model. In the first place, the wording of Art. 23(1) OECD Model does not imply that the determination of whether "income ... may be taxed in the other Contracting State ... in accordance with the provisions of this Convention" is to be made exclusively from the source state's point of view. Rather, Art. 23 OECD Model focuses on the residence state, such that the persons applying the DTC in the residence state must establish whether the income may be taxed "in accordance with the provisions of this Convention" in the other contracting state, irrespective of the domestic legal situation in that state. This is, for example, the advantage of the exemption method, "since it relieves the State of residence from undertaking investigations of the actual taxation position in the other State" (OECD Commentary on Art. 23, para. 34). This advantage would not exist if the persons applying the DTC in the residence state had to take into account the domestic legal situation in the source state in order to recognize the right to the exemption. In addition, the exceptions to the characterization of the source state occasionally contained in the allocation rules (e.g. Art. 6(2) and Art. 10(3) OECD Model) would become superfluous if Art. 23(1) OECD Model would lead in every case to the reference to the characterization of the source state. Finally, the exemption by the residence state does not always result from Art. 23 OECD

Model but occasionally from the allocation rule itself, as Art. 19 OECD Model demonstrates.

However, the OECD Commentary on Art. 23 assumes the binding effect of the characterization of the source state **only when it originates in its domestic law** (OECD Commentary on Art. 23, para. 32.3; cf. also para. 32.5). It would therefore be necessary to distinguish between those cases in which the source state wins the characterization under the context of the treaty and those cases in which the source state is required to refer to domestic law definitions. Only in the latter should the source state's characterization have a binding effect. However, this presupposes that the demarcation between the two groups of cases is clear. In practice, the situation is the reverse. The question of whether the context of the treaty requires a certain result or not can be raised in every case. The issues that arise as regards Art. 3(2) OECD Model would then play a role in the interpretation of Art. 23(1). 127

Example 128

In LU: CA 23 Apr. 2002, case 14442, the Cour Administrative had to determine which allocation rule, of those contained in the France–Luxembourg DTC, was applicable. Under the facts, a Luxembourg resident company owned real estate in France and had applied, to the income deriving therefrom, Art. 3 (immovable property) of the France–Luxembourg DTC, which granted exclusive taxing rights to France. The company did not, therefore, pay tax to Luxembourg on this income. Moreover, the company did not pay any tax to France because according to Conseil d'État jurisprudence, based on the interpretation of the treaty itself and not on French domestic law, income derived from immovable property owned by a company is covered by Art. 4 of the France–Luxembourg DTC on business profits. In this case, Art. 4 Luxembourg–France DTC attributed exclusive taxing rights to Luxembourg since the Luxembourg resident company did not have a PE in France. Confirming the decision of the lower court, the Cour Administrative held that the characterization of the income by the source state (France) was not binding on Luxembourg, not even if double non-taxation would arise. Noticeably, the characterization given by the French Conseil d'État was not based on French domestic tax law but rather on the interpretation of the treaty.

The interpretation proposed by the OECD Commentary on Art. 23 would mean that **conflicts of qualification are resolved at the expense of the residence state**. This can be understood by the tax authorities of the source state as an invitation to extend taxing rights. However, the tax authorities of the residence state would fight against such attempts of the tax authorities of the source state through the characterization under domestic law in the interpretation of the DTC. In order to avoid the expansion of the taxing rights of the source state at the expense of the residence state, the latter will try, if needed, to reject the argument of the binding effect of the characterization of the source state if it procures taxing rights. Thus, if the interpretation proposed by the OECD Commentary with respect to Art. 23(1) was followed in practice, conflicts of qualification and the double taxation arising from them would not only remain but could even increase. 129

130 **Example**

A Belgian professor holds a 2-day lecture as guest professor at an Austrian public university. According to Sec. 25(1)(5) of the Austrian Income Tax Act, the income that the scientist derives from this activity is income from employment. Referring to Art. 3(2) of the Austria–Belgium DTC, the Austrian tax authorities use this characterization on the treaty level and apply Art. 19 of the treaty (cf. Hofbauer, in Lang (ed.), Interpretation, 32). Consequently, the Austrian tax authorities believe that the income is taxable in Austria and expect the Belgian authorities to follow this characterization. However, it will be difficult to explain to the Belgian authorities that a 2-day lecture held in Austria should constitute employment in terms of the DTC and it is unlikely that they will understand the Austrian legal situation. Since Belgium would lose its right to tax if it followed the Austrian domestic characterization, the Belgian tax authorities may prefer to characterize the income based on the tax treaty only, pursuant to which they will apply Art. 14 of the DTC, as opposed to Art. 15 or 19. If Austria is not obliged to interpret the DTC according to Austrian law, the OECD Commentary provides that Belgium is not bound by the characterization of the source state. In this way Belgium would, due to the lack of a fixed base in Austria, secure its taxing right. This would result in double taxation (cf. Gassner/Lang, in: Vanistendael (ed.), Liber amicorum Hinnekens, 219 et seq.).

131 It is doubtful, whether the **interpretation of DTCs** should be based on the view stated in the OECD Commentary on Art. 23 that the residence state is legally bound in certain cases by the qualification of the source state. According to the opinion represented here (cf. m.no. 90 et seq.), this view can only be taken into consideration with respect to those DTCs that were negotiated and completed after the publication of the 2000 OECD Model and the Commentary. In addition, for the interpretation of these DTCs, the OECD Commentary is not the single means of interpretation. Remarkable systematic and teleological arguments counter the opinion set out in the Commentary on Art. 23 (cf. m.no. 118). In addition, the OECD Commentary itself does not clearly express which situations are covered by the binding effect of the characterization of the source state (cf. m.no. 126). For all these reasons, it follows that the binding effect of the characterization of the source state on the residence state cannot be relevant for the interpretation of even the more recent DTCs.

132 The interpretation of Art. 23(1) OECD Model proposed by the OECD Commentary also addresses the purpose of **avoiding double non-taxation** through the uniform application of the DTC definitions in both contracting states, to the extent that the conflict is due to differences in the domestic law between the source state and the residence state (OECD Commentary on Art. 23, para. 32.6 read in the light of para. 32.3).

133 In line with the purpose of avoiding cases of double non-taxation, a new **paragraph 4** was included in Art. 23A OECD Model in 2000. According to this new provision, the exemption shall not be granted by the residence state where the other contracting state applies the provisions of the convention to exempt income (or capital) from tax or applies the provisions of para. 2 of Art. 10 or Art. 11

OECD Model. The rule in Art. 23(4) OECD Model gives the residence state the right to switch from the exemption to the credit method when the interpretation of facts or of the provisions of the DTC leads the source state to exempt or to impose nominal taxes (because it applies Art. 10(2) or Art. 11(2) OECD Model) on a certain item of income.

4.3.3. The relevance of later commentaries

Some recent DTCs contain a **specific interpretation rule** which establishes that later commentaries are to be taken into account. In one of the DTCs recently concluded by the Netherlands, for example, this rule reads as follows: "It is understood that the provisions of the Convention which are the same or substantially the same as the corresponding provisions of the OECD Model Tax Convention on Income and on Capital, shall be interpreted according to the OECD Commentary on these provisions at the moment of signing the Convention and to subsequent clarifying modifications of the OECD Commentary on these provisions" (Protocol to the Bahrain–Netherlands DTC, para. A.1.). This provision results from the Netherlands' treaty policy according to which tax treaties have to be interpreted in a dynamic way (cf. De Bont, in Lang (ed.), *Interpretation*, 246 et seq.). In the DTCs recently signed by Belgium, a slightly different rule can usually be found: "In the interpretation of the provisions of the Agreement which are identical or in substance similar to the provisions of the OECD Model Tax Convention, the tax administrations of the Contracting States shall follow the general principles of the commentary of the Model Convention provided the Contracting States did not include in that commentary any observations expressing a disagreement with those principles and to the extent the Contracting States do not agree on a divergent interpretation in special circumstances" (para. 2 of the Protocol to the Belgium–Tajikistan DTC; para. 1 of the Protocol to the Belgium– Moldova DTC; similar also para. 8 of the Protocol to the Belgium–Isle of Man DTC). 134

Some recent **Austrian tax treaties** also include a specific interpretation rule, which usually reads as follows: "It is understood that provisions of the Convention which are drafted according to the corresponding provisions of the OECD Model Convention on Income and on Capital shall generally be expected to have the same meaning as expressed in the OECD Commentary thereon. The OECD Commentary as it may be revised from time to time – constitutes a tool of interpretation in the sense of the Vienna Convention of 23 May 1969 on the Law of Treaties" (cf. e.g. para. 6 of the Protocol to the Austria–Bulgaria DTC 2009; para. 1 of the Protocol to the Austria–Bosnia and Herzegovina DTC 2008; para. 5 of the Protocol to the Albania–Austria DTC 2007). 135

The meaning of this rule is unclear. It is unquestionably intended to **ensure that the OECD Commentary is taken into account** but it is not clear whether it pro- 136 vides the required authority to always refer to the latest version of the OECD Commentary (e.g. this is what the Austrian tax authorities held, cf. Loukota, *SWI* 1995, 450 et seq.). In fact, its wording is not clear since it does not specify the version of the Commentary to which a reference should be made. A clear conclusion cannot even be derived from the provision which reads that the OECD Commentary – as it may be revised from time to time – constitutes a means of interpretation in the sense of the VCLT. This phrase can be read as merely a description that the Commentary may be revised from time to time without saying which version should be taken into account.

5. Treaty abuse

5.1. Denial of treaty benefits

Great controversy exists among tax scholars with respect to whether tax authorities may prevent the **improper use of DTCs**. The discussion focuses, on the one hand, on what constitutes abuse and is thus undesirable and, on the other, on the rules empowering tax authorities not to grant treaty benefits. In 2017, a new title, preamble and Art. 29 on the entitlement to treaty benefits were added to the OECD Model in order to emphasize that the object and purpose of the OECD Model is not only to prevent double taxation, but also to prevent tax evasion and tax avoidance. 137

5.2. The application of domestic anti-abuse principles?

In most countries, taxes cannot be avoided or reduced through abuse. **Domestic tax laws** contain provisions or principles pursuant to which transactions are disregarded or recharacterized if they are abusive. Often, an abuse exists when the arrangement or transaction is artificial or uncommon and it was entered into for the main or one of the main purposes of obtaining a tax benefit. 138

The courts of some countries apply the principle of "**substance over form**" to disregard the legal form of a transaction in favour of its true economic substance (e.g. in the US). In several civil law countries a general prohibition against the abuse of law ("fraus legis") exists (e.g. in France and the Netherlands). Finally, many countries have enacted a general anti-avoidance rule (GAAR), which permits the recharacterization of transactions designed to circumvent the tax laws in order to achieve a tax benefit. 139

Domestic anti-abuse legislation does **not**, in my opinion, apply to **deny treaty benefits**. DTC law and domestic law are, for the purposes of interpretation, separate legal systems. When domestic anti-abuse rules apply to extend the taxable basis, the treaty protection still exists. DTCs set out the situations in which the domestic right to tax is reduced, eliminated or maintained. This function would be lost if it were to be interpreted by reference to domestic anti-abuse rules. Consequently, domestic anti-abuse rules may not be applied to DTCs. This conclusion is affirmed by the consequences that would arise if these rules were applied to DTCs. If the tax authorities of each contracting state interpreted a provision of a DTC in the light of its own domestic anti-abuse rules, it would lead to two different interpretations of the provision because anti-abuse rules differ from country to country. This is not in line with the object and purpose of DTCs. Thus, in addition to the above systematic arguments, teleological reasons oppose the application of domestic anti-abuse rules to DTCs. 140

141 **Example**

The taxpayer was a company resident in the Netherlands, whose shares were owned by an individual resident in Belgium. The individual also held shares in a second company, C NV, which was also resident in the Netherlands. If the taxpayer were to have distributed dividends to the individual, Dutch withholding tax of 25% would have applied. This rate would be reduced to 15% under Art. 10 of the Belgium–Netherlands DTC. The individual instead sold the shares of the taxpayer to C NV in return for cash and the assumption by C NV of a debt owed by the individual to the taxpayer. The taxpayer then distributed the dividends to C NV. Dutch withholding tax did not apply since both companies were residents of the Netherlands. C NV then paid off the debt to the taxpayer. The tax authorities were of the view that the sale of the shares in combination with the dividend distribution and payment of the debt were carried out in order to avoid the Dutch withholding tax on dividends. They relied on the abuse of law doctrine to recharacterize the dividend distribution to C NV as a dividend distribution to the Belgian resident and imposed a 15% withholding tax on this distribution. However, the Supreme Court of the Netherlands allowed the taxpayer's appeal. It acknowledged that Art. 10 of the Belgium–Netherlands DTC allows the Netherlands to levy dividend withholding tax on dividends distributed by a Dutch company to a resident of Belgium, but stated that there was nothing in the DTC that allowed a dividend distribution by a Dutch resident to another Dutch resident to be recharacterized as a dividend distribution by a Dutch resident to a Belgian resident. Art. 10 of the Belgium–Netherlands DTC therefore did not permit the dividend to be taxed as though it had been paid to a Belgian resident (NL, HR 6 Dec. 2002, Case 36.773).

5.3. The application of abuse rules of international law?

142 DTCs are part of the domestic law of the contracting states. They are also part of international law as international law treaties (cf. m.no. 20). Scholars have tried to determine the extent to which the denial of treaty benefits in "abuse cases" can be supported by principles of international law. Vogel (*StuW* 1985, 376) came to the conclusion that **international law contains a prohibition** against abuse of law. Namely, the principle of good faith in relationships between states prevents a contracting state from interpreting law unfairly in its favour. In addition, most states recognize the possibility of considering the "substance" over the "form", if the result would otherwise be contrary to principles of justice. The principle of good faith is binding on states and consequently can be relied upon by the citizens. Therefore, treaty benefits can be denied in cases of abuse.

143 Many national legal systems also prohibit abuse of law in **different forms**. They usually rely on specific anti-abuse rules, from which, however, a **general prohibition against abuse of law** cannot be derived. The policy considerations underlying those specific anti-abuse rules are unequivocally subordinate to international law and in particular to international law treaties. Therefore, in order to restrict tax treaty law, the specific anti-abuse rules would have to be at least on the same level as international law treaties.

When a general principle of abuse of law exists in a national legal system, it cannot restrict tax treaty law as well. General principles of law are norms of international law on international law subjects. According to international law scholars, human beings can be international law subjects only in exceptions. In the area of DTCs, however, human beings are not international law subjects. Therefore, a general principle of law **cannot be binding on taxable persons** (cf. Gassner/Lang, in Gassner/Lang/Lechner (eds.), *Entwicklungen*, 58). Thus, international law does not provide a legal basis to apply anti-abuse domestic rules in the treaty context. 144

5.4. Art. 29(9) OECD Model – The Principal Purpose Test

In 2017, a general anti-abuse rule was introduced in Art. 29(9) OECD Model. 145
The provision is generally known as the principal purpose test and provides that a treaty benefit will not be granted if it is reasonable to conclude that obtaining that benefit was one of the principal purposes of any arrangement or transaction. The essential requirement for the application of the provision is the presence of a subjective element: obtaining a treaty benefit must be one of the main purposes of the taxpayer. The problem with this requirement is that it is impossible to prove the intentions of a taxpayer with certainty. Of course, indications on the intention of a taxpayer can be derived from an analysis of objective facts, yet this remains only an approximation of the true intentions of the taxpayer. Therefore, Art. 29(9) OECD Model does not require that the tax authorities deliver full proof for the provision to apply, but it is sufficient that it is reasonable to conclude that one of the main objectives of the taxpayer was obtaining a treaty benefit.

Besides a subjective element, Art. 29(9) OECD Model contains an objective ele- 146
ment for the provision to apply that is formulated as an exception: even if the subjective requirement is fulfilled, treaty benefits will not be denied if it can be established that granting the benefit would be in accordance with the object and purpose of the relevant treaty provision. It is of no relevance for the interpretation of Art. 29(9) OECD Model that the objective element is formulated as an exception, because whether a certain element of a provision is formulated as an exception or an additional requirement solely depends on the legal drafting technique used. Where for the subjective element the wording "reasonable to conclude" is used, for the objective element to be fulfilled it must "be established", which is generally considered as a higher threshold. The objective element puts the emphasis on the object and purpose of the relevant provisions. This is a mere confirmation of the current status of legal methodology according to which the object and purpose of a provision must always be taken into account for its interpretation. Art. 31 VCLT confirms the importance of the object and purpose in the interpretation process with respect to international law treaties.

147 Against this backdrop, it can be concluded that Art. 29(9) OECD Model has merely a "signalling function" (see in detail Lang, Bulletin 2020, (Volume 74), No. 4/5, pp. 264–268). The provision reminds us that the interpretation of DTCs does not end with the letter of the law, but requires to take into account the object and purpose of each provision. This is particularly important if one of the main purposes of the taxpayer is to obtain a benefit. Therefore, Art. 29(9) emphasizes this situation. However, this does not mean that in other situations the object and purpose of the provision is not relevant. The legal effect of Art. 29(9) is therefore small. The provision merely provides us guidance for the interpretation of other provisions but should not be read as an exception to those other provisions or as a separate legal basis for not granting tax treaty benefits.

148 Not all DTCs contain a provision based on Art. 29(9) OECD Model. The OECD Commentary holds that also with respect to those DTCs where the benefits of the DTC do not have to be granted if the main purpose of a transaction or arrangement was to secure a tax benefit and obtaining that benefit would be against the object and purpose of the relevant treaty provisions. As explained in the previous paragraphs, the relevance of this statement is limited, and the improper use of a DTC is exclusively a matter of interpretation.

6. The structure and system of DTCs

6.1. Applying the convention

The structures and systems of **all DTCs show similarities**. Tax treaties usually contain rules relating to the personal and substantive scope. The allocation of taxing rights over the persons and taxes covered is dealt with in one of the allocation rules. The avoidance of double taxation is almost always dealt with in the method article. Other provisions supplement the treaties. 149

Insofar as the treaty follows the OECD Model, the **personal scope** of a DTC is established by Art. 1 and Art. 4 (cf. m.no. 177 et seq.). Under Art. 1 OECD Model, the convention is applicable to persons who are residents of one or both contracting states. According to Art. 3(1) OECD Model, a person includes an individual, a company and any other body of persons. However, a PE is not regarded as being a person. Under Art. 4(1) OECD Model, any person who, under the laws of that state, is liable to tax therein by reason of his domicile, residence, place of management or any other criterion of a similar nature, is considered a "resident of a Contracting State". Persons who are liable to tax in that state in respect only of income from sources in that state or capital situated therein are not considered "residents of a Contracting State". It is inferred from this article that in case of worldwide tax liability in one of the two states a DTC is in any event applicable. 150

The **substantive scope** is established by Art. 2 (cf. m.no. 220 et seq.). Art. 2(1) OECD Model states that the convention shall apply to taxes on income and on capital imposed on behalf of a contracting state or of its political subdivisions or local authorities, irrespective of the manner in which they are levied. Usually, Art. 2 also lists the taxes in force at the time the treaty is concluded, which fall into the substantive scope of the treaty, and establishes that the convention is applicable to any identical or substantially similar taxes that are imposed after the date of signature of the convention in addition to, or in place of, the existing taxes. 151

If the convention is applicable to both the person and the taxes, the **allocation rules** must be applied (cf. m.no. 229 et seq.). With respect to the taxation of income, the allocation rules can be found in Art. 6 to Art. 21 OECD Model (with the exception of Art. 9). With respect to the taxation of capital, the allocation rules are set out in Art. 22 OECD Model. The legal consequences of the allocation rules differ: some allocation rules reduce source taxation; others entirely remove the taxing rights of the source state. The restriction of taxing rights of the residence state is not generally found in an allocation rule but rather in the method article. 152

The **method article** (Art. 23 OECD Model) contained in DTCs provides the manner in which double taxation will be eliminated (cf. m.no. 397 et seq.): either the 153 exemption method or the credit method will be applied. The exemption method interferes with the taxable base, so that certain income or assets become tax exempt. The credit method obliges the residence state to credit the taxes levied by the source state in accordance with the allocation rules.

6.2. Persons covered

154 DTC provisions that reproduce Art. 1, Art. 3 and Art. 4 OECD Model cause the DTC to be applicable if **worldwide tax liability** exists in at least one of the two states or if a person meets there the requirements which typically could lead to worldwide tax liability. Consequently, the law of the contracting states has to be taken into account in this respect. In the case of worldwide tax liability in one of the two states, the other contracting state is obliged to apply the DTC.

155 On individuals DTCs are applicable even if worldwide tax liability exists in both states. In this case, a choice between the two contracting states must be made in order to determine the residence state for tax treaty purposes, since the functioning of the allocation rules and the method article requires that there **is only one residence state**. The criteria under which the residence state is established are found in Art. 4(2) OECD Model (cf. m.no. 204 et seq.). Permanent home, centre of vital interests, habitual abode and nationality arise in sequence. However, as far as persons other than individuals are concerned, treaty entitlement in cases of dual residence is not automatically granted. It depends on the existence of a mutual agreement (cf. m.no. 217 et seq.).

156 The determination of the residence state is **for treaty purposes only**. The residence in just one of the two states does not automatically mean that in the other state taxes are levied under the limited tax liability rules. Domestic full tax liability rules of the source state may remain applicable. The amount of tax might still be determined according to the residence taxation rules and not according to non-residence taxation rules.

157 The DTC signed between two states, however, is not applicable in cases of **limited tax liability in both states**. In these cases, a taxable person can only rely on DTCs potentially existing between the states in which he/she/it is subject to limited taxation and the state where he/she/it is subject to full tax liability. If such DTCs do not exist, double taxation can only be avoided by unilateral measures.

158 **Example**

An individual is resident in Switzerland. She receives dividends from a corporation incorporated in France with its place of effective management in the Netherlands. Both France and the Netherlands tax the dividends paid to the individual. However, the France-Netherlands DTC does not apply since the individual is subject only to limited tax liability in both states. Double taxation can only be avoided by the application of the France-Switzerland DTC and the Netherlands-Switzerland DTC.

6.3. Taxes covered

Pursuant to DTC provisions that reproduce Art. 2(1) OECD Model, the treaty is applicable with respect to **taxes on income** imposed on behalf of a contracting state or its political subdivisions or local authorities. The manner in which they are levied is irrelevant. In general, taxes imposed on total income or on elements of income are covered. In addition, Art. 2 OECD Model sets out a list of the taxes in force at the time the treaty was concluded to which the DTC shall apply. An adjustment clause usually supplements this provision. Pursuant to this clause, the OECD Model is also applicable to any identical or substantially similar taxes that are imposed after the date of signature of the convention in addition to, or in place of, the existing taxes. 159

Pursuant to DTC provisions patterned after Art. 2 OECD Model, the treaty is also applicable to **taxes on capital** imposed on behalf of a contracting state or its political subdivisions or local authorities. As with taxes on income, the manner in which taxes on capital are levied is irrelevant. In general, taxes imposed on total capital or on elements of capital are covered. When taxes on capital are included in the substantive scope of a DTC, the treaty can still have an impact when those taxes have been abolished in the domestic law of one of the contracting states: as long as the other contracting state keeps levying taxes on capital, the treaty benefits are available to taxable persons despite the fact that the former state has waived levying taxes of that kind. 160

6.4. Allocation rules

The allocation rules of DTCs (patterned after Arts. 6 to 8 and 10 to 21 OECD Model for taxes on income and Art. 22 OECD Model for taxes on capital) shall apply only if the personal and substantive scope of the treaty are fulfilled. Thus, the personal and substantive scope must first be examined. In most cases, the allocation rules do **not ensure that double taxation is avoided**. The limitation of the taxing rights of the residence state is provided for in the method article. 161

Example 162

Pursuant to Art. 7(1) of the Italy–Spain DTC, business profits of an enterprise of a contracting state are taxable in the other contracting state if the enterprise carries on business in that other state through a PE. If the enterprise carries on business as aforesaid, the profits of the enterprise may be taxed in the other state but only so much of them as is attributable to that PE. The profits that an Italian company makes through its PE in Spain can therefore be taxed in Spain. This does not mean, however, that Italy cannot tax these business profits. Art. 7(1) does not address Italy's right to tax. The method article (Art. 22 Italy–Spain DTC) does not deprive Italy of its right to tax but rather provides that Italy will credit the tax paid to Spain on the business profits.

The allocation rules impose **limitations on the taxing rights of the source state**. 163
This is frequently the case with dividends, interest and royalties. The allocation

rules often state that the source state's tax cannot exceed a certain rate. The avoidance of the remaining double taxation is dealt with in the method article.

164 **Example**

Under Art. 10(1) of the Australia–Japan DTC, dividends paid by a company that is a resident of a contracting state to a resident of the other contracting state may be taxed in that other contracting state. Australia may therefore tax dividends received by an Australian resident from a Japanese company. Japan's taxing right is not restricted by this provision. Art. 10(2) Australia–Japan DTC provides that the dividends may also be taxed in the contracting state of which the company paying the dividends is a resident but the tax cannot exceed 10% of the gross amount of the dividends. Thus, Japan's right to tax is restricted to 10%. The double taxation of this 10% is avoided through the method article (Art. 25 Australia–Japan DTC), which provides that Australia will give a credit for the tax paid to Japan.

165 In some cases, however, the allocation rule **excludes the taxing rights** of one of the two states entirely. This is usually the case when the allocation rules state that certain income "shall be taxable only" in the other state. In this case, the former state no longer has any taxing rights.

166 **Example**

Pursuant to Art. 7 of the Belarus–Denmark DTC (royalty article), royalties arising in a contracting state and paid to a resident of the other contracting state shall be taxable only in that other state. Thus, royalties arising in Denmark and paid to a resident of Belarus can only be taxed in Belarus.

167 All items of income are to be assigned to one single allocation rule. In cases in which none of the allocation rules established in Art. 6 to Art. 8 and Art. 10 to Art. 20 OECD Model apply, the **blanket clause** in Art. 21 (1) OECD Model (other income) is applicable: all items of income not dealt with in the foregoing articles of the DTC are covered by this clause. Art. 22(4) OECD Model regarding taxes on capital has a similar function. Nearly all DTCs include such other income provisions as foreseen by the OECD Model.

168 Some allocation rules require a cross-border situation between the two contracting states: the allocation rule is only applicable if the person receiving the income or owning the capital resides in one contracting state and the source of income or capital is located in the other contracting state. However, other allocation rules only require the residence of the taxpayer in one of the contracting states and are applicable irrespective of where the source of income or capital is located.

169 **Example**

Dividends are covered by Art. 10 OECD Model. The provision applies only to dividends arising in a contracting state and paid to an individual resident in the other contracting state. Thus, dividends received by a resident of Belgium from a company resident in Belgium or in a third country are not covered by Art. 10 OECD Model. In such a case, Art. 21(1) OECD Model applies. This rule gives the exclusive right to tax to the residence state and prevents the other contracting state from levying a tax on these dividends.

Example 170

The allocation rule for business profits in Art. 7 OECD Model does not require the existence of a PE in the other contracting state in order to apply. If a German company serves the Dutch market remotely without establishing a PE in the Netherlands, it still obtains business profits conducted in the Netherlands. According to Art. 7(1) of the Germany–Netherlands DTC, those profits are taxable only in Germany. In this case, the source taxing right of the Netherlands in the second half of Art. 7(1) is not applicable due to the lack of a PE.

Each item of income or element of capital can **only be covered by one** allocation rule, not by several. The application of the method article presupposes that only one allocation rule is applicable. Should two or more allocation rules receive consideration, it is essential to clarify through interpretation which allocation rule is to be applied. In some cases the allocation rules contain express priority provisions. If this is the case, these treaty provisions state which allocation rule is to be given priority in the conflict. 171

Example 172

A Dutch company receives dividends from Iceland. Under Art. 7 of the Iceland–Netherlands DTC, the profits of the Dutch company cannot be taxed by Iceland unless the Dutch company has a PE in Iceland. Dividends, however, are covered by Art. 10. Art. 7(7) of the applicable treaty provides that where profits include items of income which are dealt with separately in other articles, the provisions of those articles shall not be affected by the provisions of Art. 7. Thus, Art. 7 provides that Art. 10 Iceland–Netherlands DTC is to be given priority and Iceland will be entitled to levy source taxation on the dividends.

6.5. Methods for elimination of double taxation

Generally, in the allocation rules, the taxing rights of one of the two contracting states are partially restricted. Therefore, the manner in which double taxation is avoided is set out in the method article. In continental Europe, the **exemption method** is often adopted: the residence state excludes from the taxable base the income derived or the capital owned in the other state. In this case, the taxing rights lie only with the source state. The residence state may nevertheless take the exempt income or capital into account in calculating the amount of tax on the remaining income or capital of the taxable person. This proviso safeguarding progression ensures the mitigation of the advantages that are created through the allocation of income to different states and the corresponding classification of income into low-tax brackets in both states. 173

Example 174

A Belgian entrepreneur has a place of business in Brussels and another in Amsterdam. In each place of business, he earns business profits of EUR 30,000. Pursuant to Art. 7(1) of the Belgium-Netherlands DTC, the business profits earned in Amsterdam may be taxed by the Netherlands. Art. 23(1) of that DTC precludes Belgium's right to tax these profits, but the DTC also allows these profits to be taken into account in determining the tax due on the remaining income. Consequently, only the income of EUR 30,000 in Belgium is subject to tax in this state but the applicable rate of tax is the one that would be applied to income of EUR 60,000.

175 The second method is the **credit method**. It is especially common for countries like the US, most Asian or African countries and countries belonging to the Commonwealth. It is also adopted in almost all DTCs to avoid double taxation on dividends and interest and, in some DTCs, to avoid double taxation on royalties. Under the credit method, the taxable base in the residence state remains unchanged. In other words, the foreign income is still included in the domestic taxable base. However, the taxes levied in the source state are credited on the taxes levied in the residence state.

176 **Example**

A Maltese corporation receives dividends of EUR 10,000 from a 5% holding in an Irish corporation. Pursuant to Art. 10(1) Ireland–Malta DTC, Malta may tax these dividends. Under Art. 10(2), Ireland may also tax the dividends to a maximum of 15%. Under Art. 22(2), Malta will give a credit for Irish tax at source. In Malta, the EUR 10,000 are subject to corporate tax of 35%, and tax of EUR 3,500 is payable. The Irish tax at source amounts to EUR 1,500, which is credited on the Maltese tax due so that it amounts to EUR 2,000.

7. Persons covered

7.1. Full tax liability as a prerequisite for the application of the DTCs

7.1.1. Full tax liability

Pursuant to treaty provisions patterned after Art. 1 OECD Model, DTCs are applicable to persons who are residents of one or both contracting states. Art. 4 OECD Model serves as a basis for treaty provisions defining the **concept of residence**. Under these provisions, a resident is "any person who, under the laws of that State, is liable to tax therein by reason of his domicile, residence, place of management or any other criterion of a similar nature, and also includes that State and any political subdivision or local authority thereof as well as a recognised pension fund of that State. This term, however, does not include any person who is liable to tax in that State in respect only of income from sources in that State or capital situated therein." In practice, this wording indicates that full tax liability in one of the two contracting states leads to treaty entitlement. 177

Example 178

A corporation is established in the Netherlands and is subject to full tax liability therein. It derives income almost exclusively from Dutch sources but it also holds an 11% participation in a Japanese company from which it receives dividends. With respect to those dividends, the Dutch company benefits from the Dutch domestic participation exemption regime, according to which the dividends are fully excluded from the taxable base. Therefore, the Dutch company is subject to taxation only on Dutch-source income. Nevertheless, the Dutch company is a resident of the Netherlands under the DTC between Japan and the Netherlands so that the DTC is applicable. In fact, full tax liability in the Netherlands is sufficient for these purposes. Therefore, the Dutch company can also benefit from the reduction of Japanese taxation at source on the dividends according to the provisions on dividends included in the DTC between Japan and the Netherlands.

Any taxable person who is liable to tax in one of the two contracting states by reason of his domicile, residence, place of management "or any **other criterion of a similar nature**" is entitled to treaty benefits. The meaning to be attributed to "similar" is controversial. According to one opinion, every characteristic which leads to full tax liability is similar (cf. Huemer, *Steuerpflicht*, 99 with further references). According to another view, the characteristics mentioned in Art. 4(1) OECD Model are locality-related; hence, it is crucial that the "criterion of a similar nature" also is a locality-related criterion (Vogel, *DTC* Art. 4, m.no. 28). 179

Example 180

In some countries, persons are deemed to be residents by other criteria, even though they have no physical home or location in the state. In the United States, for example, nationality attracts full tax liability. Some DTCs include these additional criteria in Art. 4(1) (Vogel, *DTC* Art. 4, m.no. 29). If the DTC does not, however, include these additional criteria, deemed residents of the state who are resident in third countries may or may not be entitled to treaty benefits of DTCs concluded by that state. If a court believes that the term "other criterion of a similar nature" refers only to characteristics of a locality-related nature, a deemed resident of the state who is resident in State A will not be entitled to benefits of DTCs concluded between State A and the state of the deemed residence. If, on the other hand, the court is of the view that the phrase refers to every characteristic which leads to full tax liability, the deemed resident will be entitled to the benefits of the DTC concluded between State A and the state of the deemed residence.

7.1.2. Effects of the DTC non-discrimination rules

181 The non-discrimination rules, and in particular the non-discrimination rules regarding PEs, may sometimes have similar effects for non-resident taxpayers as if the treaty were applicable. According to Art. 24(3) OECD Model, the taxation of a PE which an enterprise of a contracting state has in the other contracting state shall not be less favourably levied in that other state than the taxation levied on enterprises of that other state carrying on the same activities (m.no 483 et seq.). If an enterprise of that state would therefore be entitled to the treaty benefits, the PE of the enterprise would have to be treated identically. However, this does not mean that the treaty becomes applicable. Therefore the state where the income arises which is attributed to the PE is only bound by its treaty with the state of residence of the taxpayer.

182 **Example**

A company resident in Slovenia has a PE in Poland. Royalties from Czech sources are attributable to this PE. Under both the Czech Republic-Poland DTC and the Czech Republic-Slovenia DTC a withholding tax of 10% is levied on royalty income. The Czech Republic-Poland DTC is inapplicable since the Slovenian company is not a resident of either contracting state. However, Art. 25(2) (non-discrimination clause) of the Poland-Slovenia DTC provides that the taxation of a PE, which an enterprise from Slovenia has in Poland, shall not be less favourable than the taxation levied on enterprises of Poland carrying on the same activities. According to the view mentioned above, Poland must treat the PE of the Slovenian company no less favourably than it would treat PEs of Polish enterprises. In taxing the business profits of the PE, Poland must therefore allow the PE a credit for the tax paid in the Czech Republic.

7.1.3. Effects of other DTCs

183 A DTC allocates taxation rights between the two contracting states. A treaty imposes obligations on these two countries, but not on third countries. Usually, a DTC does not have effects on third countries.

184 Nevertheless, the applicability of a certain DTC might be influenced by a DTC concluded by one contracting state with another state. This might occur **because of the residence tiebreaker rules** which are contained in the latter DTC (cf. e.g. the IRS Revenue Ruling 2004-76). In case of such a tiebreaker clause the "losing" state is left with taxation rights for income or capital more or less from its own

sources. Third-country income or capital may usually not be taxed in that state, but only in the "winning" state. The OECD therefore takes the view that the "losing" state does not provide residence to this taxpayer under its other treaties either. Such a taxpayer is therefore not entitled to any of the other treaties concluded by that state. Grounds for this interpretation are found in the second sentence of Art. 4(1) OECD Model, according to which the term "resident of a Contracting State" "does not include any person who is liable to tax in that State in respect only of income from sources in that State or capital situated therein". Due to the 2008 amendments to the OECD Model, the Commentary on Art. 4 OECD Model (2017 OECD Commentary at para. 8.2) now reads as follows: "According to its wording and spirit the second sentence also excludes from the definition of a resident of a Contracting State ... companies and other persons who are not subject to comprehensive liability to tax in a Contracting State because these persons, whilst being residents of that State under that State's tax law, are considered to be residents of another State pursuant to a treaty between these two States". Such an interpretation, however, is questionable (cf. also Vann, in Maisto (ed.), *Residence of Companies*, 252 et seq.), in particular if one takes the view that each treaty should be interpreted separately.

7.2. Treaty entitlement of corporate entities that are subject to limited tax liability

7.2.1. Public law corporations

It has occasionally been questioned whether public law corporations that are **subject only to territorial taxation** are entitled to treaty benefits. Vogel correctly points out that the condition for tax treaty entitlement is not that the person is actually taxed without restriction but that the person merely shows those connections to the contracting state that can lead to full tax liability (Vogel, *DTC* Art. 4, m.no. 23 et seq.). Therefore, states and their political subdivisions or local authorities are also entitled to treaty benefits. 185

Example 186

A Dutch municipality holds shares in a Swiss corporation. The dividends received from this participation are not received in connection with a business carried on by the municipality. The Dutch municipality is nevertheless entitled to the 15% withholding tax rate provided by Art. 10(2) of the Netherlands–Switzerland DTC.

In 1995, the OECD Committee on Fiscal Affairs changed Art. 4(1) OECD Model in this respect, expressly including states and their political subdivisions or local authorities among persons entitled to treaty benefits. It is doubtful, however, whether **public law corporations** that are **not at the same time political subdivisions** or local authorities are entitled to treaty benefits. Since the OECD Committee on Fiscal Affairs merely mentioned states and their political subdivisions or local 187 authorities, it could be argued that the reverse conclusion is applicable to public law corporations, i.e. that public law corporations do not have any tax treaty entitlement. However, the intention of the OECD Committee on Fiscal Affairs was obviously not to go in this direction and such reverse conclusion shall not be drawn.

7.2.2. Corporate entities that are exempt from full tax liability

188 Corporate entities that are exempt from full tax liability are also **regarded as being entitled** to tax treaty benefits. The same considerations that apply to public law corporations apply to these corporations. The fact that these exempt corporations are not expressly mentioned in Art. 4(1) OECD Model, in contrast to states and their political subdivisions or local authorities, does not alter this conclusion.

189 **Example**

In High Court, 26 Aug. 2015, Serco BPO Pvt. v. Authority for Advance Rulings, two Mauritian companies acquired shares in an Indian company. The Mauritian companies had Mauritian tax residence certificates but were tax exempt in Mauritius. The question was whether the Indian company had to withhold taxes on payments made to the Mauritian companies under the DTC between India and Mauritius. The High Court held that, firstly, the tax residence certificates established that the two Mauritian companies were indeed residents of Mauritius and that, secondly, the mere fact that the Mauritian companies were tax exempt did not render them non-residents of Mauritius pursuant to Art. 4 of the treaty. Whether or not a person is actually liable to tax is irrelevant in the Court's view.

7.3. Treaty entitlement of partnerships and/or partners

190 Partnerships are “persons”. This is because Art. 3(1)(a) OECD Model states that the term “**person**” includes individuals, companies and any other body of persons. Under Art. 3(1)(b) OECD Model, the term “company” means any body corporate or any entity that is treated as a body corporate for tax purposes. However, in order to be entitled to tax treaty benefits, such a person must also be a resident of one or both of the two contracting states under Art. 4(1) OECD Model. Accordingly, a person has to be “liable to tax”. Thus, liability to tax in one of the two contracting states is a condition of treaty entitlement.

191 According to prevailing opinion, partnerships are not entitled to tax treaty benefits if they are not tax subjects for income tax purposes. The application of the tax treaty is therefore obtained “through” partnerships. Consequently, the person **entitled to tax treaty benefits** is not the partnership but **rather the partner(s)**.

192 **Example**

An Italian partnership has three partners and a place of business in Spain. One partner is resident in Germany, another in Switzerland and the third in Italy. With respect to the Italian partner’s income, the Italy-Spain DTC applies; with respect to the Swiss partner’s income, the Spain-Switzerland DTC applies; with respect to the German partner’s income, the Germany-Spain DTC applies.

The above conclusion, however, was controversial if a partnership is **characterized in different ways** in two states, e.g. if it is characterized as a taxable entity in one state and is treated as transparent for tax purposes in the other state. Therefore, Art. 1(2) was introduced in the 2017 OECD Model. This provision stipulates that income derived by or through an entity or arrangement that is treated as wholly or partly fiscally transparent under the tax law of either contracting state shall be considered to be income of a resident of a contracting state. This treatment, however, is subject to the income being treated as the income of a resident of one of the contracting states for taxation purposes. According to the Commentary on Art. 1 OECD Model (2017 OECD Commentary at para. 5) this ensures that treaty benefits are granted in appropriate cases and that benefits are not granted where neither contracting state treats, under its domestic law, this income as income of one of its residents. 193

Example 194

State A and State B have concluded a treaty identical to the OECD Model. State A considers that an entity established in State B is a company and taxes that entity on interest that it receives from a debtor resident in State A. Under the domestic law of State B, however, the entity is treated as a partnership and the two members in that entity, who share equally all its income, are each taxed on half of the interest. One of the members is a resident of State B and the other one is a resident of a country with which State A and B do not have a treaty. Art. 1(2) OECD Model provides that in such case, half of the interest shall be considered, for the purposes of Art. 11 OECD Model, to be income of a resident of State B (2017 OECD Commentary on Art. 1 at para. 6).

Before Art. 1(2) was introduced into the OECD Model, this position was already taken by the OECD. The OECD Committee on Fiscal Affairs created a Working Party that produced a report on this topic. The OECD's position makes the tax treaty entitlement in the source state dependent on the tax treatment of the partnership in the state in which it is established: if the partnership is treated as a tax subject in the latter state, it should be entitled to treaty benefits, otherwise the partners should be entitled to tax treaty benefits if they are resident there (cf. OECD Partnership Report). However, there is only a clear basis for such treatment in DTCs which contain a provision identical or similar to Art. 1(2) OECD Model. If a DTC does not contain such a clause, conflicts of qualification will continue to arise. 195

Example 196

A partnership with a head office in State P receives dividends from a company resident in State S. The partners of the partnership are resident in State R. States S and R treat the partnership as a taxable entity while State P treats it as transparent. According to the opinion set out in the OECD Partnership Report, the P–S DTC is not applicable because the partnership is not a resident of State P since State P treats it as transparent. The partners are resident in State R but since State R considers the income to be received by the partnership and not the partners, the R–S DTC cannot apply. The tax in State S is therefore not restricted since neither DTC applies.

197 Some DTCs contain **special provisions** for partnerships, different from Art. 1(2) OECD Model. These DTCs set out the conditions under which the partner(s) are entitled to tax treaty benefits. In some DTCs, it is sometimes stated that, under certain conditions, partnerships are entitled to tax treaty benefits. For example, under Art. 28(6) of the DTC between Austria and Switzerland, partnerships (general partnerships, collective companies, limited partnerships), which are established under the law of a contracting state and which have their seat in that state, "may claim the tax relief, granted in Art. 10, 11 and 12 of the Convention, from the other State, provided that at least three quarters of the profit of the association is benefiting persons who are residents of the first-mentioned State".

7.4. Treaty entitlement and limitations

198 Before the 2017 OECD Model, treaty entitlement generally only depended on the residence status. Further restrictions were not found in the OECD Model. In the OECD Model 2017, however, a new Art. 29 was inserted. This provision incorporates the minimum standard agreed to as part of the work on BEPS Action 6. Its aim is to avoid granting treaty benefits in cases of treaty shopping. Art. 29 OECD Model contains seven specific anti-abuse rules in paras. 1–7 (Limitation on benefits) and a general anti-abuse rule in para. 9 (Principal purpose test). The provisions to be included in the article will depend on how the contracting states want to implement the minimum standard, therefore different variations of paras. 1–7 and 9 can occur.

199 **Example**

Art. 29(4) OECD Model contains the so-called derivative benefits test. It entitles companies and entities that are residents of a contracting state but not a qualifying person under Art. 29(2) OECD Model to treaty benefits in respect of an item of income if, at the time when the benefit otherwise would be accorded and on at least half of the days of any twelve-month period that included that time, persons that are equivalent beneficiaries own, directly or indirectly, at least 75% of the shares of the resident. Equivalent beneficiaries are persons who would have been entitled to equivalent or more favourable benefits from the state of source if they had received the income directly (2017 OECD Commentary on Art. 29 at para. 82).

200 **Example**

Art. 29(6) OECD Model contains a discretionary relief clause. If a resident of a contracting state is neither a qualified person pursuant to Art. 29(2) OECD Model nor entitled to benefits under the previous paragraphs of Art. 29 OECD Model, the person can request the competent authority of the state in which benefits are denied to grant these benefits. The resident must demonstrate that neither its establishment, acquisition or maintenance, nor the conduct of its operations had as one of its principal purposes the obtaining of treaty benefits. The competent authority must consult with the other contracting state's competent authority whether treaty benefits shall be granted (2017 OECD Commentary on Art. 29 at para. 101).

Art. 29(8) OECD Model contains a specific anti-abuse provision with respect to triangular cases. The rule denies treaty benefits where the income of an enterprise of that state that is attributable to a PE situated in a third jurisdiction, and that PE was only created because that third jurisdiction does not tax, or offers preferential treatment, to that income. The rule does not apply if the income bears a significant level of tax in the PE state or there is business actively conducted in the PE. 201

Example 202

Company ACo, resident of State A, sets up a PE in State C, which imposes no tax on the profits of the PE. The profits attributable to the PE are exempt from tax in State A, according to the DTC between A and C. ACo derives royalty income from State B, which is included in the profits attributable to the PE. State B is obliged to limit its withholding tax on the royalty income under the A-B DTC which is drafted after the OECD Model. The royalty income would now be subject to no tax in State C and to a reduced amount of withholding tax in State B. This benefit (limitation in State B) is denied unless the PE actively conducts business.

If none of the specific anti-abuse provisions in Art. 29(1) to (8) OECD Model is applicable, the principal purpose test (PPT) in Art. 29(9) OECD Model might come into play. This provision applies if it is reasonable to conclude, having regard to all facts and circumstances, that obtaining a benefit was one of the principal purposes of any arrangement or transaction that resulted directly or indirectly in that benefit. Benefits will not be denied if it is established that granting that benefit in the specific circumstances is in accordance with the object and purpose of the relevant provisions of the convention. The provision emphasizes the need for a purposive interpretation. Therefore Art 29(8) OECD Model has in my view only a "signalling function" and should not serve as a legal basis to deny treaty benefits (m.no 145 et seq.). 203

7.5. Residence state in the case of dual residence

7.5.1. Necessity of determining the residence state

7.5.1.1. Allocation rules

DTCs use the concept of "residence" for different purposes. Under Art. 1 and Art. 4(1) OECD Model, residence is a condition for the application of the tax treaty. Persons who are residents of one or both of the contracting states are regarded as being entitled to treaty benefits. For the purposes of these provisions, a person can be a resident of both contracting states. In other words, it is not necessary to award one of the two states the priority of rank. 204

Things are different under the allocation rules of DTCs. These rules pre-suppose that only one of the two states is the residence state. If both states under Art. 1 and Art. 4(1) OECD Model are regarded as residence states, a rule must exist to **determine** which state is the **residence state** in order for the allocation rules to apply properly. 205

206 **Example**

An individual, who is resident both of Finland and of Switzerland, receives dividends from sources in Switzerland. Pursuant to Art. 10(2) of the Finland–Switzerland DTC, the tax at source is restricted to 10%. However, the application of Art. 10 of that DTC requires that the company paying the dividends and the person receiving the dividends are residents of different contracting states. In other words, Art. 10 Finland–Switzerland DTC applies only if the application of the tiebreaker rules of Art. 4(2) of the Finland–Switzerland DTC leads to the recipient of the dividends being a resident of Finland (for the tiebreaker rules cf. in detail m.no. 209).

7.5.1.2. Method article

207 The same arguments apply for the purposes of the method article. This article applies to persons who are residents of a contracting state and derive income that may be taxed in the other contracting state. The differentiation from "a" and "the other" contracting state requires that **only one of the two states be the residence state**. Otherwise, the application of the tax treaty fails.

208 **Example**

A corporation incorporated in Greece and managed in Romania receives royalties from Romania. The corporation is considered a resident of both Greece and Romania under the applicable domestic laws. Under Art. 25 of the Greece–Romania DTC (method article), the state of residence of the recipient of the royalties must grant a deduction from tax on income with respect to tax paid in the other contracting state. If Art. 25 of the DTC were applied on the basis of the domestic definition of residence, Greece would be bound to grant such a deduction for the taxes paid in Romania. However, under Art. 4(3) of the DTC (which corresponds to the pre-2017 version of the OECD Model, see in more detail m.nos 218, 219, 284), the corporation is deemed to be a resident of Romania since its place of effective management is in Romania. Since Greece is not the state of residence of the corporation under the DTC, it is not required to grant a deduction for tax paid with respect to the royalties earned in Romania.

7.5.2. Criteria

7.5.2.1. Permanent home

209 A DTC provision patterned after Art. 4(2) OECD Model provides a list of criteria for establishing, as far as individuals are concerned, how "residence" is to be determined for the purposes of the allocation rules and of the method article. These provisions are known as **"tiebreaker rules"**. The very first criterion that applies for determining residence for the purposes of the allocation rules and the method article in the case of dual residence is the permanent home. If an individual is a resident of both contracting states under Art. 4(1) he/she is resident, for treaty purposes, only in the state where he/she has a permanent home.

210 **Example**

An Australian citizen works as an IT consultant and receives income from the US. He does not own immovable property in Australia but lives at his parents' home, for which he has a key to access at all times. Also, he uses this address as his home address in several documents. He originally comes from Malaysia, where he has a rental apartment. The taxpayer argues that he does not have a permanent home available to him in Australia and that he therefore is a resident of Malaysia under Art. 4(2) of the Australia-Malaysia DTC. However, the Court finds that the taxpayer also has a permanent home in Australia because he has the actual power of disposition over his parents' home by being able to move out at will (AU: Administrative Appeals Tribunal Perth, 21 Dec. 2016, 2016 ATC 10-443).

7.5.2.2. Centre of vital interests

If an individual owns a permanent home in both contracting states, that person will be a resident of the state with which his/her **personal and economic relations** are closer, i.e. the state where his/her centre of vital interests is established. Personal relations will be found in the person's family life as well as in social and religious interests and activities. Economic relations exist with activities linked to a locality or source of income. Priority cannot be given to either personal relations or economic relations because the concept is indivisible. In some countries, however, court decisions give priority to personal relations in cases of doubt (Vogel, *DTC* Art. 4; AT, VwGH 25 Feb. 1970, 1001/69; AT, VwGH 22 Mar. 1991, 90/13/0073). 211

Example 212

An individual has homes in both Germany and Canada. The person earns income from sources in both states. The person's spouse and children reside primarily in the German home and the individual's social and cultural activities are centred in Germany. According to a Canadian judgment, the person is a resident of Germany for purposes of the Canada–Germany DTC since his centre of vital interests is in Germany (CA, FCA 18 Aug. 2006, Hertel v. MNR, 93 DTC 721).

7.5.2.3. Habitual abode

Under certain conditions, the person's habitual abode will be determinative. Under Art. 4(2)(b) OECD Model, this is the case if the state in which the individual has his/her centre of vital interests cannot be determined or if he/she does not have a permanent home available to him/her in either state. In the literature, the habitual abode is seen to be in the **country in which one "normally lives"** (Vogel, *DTC* Art. 4, m.no. 80); however, the OECD Commentary on Art. 4 appears to put the focus on the state in which the person spends more time. 213

Example 214

The French Cour Administrative d'Appel considered the case of a taxpayer who lived permanently in Ivory Coast where he worked. His wife and children lived in France and he visited France one or two months per year. Art. 2 of the France–Ivory Coast DTC provided that "an individual shall be deemed to be domiciled in the place in which he has his 'permanent home', that expression being understood to mean the centre of vital interests, i.e. the place with which his personal relations are closest". The Cour Administrative d'Appel stated that it was impossible to determine the place of his permanent home since his family lived in France but he was permanently in Ivory Coast for work. It proceeded to the next test, where he principally resides, and concluded that the taxpayer was a resident of Ivory Coast (FR, CAA 28 Dec. 1995, 94PA01491).

7.5.2.4. Nationality

215 According to Art. 4(2)(c) OECD Model, if the individual has a habitual abode in both states or in neither of them, he/she shall be deemed to be a resident only of the state of which he/she is a national. As indicated by Art. 3(1)(g) OECD Model, insofar as individuals are concerned, the term "national" means any individual possessing the **nationality or citizenship of a contracting state**. Thus, nationality or citizenship under domestic law is decisive.

216 **Example**

The French Conseil d'État considered the case of a taxpayer who had permanent homes in both France and Germany. The individual worked in Germany but spent weekends and holidays in France with his family. The centre of vital interests of the taxpayer was equally divided between the two states and the habitual abode could not be determined because of the frequent trips between France and Germany. The Court used the nationality tiebreaker rule to determine that the taxpayer was a resident of France (FR, CE 26 Jan. 1990, 69.853).

7.5.2.5. Mutual agreement procedure

217 If the application of the above criteria does not lead to a clear determination, reference must be made to Art. 4(2)(d) OECD Model (mutual agreement procedure): if the individual is a national of both states or of neither of them, the competent authorities of the contracting states shall settle the question by mutual agreement. For the decisions of the authorities, no restrictions exist with respect to the content. In the literature, it has been argued that in this case the competent authorities have an **obligation to reach a mutual agreement** (cf. Vogel, *DTC* Art. 4, m.no. 84). However, there is no indication with respect to how the obligation to reach a mutual agreement could be enforced.

7.5.2.6. Place of effective management

218 For **legal entities**, there are no such tiebreaker rules to determine the residence in cases of dual residency. Art. 4(3) OECD Model establishes that if a company is resident in both contracting states under domestic law, the competent authorities of both contracting states shall endeavour to determine by mutual agreement where the company should be deemed to be resident for treaty purposes. Unless such mutual agreement is concluded, such a dual-resident company does not obtain treaty benefits. The competent authorities shall take into account the company's place of effective management, the place where it is incorporated or otherwise constituted and any other relevant factors. If the competent authorities do not come to a mutual agreement, the company is not entitled to any treaty benefits. Such provision is apparently designed to prevent shareholders from deliberately creating dual-resident companies for tax planning purposes (Vogel, *DTC* Art. 4, m.no. 287). This provision, however, has only been introduced into the OECD Model with the 2017 Update. Before that, only one single criterion was set

out in Art. 4(3) OECD Model: if a person other than an individual is a resident of both contracting states, it will be considered a resident of the state where its "place of effective management" is situated. This concept is an autonomous concept in tax treaties. There is extensive consensus among scholars on this conclusion (Vogel, *DTC* Art. 4, m.no. 106). Many existing treaties still apply this former version of Art. 4(3) OECD Model.

Example 219

A Maltese company, X Malta Ltd., owned 100% of a Swedish company, X AB. After a reorganization of the business of X AB, this company no longer had an establishment in Sweden and was subject to full tax liability in Malta under Maltese domestic legislation. X AB however still had its seat in Sweden. X AB raised the question before the Swedish Council for Advance Tax Rulings whether, after the reorganization, its place of effective management was in Malta. If so, it would be a resident of Malta pursuant to Art. 4(3) of the DTC between Malta and Sweden. In reaching its conclusion, the Swedish Council for Advance Tax Rulings decided that under the domestic laws of Malta and Sweden, X AB was a resident of both Sweden and of Malta. The Council then considered Art. 4(3) DTC Malta/Sweden, which was patterned after the OECD Model and gave relevance to the place of effective management. Since all of X AB's management functions were exercised in Malta, the Swedish Council for Advance Tax Rulings considered that the place of effective management of X AB was located in Malta and, therefore, company X AB was a resident of Malta for treaty purposes. These conclusions were confirmed by the Regeringsrätten (SE, RR 24 Apr. 2008, RÅ 2008 ref 30 (6639-06)). The Malta-Sweden DTC follows the old version of Art. 4(3) OECD Model.

8. Taxes covered

8.1. Taxes on income

220 The OECD Model covers **taxes on income and on capital**. The manner in which they are levied is irrelevant. The taxes must be imposed on behalf of a contracting state or of its political subdivisions or local authorities. The OECD Model provides for a general definition of taxes on income: all taxes imposed on total income or on elements of income, including taxes on gains from the alienation of movable or immovable property, as well as taxes on the total amounts of wages or salaries paid by enterprises. For the qualification of a tax as tax on income or capital the whole structure of the tax is important.

221 DTCs regularly contain an **exemplary list** of taxes on income to which the treaty is applicable. When DTCs are patterned after the OECD Model, this list is found in Art. 2(3) and is introduced by the following sentence: "The existing taxes to which the Convention shall apply are in particular: …". The use of the term "in particular" clarifies that the list is not exhaustive but merely serves to illustrate the general definition found in Art. 2(1) and (2) OECD Model. The treaty remains applicable even if one country stops levying a certain tax which is listed.

8.2. Taxes on capital

222 The OECD Model is also applicable to **taxes on capital** that are imposed on behalf of a contracting state or of its political subdivisions or local authorities. As is the case with taxes on income, the manner in which taxes on capital are levied does not play any role. The OECD Model provides for a general definition of taxes on capital. It includes all taxes imposed on total capital or on elements of capital, including taxes on capital appreciation. However, not all DTCs are to be applied to taxes on capital. Some treaties apply only to taxes on income.

223 **Example**

The taxpayer, a collective investment vehicle established in Luxembourg, was registered with the Belgian financial market regulator and thus was subject to the relevant "annual tax on collective investment vehicles" or "net asset tax" (hereafter 'NAT') in Belgium. The taxable basis for the NAT is the net asset value of the outstanding shares/units in Belgium (i.e. the total value of the assets of the fund minus expenses and liabilities). The taxpayer objected against the NAT assessment arguing that the NAT was a tax on capital within the meaning of Art. 22(4) of the treaty, which provided that taxes on capital could only be levied in the taxpayer's state of residence. Consequently, Belgium was not allowed to subject a Luxembourg resident to such a tax. Before the Brussels Court of First Instance, the Belgian tax authorities argued that the NAT could not be regarded as a 'tax on capital', since it was not a tax on a taxpayer's total capital, but rather a specific tax. The Brussels Court of First Instance (decision of 23 November 2011, No. 2008/16347/A) decided in favour of the taxpayer and concluded that, given the definition of Art. 2(2) of the treaty, the NAT should be considered as a tax on capital.

The tax authorities appealed and the case was referred to the Court of Appeal of Brussels. By its decision 2012/AR/906 of 29 November 2018, the Court of Appeal of Brussels upheld the decision by the Court of First Instance concerning the material scope of the treaty (i.e. Art. 2 'taxes covered') with regard to the NAT. The Court of Appeal observed that the text of Art. 2 of the treaty was corresponding to Art. 2 OECD Model and that the treaty in question had been assigned as an OECD confirmed treaty in the Belgian administrative guidelines on tax treaties ('Com.Conv.'). With regard to the application of Art. 2(1) of the treaty, the Court of Appeal observed that the tax authorities' argued that the term 'capital tax' ('impôt sur la fortune') was not defined in the treaty and had to be interpreted by application of Art. 3(2). Because no capital taxes were mentioned in the list of Belgian taxes in Art. 2(3) and because the concept of 'capital tax' did not exist in Belgian tax law, the tax authorities argued one had to rely on the meaning of the term under Luxembourg domestic tax law. The Court dismissed the argument: Art. 2(1) and (2) did provide for a definition of the terms 'taxes on income and on capital'. In line with the doctrine and the OECD Commentary, this definition had to be understood as giving these terms an autonomous meaning for the purpose of the treaty. The Court of Appeal then observed that the tax authorities denied that the NAT was a capital tax because the taxable event of the tax was the placement of shares of the undertakings for collective investment with Belgian investors. The tax was due however on the first of January of the next year and only if and to the extent the conditions of the share placement were still fulfilled at that date. The NAT tax base consisted only of the amounts invested by Belgian investors and represented in the capital of the undertakings for collective investments and not the assets held by the collective investment. This amount was said to be determined by taking into consideration the amount of the subscribed shares, the amount of shares repurchased, the amount of debts incurred by the collective investment, the evolution of the value of its assets, its income (income on assets, i.e. dividends and interests etc. received on its investments) and its expenses. The Court observed in conclusion that the NAT was levied annually on the collective investment's net assets and not merely on the basis of the amount subscribed to by Belgian shareholders of the foreign undertaking for collective investment. As such, the NAT was levied on elements of capital assets ('une portion du patrimoine') of the undertaking for collective investment and was within the material scope of the treaty as determined by Art. 2(2) of the treaty.

8.3. Comparability

The OECD Model and most DTCs contain clauses pursuant to which the treaty shall apply to **any identical or substantially similar taxes** that are imposed after the date of signature in addition to, or in place of, the existing taxes. These clauses seek to prevent situations in which the introduction of new taxes leads to a renegotiation of a DTC. If the newly introduced taxes are comparable to the taxes existing at the time the treaty was concluded, the treaty is applicable. 224

Example 225

In 2003, a Swiss resident taxpayer disposed of a number of shares in a company incorporated and resident in Australia. Under Art. 7(1) of the Australia–Switzerland DTC, Australia did not have any taxing rights in respect of that gain. Nevertheless, the Australian tax authorities argued that such gain was subject to the Capital Gains Tax (CGT), a tax that was introduced in 1985 after the treaty was concluded (1980). The Australian tax authorities argued CGT was not covered by treaties concluded before its introduction and Australia was therefore not restricted by the treaty between Australia and Switzerland. The Court noted that CGT was not a separate tax but merely a part of the Australian income tax under the relevant Income Tax Assessment Act and ruled that CGT was "substantially similar, if not identical, to the income tax" for the purposes of Art. 2(2) of the Treaty (AU, FCA 10 Oct. 2008, Virgin Holdings SA v. Federal Commissioner of Taxation.

8.4. Inheritance and gift taxes

226 In addition to the OECD Model on Income and on Capital, there is an OECD Model in the area of inheritance taxation. This OECD Inheritance Tax Model was published in 1966 and modified in 1982 (cf. m.no. 533). In the course of this modification, gift taxes were included in the substantive scope of the OECD Inheritance Tax Model; therefore, most DTCs consequently cover income and capital taxes only. However, there are some **"combined" treaties** which also deal with inheritance and gift taxes, e.g. the Sweden–Germany DTC and the Algeria–France DTC.

9. Allocation rules

9.1. Income from immovable property

9.1.1. Immovable property

Income from immovable property is dealt with by treaty provisions patterned after **Art. 6 OECD Model**. The concept of immovable property is set out in Art. 6(2) OECD Model: "The term 'immovable property' shall have the meaning which it has under the law of the Contracting State in which the property in question is situated. The term shall in any case include property accessory to immovable property, livestock and equipment used in agriculture and forestry, rights to which the provisions of general law respecting landed property apply, usufruct of immovable property and rights to variable or fixed payments as consideration for the working of, or the right to work, mineral deposits, sources and other natural resources". This definition partly refers to the domestic law of the state where the property is situated. However, the terms used in the definition have to be interpreted as far as possible within the context of the OECD Model. 227

Art. 6 OECD Model covers income arising from the immediate **utilization of the property** and the rental or lease of the property, as well as income arising from any other use of real estate. The general rule applies irrespective of the form of exploitation of the immovable property. However, capital gains deriving from the sale of the immovable property are not covered. Nonetheless, Art. 13(1) OECD Model states that the place where the property in question is situated is also decisive for the allocation of taxing rights on such capital gains. 228

9.1.2. Allocation of taxing rights

Pursuant to treaty provisions patterned after **Art. 6(1) OECD Model**, income derived by a resident of a contracting state from immovable property situated in the other contracting state may be taxed in the latter state. Consequently, the state in which the immovable property is situated has the right to tax. Art. 6 OECD Model does not address the taxing rights of the residence state. The question whether the residence state may also tax the income and grant credit for the taxes levied in the source state, or must instead exempt such income, is decided in the method article. 229

Example 230

An individual resident in China rents out real estate situated in Austria. Under Art. 6 of the China –Austria DTC, Austria has the right to tax this rental income. Art. 6 does not address the taxation rights of China. Thus, Art. 24 (corresponding to Art. 23 OECD Model) has to be consulted. Under this provision, China must apply the credit method in order to avoid double taxation.

231 The allocation rule of Art. 6 OECD Model only comes into effect if the recipient of the income is resident in a contracting state and the immovable property is situated in the other contracting state. Art. 6 is therefore inapplicable if the immovable property is situated in the contracting state of which the recipient of the income is a resident or if the immovable property is situated in a third country.

232 **Example**

An individual resident in Japan receives income from the rental of a Japanese property. Since the residence state of the recipient of the income and the situs state of the property are the same, Art. 6 OECD Model does not apply (all Japanese DTCs follow the OECD Model with respect to that criteria of immovable property). In the absence of other allocation rules, Art. 21 (other income) applies. This, however, does not change the fact that Japan has the right to tax.

233 Art. 6(4) OECD Model contains a **priority rule** for cases in which immovable property, from which the income is earned, is used in the exercise of a business or the performance of independent personal services. Where Art. 7 OECD Model or Art. 14 of the former OECD Model are also applicable, the allocation rule regarding immovable property takes precedence and the situs state has the right to tax.

234 **Example**

A Dutch enterprise holds Indian real estate in its business property. The income derived from this property could be qualified as income from immovable property and as business income. Art. 6(4) of the India–Netherlands DTC, however, provides that Art. 6 takes precedence. India therefore has the taxing right irrespective of the existence of a PE in India. According to Art. 23(2) (method article), the Netherlands has to exempt the income derived from India.

9.2. Business profits

9.2.1. Profits of an enterprise

235 **Art. 7 OECD Model** regulates business profits and thereby requires the existence of an enterprise. The Commentary on Art. 3 indicates that the Model "does not contain an exhaustive definition" – neither of the term "enterprise" (cf. OECD Commentary on Art. 3, para. 4) nor of the term "business" (cf. OECD Commentary on Art. 3, para. 10.2). It is therefore occasionally concluded that it is necessary to refer to domestic law in order to define this term (cf. Avery Jones et al., *Bulletin – Tax Treaty Monitor* 2003, 237 et seq.). However, it can be more convincingly argued that both terms are dealt with in Art. 3(1) OECD Model under the heading "General Definitions" and even for only exhaustive definitions would count for the purposes of Art. 3(2) OECD Model the terms need to be interpreted within the context of the DTC.

236 In 2000, the OECD Fiscal Committee **deleted Art. 14 OECD Model** without replacing it (cf. also m.no. 320). The OECD Fiscal Committee was of the view that Art. 14 OECD Model had essentially the same legal consequences as Art. 7 OECD

Model and was therefore superfluous. Thus, all income formerly covered under Art. 14 OECD Model should now be assigned to Art. 7 OECD Model. However, it will still take some time for the change in the OECD Model to be implemented in bilateral agreements.

9.2.2. Allocation of taxing rights

The profits of an enterprise of a contracting state shall be **taxable only in that state**. According to Art. 7(1) OECD Model, the only exception arises when the enterprise carries on business in the other contracting state through a PE situated therein. In cases in which there is no PE situated in the other state, Art. 7(1) OECD Model gives exclusive taxing rights to the residence state, in which case the method article is not required. 237

Example 238

A Spanish company provides advisory services in Portugal but does not have a PE in Portugal. Under Art. 7(1) Portugal–Spain DTC, Spain has the exclusive taxing right. The method article does not need to be consulted.

If the company carries on business in the other contracting state through a PE situated therein, Art. 7(1) OECD Model provides that the **PE state also has the right to tax**. The PE state may tax the profits **that are attributable to the PE**. Art. 7(1) OECD Model does not preclude the residence state from taxing this income. 239

Example 240

A Swedish company has one PE in Norway and one in Denmark. Business profits amounting to SEK 1 million can be attributed to both PEs. According to Art. 7(1) of the Nordic Convention (NC), Norway and Denmark may tax the profits attributable to the PEs situated in their countries. This provision, however, does not remove Sweden's taxing right. The method article (Art. 25 NC) provides for the credit method. Sweden must allow a credit for taxes paid in Norway and in Denmark against the taxes payable in Sweden in order to avoid double taxation.

The general rule that a PE state may only tax profits attributable to the PE is slightly amended in the UN Model: **Art. 7(1)(b) and (c)** provides for the **"limited force of attraction principle"**, which permits that the enterprise, once it carries out business through a PE in the source state, can be taxed on business profits in that state arising from transactions of the same or similar kind outside the PE (Vogel, *DTC* Art. 7, m.no. 34). 241

Art. 7 OECD Model uses the concept of business profits of an **"enterprise of a Contracting State"**. This term is defined in Art. 3(1)(d): it is assumed to be an enterprise that is carried on by a resident of a contracting state. If there is no PE in the other contracting state to which the business profits are attributable, the residence state of the person who runs the enterprise has the exclusive taxing right with respect to the business profits. 242

243 **Example**

An individual resident in Estonia runs a grocery store in Riga, Latvia. In terms of treaty law, this activity is an Estonian enterprise because it is run by an Estonian resident (Art. 3(1)(f) Estonia–Latvia DTC). The grocery store, however, constitutes a Latvian PE and, consequently, Latvia may tax the income attributable to the PE (Art. 7 and Art. 5 Estonia–Latvia DTC).

244 The concept of PE is important for the allocation of taxing rights. With respect to the concept used in the OECD Model, only the definition contained in Art. 5 OECD Model is decisive. A PE must be a **fixed place of business** through which the business of the enterprise is wholly or partly carried on. The requirement of a fixed place of business means that the taxation of the profits of an enterprise in the other contracting state is only allowed when there is an **intensive economic connection** to that state (Vogel, *DTC* Art. 5, m.no. 21) or a **"physical location at the disposal of the enterprise"** (Baker, *DTC* 5 B.06).

245 **Example**

A company resident in Mexico concluded a contract with an individual resident in Canada under which the individual provided training to the company's staff over a 20-month period. The training is undertaken at the company's premises. There, the individual meets the employees and is allowed to use an office to prepare his courses. The individual is given full access to the company's premises during business hours for the purpose of the contract. The Canadian individual constitutes a Mexican PE since he was present at the company's premises during the training period and had an office available for the preparation of his training activities (Art. 7 and Art. 5 Mexico–Canada DTC).

246 A place of business encompasses all things (physical objects) that serve the enterprise (GE, RFH 30 Apr. 1935). In borderline cases, a single object may suffice (Vogel, *DTC* Art. 5, m.no. 22). According to this definition, a PE does not necessarily need to be a room. It is crucial, however, that the place of business be not only temporarily at the disposal of the person; the actual possibility of disposal is sufficient. Thus, if the premises are at the person's disposal only from time to time, this does not suffice to constitute a PE. Furthermore, a PE must be a **"permanent" place of business**. The place of business must be created "with a certain degree of permanence" (Vogel, *DTC* Art. 5, m.no. 27). In some DTCs, a time limit of six months is provided as a guideline. Finally, a connection to a certain point of the earth's surface must exist (Vogel, *DTC* Art. 5, m.no. 23).

247 **Example**

A company resident in Germany tested a software for cars at the same place in Sweden for several years. Each year, the activities that the company performed in Sweden lasted only for three or four months. Even though each particular activity lasts less than six months per year, the court still ruled that the German company had a fixed place of business in Sweden. According to the court, activities of a recurrent nature may lead to the existence of a fixed place of business despite the permanence test (cf. Swedish Kammarrätten i Göteborg of 24 Oct. 2016, case 2276-15).

A **list** in Art. 5(2) OECD Model provides examples of what is meant by "PE". According to this paragraph, a PE especially includes a place of management, a branch, an office, a factory, a workshop, a mine, an oil or gas well, a quarry or any other place of extraction of natural resources. It is unclear whether the examples mentioned in Art. 5(2) OECD Model are in every case regarded as PEs. According to prevailing opinion, the examples have to be seen in the light of the general definition of "PE" in Art. 5(1) OECD Model. They can therefore only constitute PEs if the requirements of the general definition are fulfilled (cf. OECD Commentary on Art. 5, para. 45; also Vogel, *DTC* Art. 5, m.no. 52; also Baker, *DTC* 5 B.14). 248

Example 249

A self-employed IT consultant, resident in Uruguay, provided services to a German company. The IT consultant was provided with a workplace in the company, but he could use it only during office hours. Besides, the IT consultant organized some of his work from his private living room in Germany. The tax court therefore regarded the living room of the IT consultant as a "place of management" according to Art. 5(2)(a) Germany–Uruguay DTC. In contrast to the prevailing opinion, the court explicitly stated that Art. 5(2)(a) extended the scope of Art. 5(1) and that a fixed place is not required for a place of management. As a result, Germany is allowed to tax the income earned from the services rendered in Germany (cf. German Finanzgericht München, 9K 3041/15, IStR 2017, 749, 31 May 2017).

Building sites and construction or installation projects are specifically mentioned in Art. 5(3) OECD Model. They are only regarded as PEs when they last longer than 12 months. Mentioning building and construction sites explicitly does not widen the PE concept but merely explains it. Since the permanence of the PE is uncertain in these cases, the treaty clarifies when a sufficiently solid connection of a normally temporary activity can be assumed in order to classify the arrangement as a PE. The 12-month period is therefore of importance where the existence of a PE is otherwise doubtful. **Art. 5(3)(a) UN Model** differs from the OECD Model in two ways: firstly, the scope of the provision is wider since it expressly includes "assembly projects" and "supervisory activities" in connection with building sites, construction, installation or assembly projects to constitute a PE; secondly, the required duration is reduced to 6 months. 250

Art. 5(4) OECD Model excludes **preparatory and auxiliary activities** from the definition of a PE. The taxation by the state in which such activities are performed is not as evidently legitimate as taxation of more direct activities. Furthermore, in practice, it is especially difficult to determine the share of business profits that should be allocated to these auxiliary activities (Vogel, *DTC* Art. 5, m.no. 110). 251

Example 252

According to Art. 5(4)(d) OECD Model, a fixed place of business the only purpose of which is to obtain information for the company is not regarded as a PE. Consequently, newspapers that provide their correspondents with offices do not establish PEs in those states. As long as the company only acquires the information, a PE is not constituted.

However, if the information is processed in a fixed place of business – in the sense of an evaluation or editorial department – the enterprise constitutes a PE. Thus, editorial departments of newspapers are not exempt under Art. 5(4) OECD Model (Vogel, DTC Art. 5, m.no. 115).

253 An **agent** can also be regarded as a PE. The requirements are set forth in Art. 5(5) OECD Model: the agent must habitually conclude contracts, or habitually plays the principal role leading to the conclusion of contracts that are routinely concluded without material modification by the enterprise; if, however, the activities of the agent are restricted to the preparatory and auxiliary activities as per Art. 5(4) OECD Model, the agent does not constitute a PE for the enterprise. According to the concept of Art. 5(5)(b) UN Model, a person that does not habitually conclude contracts nor plays the principal role leading to the conclusion of such contracts is nonetheless considered a dependent agent in the case that the person habitually maintains a stock of goods or merchandise to regularly deliver on behalf of the enterprise. However, as Vogel points out, constituting a PE in such a way can easily be avoided (Vogel, *DTC* Art. 5).

254 **Example**

Google Ireland Limited provided online services in France. Customers could buy advertisement space on the home page of the search engine Google and pay a fee in accordance with the number of users clicked on the advertisement. Google France SARL advised and assisted the customers with regard to the placement of the advertisements. The French court held that Google France SARL did not have the authority to conclude contracts because all the contracts between the customers and Google Ireland Limited were validated by Google Ireland and all advertisements were only accessible after validation of the contracts. Therefore, the court ruled that Google Ireland did not have a dependent agent PE in France (cf. French Tribunal Administratif de Paris of 12 July 2017, Société Google Ireland Limited, n° 1505178/1-1).

255 In contrast to the OECD Model, the UN Model includes an additional provision on PEs of insurance companies (**Art. 5(6) UN Model**), stipulating that an insurance company collecting premiums in another state is regarded to have a PE in that other state.

256 If an enterprise carries on business through an agent of independent status, this will not constitute a PE provided that the person acts in the ordinary course of his/her business. This provision exists merely for clarification: a person who is acting in the course of his/her own business does not thereby constitute a PE for another person. This is not the case when he/she pursues the interests of someone else. Art. 5(6) OECD Model clarifies this (Vogel, *DTC* Art. 5, m.no. 161). The corresponding provision in the UN Model is Art. 5(7). It also specifies that an agent is not regarded to be independent if his/her activities are devoted wholly or almost wholly to one or more enterprises to which it is closely related.

Art. 5(7) OECD Model emphasizes that a **subsidiary** does not automatically constitute a PE of the parent company. However, if the requirements of Art. 5 OECD Model are met, a subsidiary can constitute a PE of the parent in the same way as any other company would. 257

Example 258

An Irish computer manufacturer has 100% share in an Icelandic subsidiary. This subsidiary has the authority to conclude contracts in the name of the parent company and habitually exercises this authority. The subsidiary consequently constitutes an agency PE for the Irish parent and the parent becomes liable to tax in Iceland in respect of the profits attributable to the Icelandic agent (Art. 7(1) and Art. 5(5) of the Iceland–Ireland DTC). Of course, the Icelandic subsidiary, as a resident of Iceland, is also subject to tax in Iceland.

For **services** no special provisions exist; they are to be treated like every other type of business income. Therefore, profits arising from providing services may only be taxed in the source state if they are attributable to a PE. However, the OECD Commentary on Art. 5 mentions that contracting states may include a "service PE provision" in their DTCs in order to secure the taxing right of the source state with respect to profits from services provided therein. Such a provision expands the circumstances under which a PE arises because of the provision of services, by deeming services to be carried out through a PE, if certain thresholds are met. A sample provision can be found at para. 144 of the OECD Commentary on Art. 5: a PE will be constituted if the service provider is present in the source state for more than 183 days within a 12-month-period and if the enterprise derives more than 50% of its gross revenues from the provision of this service. **Art. 5(3)(b) UN Model** includes a provision similar to the concept proposed in the 2017 OECD Commentary on Art. 5, para. 144. Thus, an enterprise is deemed to have a PE in the other contracting state due to the performance of services for a period or periods aggregating more than 6 months within any 12-month period. There exists no threshold as regards the amount of gross revenue derived from the provision of these services. 259

Art. 7 OECD Model contains rules regarding the attribution of profits to a PE. Those rules are relevant not only for the state where the PE is situated, but also for the state of residence of the enterprise as this state shall provide double tax relief in accordance with Art. 23 A or B. According to Art. 7(2) OECD Model, the profits that are attributable to a PE are those that it might be expected to make, in particular in its dealings with other parts of the enterprise, if it were a separate and independent enterprise engaged in the same or similar activities under the same or similar conditions. The profits attributable to a PE should be calculated under the arm's length principle taking into account the functions performed, assets used and risks assumed by the enterprise through the PE and through the other parts of the enterprise. 260

261 The scope of this virtual independence of a PE is controversial. According to one opinion, only an absolute independence of the PE fulfils the requirements of the arm's length principle of Art. 7(2) OECD Model. However, other authors assume a limited independence of the PE, whereby the PE is regarded as a dependent part of the enterprise. Costs can only be taken into account when they have an effect on the expenses of the whole enterprise (GE, BFH 20 Jul. 1988, I R 49/84).

262 As there was a considerable variation in the interpretation of the attribution, the OECD has worked on a report regarding the attribution of profits to PEs, in which the **"functionally separate entity approach"** is considered as the guiding principle in the interpretation of Art. 7 OECD Model. Under the so-called "authorized OECD approach (AOA)", a functional analysis has to be carried out before transactions within various parts of a single enterprise ("dealings") have to be priced at arm's length, giving rise to a profit element. The OECD Transfer Pricing Guidelines that have been developed for transactions between associated enterprises (Art. 9 OECD Model) shall be applied by analogy also for the purposes of Art. 7 OECD Model (cf. m.no. 464 et seq.). It is arguable whether this only has relevance for treaties concluded after the OECD Model Update 2008 was released.

263 In the update of the OECD Model 2008, only changes in the Commentary on Art. 7 OECD Model were enacted to include the interpretation of the AOA. As the OECD Model was not changed, the separate entity approach could not be enacted completely. As a second step in the implementation of the AOA into DTCs, in the 2010 update of the OECD Model, changes in the wording of Art. 7 OECD Model as well as changes in the Commentary were included. The AOA is therefore fully implemented if DTCs are negotiated on the basis of the Art. 7 OECD Model 2010.

264 Art. 7(4) OECD Model 2017 (Art. 7(7) OECD Model 2008) is a rule that explains how Art. 7 OECD Model applies. According to this rule, other **allocation rules** of the OECD Model **take precedence over Art. 7** OECD Model. As a result, Art. 7 OECD Model is overridden and only applies when other allocation rules do not.

265 **Example**

A South African enterprise receives dividends from Tanzania. Pursuant to Art. 7(7) of the South Africa–Tanzania DTC, which corresponds to Art. 7(4) of the 2017 OECD Model, the dividend income falls within the scope of Art. 10 and not of Art. 7 of that DTC. Even though there is no PE in Tanzania, the source state has a taxing right. The situation would be different if the enterprise had a PE in Tanzania, to which the shares, in respect of which the dividends were paid, were connected. In this case, the PE proviso of Art. 10(4) would apply (cf. m.no. 285). This is a special provision which overrides Art. 7(7) South Africa–Tanzania DTC so that Art. 7 of that DTC applies. If the South African enterprise had a PE in Tanzania to which the dividend income was attributable, Tanzania as the PE state would have the right to tax the dividends under Art. 7(1).

9.3. International shipping and air transport

9.3.1. International shipping and air transport

Art. 8 OECD Model applies to the operation of ships or aircraft in international traffic. The concept of "international traffic" is defined in Art. 3(1)(e) OECD Model. It means any transport by a ship or aircraft except when the ship or aircraft is operated solely between places in a contracting state and the enterprise that operates the ship or aircraft is not an enterprise of that state. Therefore, if the ship or aircraft is located not in the state of the enterprise but in the other contracting state and is not crossing borders, Art. 8 OECD Model does not apply. 266

Example 267

An airline, tax resident in the United Arab Emirates, conducts flights between Bangkok and Phi Phi Island (both in Thailand). The profits resulting from this route are not covered by Art. 8 of the Thailand–United Arab Emirates DTC because these flights do not involve international traffic. Instead, Art. 7 Thailand–United Arab Emirates DTC applies. Provided that the income is attributable to a PE of the enterprise situated in Thailand, the PE state has a right to tax.

9.3.2. Allocation of taxing rights

Art. 8(1) OECD Model gives the exclusive taxing right to the state in which the person carrying on the business of international traffic is resident. The application of the exemption or the credit method is therefore not required and the PE principle, which would otherwise be decisive for business profits, is overruled. 268

Example 269

British Airways offers flights between Amsterdam and London and has a representative office in Amsterdam. Since Art. 8 takes precedence over Art. 7 in the Netherlands–UK DTC, the PE principle does not apply. Because the residence of British Airways is situated in the UK, the UK has the exclusive right to tax while the Netherlands may not tax at all.

Contrary to the OECD Model, the UN Model offers two alternatives for the allocation of taxing rights regarding profits of ships in international traffic. The wording of Art. 8A UN Model is the same as of the OECD Model but **Art. 8B(2) UN Model** follows a different concept: the state in which the place of effective management of the enterprise is located always has a right to tax, but if the activities of the shipping enterprise in the other state are more than casual, Art. 8B(2) UN Model grants this state a limited taxation right. The apportionment of profit is largely left to bilateral negotiations, as the UN Model merely states that the tax base is to be determined on the basis of the overall net profits from the enterprise's shipping activities and the amount of tax due in the other state shall be reduced by a certain percentage. 270

9.4. Dividends

9.4.1. Dividends

271 Dividends are regulated in **Art. 10 OECD Model**. The concept of "dividends" for purposes of the treaty is defined in Art. 10(3) OECD Model by a list of examples: income from shares, "jouissance" shares or "jouissance" rights, mining shares, founders' shares or other rights, not being debt claims, and participating in profits. All the profit-sharing rights listed in Art. 10(3) OECD Model must be "corporate rights". This becomes clear when the treaty speaks of "other corporate rights" and consequently affirms that by the term "dividends", only income from such rights is meant. The definition of dividends restricts the concept to those distributions by companies that are fiscally equal to the income from corporate rights according to the national law of the distributing company's residence state. Apparently, the OECD Model assumes that income from corporate rights can only qualify as "dividends" if it is not deductible when determining the profits of the distributing company.

272 The notion of **"corporate rights"** is therefore decisive for the dividend concept. Only "corporate rights" can qualify for the purposes of Art. 10 OECD Model. On the one hand, the concept's prerequisite is the existence of a "company". This concept is defined in Art. 3(1)(b) OECD Model. This term means any body corporate or any entity that is treated as a body corporate for tax purposes. Thus, all tax subjects that are not individuals are regarded as "companies" in DTCs. On the other hand, there must be a "share" in a company so that one can speak of dividends. This concept is not defined by tax treaty law. However, it has to be distinguished from the concept of the "receivables" ("not being debt claims"). In contrast to a creditor, a shareholder has to participate in current profits and in liquidation proceeds.

273 **Example**

An open-ended investment fund organized under and governed by Finnish law and enacted according to the EC Directive on undertakings for collective investment in transferable securities (UCITS), contemplated distributions to unit holders resident in Sweden and Canada. It applied for an advance ruling to clarify its withholding obligations. The Central Tax Committee gave its ruling on 2 Mar. 1998, holding that distributions made by investment funds were not subject to the same taxation treatment as income from shares under Finnish tax law, hence they were not" dividends" for tax treaty purposes. The ruling was appealed by the Representative of the Revenue. The Finnish Supreme Administrative Court (KHO) held that the distributions did not qualify as "dividends" for tax treaty purposes, since an investment fund is not a corporation; only the fund management company is a corporation. Moreover, the same withholding tax treatment of fund distributions and dividends under Sec. 3 of the Law on Taxation of Non-residents cannot be used to interpret the nature of distributions, since the differentiation exists due to practical reasons (FI, KHO 14 Jun. 1999, 14.06.1999/1600).

9.4.2. Allocation of taxing rights

Under Art. 10 OECD Model, the **residence state of the recipient** of the dividends has the right to tax. The source state is also entitled to tax but this tax will be restricted to a certain percentage **if the recipient is the beneficial owner of the dividend.** The taxes paid in accordance with the tax treaty in the **source state** can be credited in the residence state. This is guaranteed both by Art. 23 A(2) and Art 23 B(1) OECD Model. 274

Example 275

An individual resident in Hong Kong receives dividends from Luxembourg. Under Art. 10(1) of the Hong Kong–Luxembourg DTC, Hong Kong may tax this income. However, Luxembourg also has the right to tax but the taxes so charged shall not exceed 10%. Under Art. 22 (method article) of the treaty, the taxes withheld in Luxembourg must be credited against Hong Kong's taxes payable.

When the requirement of beneficial ownership was introduced in the OECD Model in 1977, its scope was intended to be limited to agents, nominees and conduit companies acting as a fiduciary or administrator that are obliged to immediately pass the income received to another person. However, courts all over the world started to interpret this criterion and occasionally broadened it considerably. The following three examples illustrate how different the approaches are that are applied by courts. 276

Example 277

A Canadian manufacturing company paid dividends to a holding company resident in the Netherlands. The shares of the Dutch holding company were owned by a Swedish company and a UK company as to 51% and 49% respectively. Given that the Swedish and UK companies entered into an agreement in which at least 80% of the profits of the Canadian company and of the Dutch holding company were to be distributed to them, the question was whether the Dutch holding company shall be regarded as the beneficial owner of the dividends. It was concluded that the Dutch company was the beneficial owner of the dividends since it was not part of the agreement and therefore was not obliged to automatically pass on the dividends (2009 FCA 57, The Queen v. Prevost Car Inc.).

Example 278

An Indonesian company issued bonds on the international market to raise funds for its operations and an American bank, through its registered London branch, acted as a trustee for the holders of the notes. According to Indonesian tax law, a 20% withholding tax rate applies to interest payments. However, to reduce the withholding tax rate the Indonesian company interposed a subsidiary established in Mauritius. For the purposes of the Indonesia–Mauritius DTC, a withholding tax rate of 10% on the interest paid from the Indonesian company to the Mauritian company was applicable and afterwards the latter company paid interest to the bank free of withholding tax. Since the Indonesia–Mauritius DTC was anticipated to be terminated, a Dutch company was set up to receive interest payments from the Indonesian company, which would pay the whole amount of the interest to the Mauritian company a day after receipt. This new structure allowed the Indonesian company to preserve the 10% withholding tax rate provided in the Indonesia–Netherlands DTC. The question was whether the Dutch company shall be regarded as the beneficial owner of the interest. The court interpreted the beneficial ownership concept in a broad economic manner and concluded that the Dutch interposed company was not the beneficial owner since it did not have the full privilege to directly benefit from the income (Indofood International Finance Ltd. v. J.P. Morgan Chase Bank N.A., London Branch, 2006, EWCA Civ. 158 – 2 March 2006).

279 **Example**

A US corporation owned a holding company in France which owned a subsidiary operating in Italy. In accordance with Art. 10(2) of the France–Italy DTC, the Italian subsidiary withheld 5% of dividends that is distributed to the French company. An application by the French company for a reimbursement of the dividend withheld by the Italian company was denied by the Italian Tax Authority. Because there is no definition of "beneficial ownership" in neither the Italian DTCs nor domestic law, the Italian Tax Authority relied on the OECD guidelines and existing international case law. Significant attention was given to the lack of operational substance of the French company. The French company did not have any premises, staff and equipment and its balance sheet did not record any trade receivables beyond its participation in the Italian subsidiary. Because of the lack of business substance, the French company could not be considered as having its place of effective management in France. It was also observed that it was wholly owned by a US company, a country that did not have a tax treaty with Italy providing a similar tax benefit as granted by the France–Italy DTC. The Italian Tax Authority thus concluded that the French sub-holding was a mere conduit set up to minimize tax leakage on up-streamed income. The Italian Supreme Court rejected the Italian Tax Authority's position, since it did not take into consideration the nature of the French company. The Supreme Court opined that "beneficial ownership" should be verified taking into consideration the specific characteristics of the object and the nature of the parent company, in this case a holding company, to be compliant with the DTC. Instead of concentrating on the lack of an operating structure, or the absence of employee and/or on the low management costs it was necessary to address the verification analysis on the autonomous capacity to make decisions regarding the use of the income (dividends in this case) received and to exercise power over the applicable funds. As a result, although the French company had limited activities, it was not sufficient to lead to a conclusion that the company did not have a valid residency, from a beneficiary position (Cassazione, sez. trib., Sent. 28 dicembre (21 settembre 2016), n. 27113).

280 Generally, the **source state's right to tax** is limited under Art. 10 OECD Model. The OECD Model limits the taxing rights to 15%. If, however, the recipient of the dividends is a corporation that directly holds at least 25% of the stock of the company paying the dividends, the OECD Model provides for a reduction to 5%. Different rules are found in many bilateral DTCs, like in the following example.

281 **Example**

A Russian company receives dividends from Mongolia. According to Art. 10(2) of the DTC between Mongolia and Russia, the source state may withhold taxes not exceeding 10%. The same would apply if the recipient of the dividends were an individual. Russia has the right to tax, but under Art. 24 of the Mongolia–Russia DTC, the credit method must be applied.

Unlike the OECD Model, the **UN Model** does not stipulate any rates of withholding tax but leaves the certain percentage to be established through bilateral negotiations. 282

Art. 10 OECD Model is only applicable if the recipient of the dividends resides in one contracting state and the **dividends are paid by a company resident in the other contracting state**. If the dividend originates in the residence state of the recipient, Art. 10 OECD Model does not apply. The same holds true for dividends originating in third states. 283

Example 284

An individual resident in Switzerland receives dividends from a company that has its legal seat in France but its place of effective management in Switzerland. Under the tie-breaker rule of Art. 4(3) of the France–Switzerland DTC (identical to Art. 4(3) OECD Model before the 2017 Update), the company is deemed to be a resident of Switzerland. The place of effective management takes precedence over the legal seat. Since the distributing company and the recipient of the dividends are both residents of the same contracting state, Art. 10 OECD Model is not applicable. If the recipient of the dividends holds the shares as private property, Art. 21 OECD Model (Art. 23 of the France–Switzerland DTC) applies. Under this provision, Switzerland has the exclusive taxing right and France must not deduct withholding tax.

According to Art. 10(4) OECD Model, the dividend rules are not applicable if the recipient of the dividends, being a resident in one contracting state, carries on business through a PE in the other contracting state, in which the distributing company is resident, and the shares actually belong to this PE. According to this so-called **"PE proviso"** (cf. Vogel, *DTC* pre Art. 10–12, m.no. 14 et seq.), the provisions of Art. 7 OECD Model take precedence over Art. 10 OECD Model. 285

Example 286

A tax adviser works in France and has an office there but resides exclusively in Spain. Among her business assets in France, she holds shares in a French consulting company from which she receives dividends. Under the PE proviso of Art. 10(5) of the France–Spain DTC, the provisions for dividends do not apply because the recipient's fixed base and the distributing company are both in the same state, and Art. 7 (business profits) or Art. 14 (independent personal services) is applicable. Under those provisions and the method article (credit method), the dividends may be taxed in France, whereas Spain must exempt them from taxation.

Within the EU, special provisions in respect of dividend income exist. Under the **Parent-Subsidiary Directive**, distributions of profits of a corporation resident in an EU Member State to a corporation resident in another EU Member State, under certain conditions, should not be subject to any tax at source. The limitations of the source tax contained in Art. 10(2) OECD Model therefore do not apply. Under tax treaty law this is not problematic. It is up to each DTC partner whether or not to apply the source state's taxing rights assured by the DTC under their domestic law. Therefore, it is not a violation of the DTC if the source state is forced by the Parent-Subsidiary Directive not to levy withholding taxes. 287

288 **Example**

An Italian corporation holds a 100% share in a French corporation. If the other prerequisites (e.g. holding period) are fulfilled, no tax at source can be withheld in France. However, Art. 10 of the Italy–France DTC provides for a 5% source tax. Nevertheless, France must not exercise its taxing right by reason of the Parent-Subsidiary Directive.

9.5. Interest

9.5.1. Interest

289 **Art. 11 OECD Model** regulates interest payments. Art. 11(3) OECD Model defines the term "interest" as income from debt claims of every kind. The term "debt claims" is not defined but must be contrasted with "dividend". From the list of examples provided in Art. 11(3) OECD Model, one could conclude that "debt claims" in terms of tax treaty law could also be connected with a participation in the profits of the debtor. However, if the contract also allows for a participation in the liquidation proceeds, it is likely regarded as a share, not a debt claim. In this case, the payments are dividends and Art. 10 OECD Model is applicable. The distinction between dividends and interest is not always easy and might differ from country to country. Nevertheless, for DTC purposes, only the treaty definition is relevant.

290 **Example**

A Czech company received a loan from an associated company resident in the Netherlands. The loan exceeded four times the equity of the company. The interest payments and the principal of the loan depended on the profits of the company. Following domestic thin capitalization rules, the Czech authorities requalified these payments as dividends. The company was therefore required to withhold taxes at source as though the payments had been dividends. This did not mean, however, that for the purposes of the Czech Republic–Netherlands DTC the payments were to be characterized as dividends. Art. 10(6) of the DTC contains an independent definition of dividends. Under this definition, dividends include income from "other corporate rights assimilated to income from shares by the taxation law of the State of which the company making the distribution is a resident". A loan can never be a corporate right because it does not give rise to the right to participate in the profits, control or surplus on liquidation. Consequently, the payments at hand constituted interest for the purposes of the DTC (cf. CZ, NSS 10 Feb. 2005, 2Afs 108/2004–106).

9.5.2. Allocation of taxing rights

291 According to Art. 11 OECD Model, the **residence state** of the recipient of the interest has the right to tax the interest. The **source state's** right to tax is restricted to a certain percentage only **if the recipient of the interest is the beneficial owner of the interest.** The taxes paid in accordance with the tax treaty in the source state will be credited in the residence state, as set out in Art. 23 OECD Model.

Example 292

A person resident in Syria receives interest payments from the Slovak Republic. Under Art. 11(2) of the Slovak Republic–Syria DTC, the Slovak Republic has the right to withhold source tax to a maximum of 10%. Double taxation is eliminated by means of the credit method.

Generally, the **taxing right of the source** state is limited: the OECD Model limits it to 10%. In practice, however, numerous DTCs provide for deviating source tax rates and, under some DTCs, source tax is not levied at all. The **residence state** usually retains the right to tax interest. The **UN Model** follows the same approach to interest as to dividend payments and does not provide for a certain withholding tax rate. 293

Example 294

A person resident in Hungary receives interest from a Macedonian savings account. Under Art. 11(1) of the DTC between Hungary and Macedonia, the residence state of the recipient has the exclusive right to tax if the recipient is the beneficial owner of the interest. No tax at source may be withheld. If the same person were to receive the interest payments from a Romanian source, the residence state of the recipient may also tax the interest. However, the source state may also tax the interest but if the recipient in the residence state is the beneficial owner, the withholding tax is limited to a maximum of 15% (Art. 11(2) Hungary–Romania DTC).

Art. 11 OECD Model only applies when the recipient is resident in one contracting state and the **interest arises in the other contracting state**. Consequently, if the interest arises in the residence state of the recipient of the interest, or the interest arises in a third country, Art. 11 OECD Model does not apply. 295

Art. 11(4) OECD Model contains the **PE proviso** for interest. The provisions of Art. 11(1) and (2) OECD Model are not applicable if the recipient of the interest carries on business through a PE in the contracting state in which the interest arises and the receivable, upon which the interest is paid, belongs to this PE. In this case, Art. 7 OECD Model takes precedence. **Art. 11(4) UN Model** differs from the OECD Model as this provision extends the "limited force of attraction principle" mentioned in Art. 7(1)(c) UN Model. Hence, interest payments arising from transactions of the same or similar kind outside a PE or fixed base do not fall into the scope of Art. 11 UN Model, so that Art. 7 or Art. 14 UN Model is applicable. 296

Example 297

A Maltese company has a PE in Egypt. The Egyptian PE has a bank deposit with an Egyptian bank from which it receives interest. If the bank deposit is actually connected to the PE, Art. 11 of the Egypt–Malta DTC does not apply because the PE proviso takes precedence. Consequently, Art. 7 Egypt–Malta DTC (business profits) is applicable, and the interest income is attributed to the PE and is taxed in the PE state. Malta will apply the credit method (Art. 22(1) of the Egypt–Malta DTC) to prevent double taxation.

9.6. Royalties

9.6.1. Royalties

298 Royalties are regulated by **Art. 12 OECD Model**. The concept is defined in Art. 12(2) OECD Model as payments of any kind received as consideration for the use of, or the right to use, any copyright of literary, artistic or scientific work including cinematographic films. Patents, trademarks, designs or models, plans, secret formulas or processes, or the information concerning industrial, commercial or scientific experience are specifically mentioned. However, tax treaties sometimes use other definitions for royalties.

299 **Example**

In former versions of the OECD Model (prior to 2002), Art. 12 OECD Model included remuneration for the use of, or the right to use, industrial, commercial or scientific equipment. In particular, this applied to leasing payments. The Jordan–Turkey DTC follows this former OECD Model and provides for a 12% source tax for such income. This definition also holds true for the UN Model and, apart from that, "films or tapes used for radio and television broadcasting" are explicitly mentioned.

9.6.2. Allocation of taxing rights

300 According to Art. 12 OECD Model, the residence state has exclusive taxing rights; the source state is only entitled to raise taxes **if the recipient of the royalties is not the beneficial owner of the royalties.** Consequently, Art. 23 OECD Model does not apply. However, numerous DTCs deviate from the provisions of Art. 12 OECD Model. The right to raise taxes on royalties in the source state is typically found in older DTCs, as well as in treaties following the UN Model. The taxing right of the source state is limited again as it is the case with dividends and interest payments. This allocation rule illustrates the way the **UN Model** is designed to take into account the special circumstances of developing countries, which typically are source states in respect of royalty payments. Over the past few years, the tax treaty practice of many countries has changed and more and more DTCs no longer include taxing rights for the source state.

301 **Example**

A Turkish company leases copyrights to a company resident in Bahrain and receives royalties. Under Art. 12(1) of the Bahrain–Turkey DTC, Turkey has the taxing right but Bahrain may withhold 10% tax at source (Art. 12(2)). Under the method article (Art. 22 of the Bahrain–Turkey DTC), Turkey must credit the withholding tax against the tax payable in Turkey on the royalties.

302 Royalties only fall within the scope of Art. 12 OECD Model, if they **arise in one contracting state** and are paid to a person resident in the **other contracting state**. When royalties arise in the same contracting state in which the recipient of the royalties is resident, Art. 12 OECD Model does not apply. This also holds true for royalties from third countries.

Like Art. 10 and 11, Art. 12 OECD Model contains a **PE proviso**. According to Art. 12(3) OECD Model, Art. 12(1) does not apply if the recipient of the royalties, resident in a contracting state, carries out business through a PE in the contracting state in which the royalties arise and the right or assets for which the royalties are paid belong to this PE. In this case, Art. 7 OECD Model applies and the PE state has the right to tax. 303

Example 304

A Mexican sole trader has a PE in Barbados, which developed a special technical procedure. This technique is made available to a Barbadian company. The royalties received by the Mexican company are effectively connected to the PE in Barbados and, consequently, the PE proviso applies. Instead of Art. 12, Art. 7 of the Barbados–Mexico DTC is applicable. Barbados, as the PE state, has the right to tax and Mexico must allow a credit (Art. 24(1) Barbados–Mexico DTC).

Due to royalties being exempt in the source state, there is no provision in the OECD Model dealing with where royalties are **deemed to arise**. However, since the UN Model grants the source state a limited taxation right, the question where royalties are deemed to arise is addressed in **Art. 12(5) UN Model**: it depends on where the payer is resident. Also, DTCs that are patterned after the OECD Model but still provide for a withholding tax normally include such provisions (cf. Baker, *DTC* 12 B.05). 305

9.7. Capital gains

9.7.1. Alienation

Art. 13 OECD Model regulates capital gains. The prerequisite for the application of Art. 13 OECD Model is the existence of an alienation. The concept is not defined in tax treaties. From the context of the convention, it is inferred that an alienation is the transfer of the ownership of the asset. The question of whether certain dealings are regarded as alienations has to be determined exclusively in the context of the treaty (cf. also Baker, *DTC* 13 B.04). Transactions in one of the two contracting states, which are merely put on par with alienations by means of domestic legislation, are therefore not necessarily alienations in the sense of a tax treaty. 306

Example 307

A resident of the Netherlands holds a 100% share in a Dutch company. In the year X1 he moves to Belgium and a year later (in X2) he sells all the shares to a bank, provided that it liquidated the company (liquidation clause). Under Dutch domestic law, the income arising from such alienation of shares constitutes "income from capital". Now the question was whether the Netherlands had a taxing right under Art. 13(5) of the Belgium–Netherlands DTC, which provides for a source tax of 20% (which is a deviation from the OECD Model). The Dutch tax administration argued that Art. 13(5) of the treaty did not apply because in domestic terms this income was not regarded as a capital gain. However, the Netherlands Supreme Court ruled that regardless of the classification of the income under domestic law, Art. 13 did also include the sale of shares with a liquidation clause, because the term capital gains had an independent meaning in the treaty (NL, Hoge Raad 3 Jul. 1991, Case 25.308; discussed by Smit, ET 1992, 57 et seq.).

9.7.2. Allocation of taxing rights

308 **Art. 13 OECD Model** contains five paragraphs, each of which contains an independent sub-allocation rule. Every capital gain is to be assigned to one of the paragraphs of Art. 13 OECD Model. If the application of the first four paragraphs of Art. 13 fails, the blanket clause contained in Art. 13(5) OECD Model applies.

309 The legal consequences vary: Art. 13(1) OECD Model deals with the **alienation of immovable property**. In accordance with Art. 6 OECD Model, the taxing rights are allocated to the state in which the property is situated. Whether the residence state can also assert taxing rights depends on Art. 23 OECD Model, which provides the applicable method for the elimination of double taxation.

310 **Example**

A person resident in Armenia owns Italian immovable property and sells it. Under Art. 13(1) of the Armenia–Italy DTC, the situs state (Italy), may tax the gain arising from the alienation. Art. 24 of the DTC (Art. 23 OECD Model) provides that Armenia has to deduct – from the taxes payable – the taxes paid in Italy (credit method).

311 The **concept of immovable property** is defined in Art. 6 OECD Model. Art. 13(1) OECD Model refers to this provision. The rule only applies if the immovable property is situated in one contracting state and the recipient of the capital gain is resident in the other contracting state. If the alienated immovable property is situated in the residence state of the alienator or in a third country, Art. 13(1) OECD Model does not apply. The blanket clause of Art. 13(5) OECD Model will then apply, so that the residence state of the alienator has the right to tax.

312 Capital gains from the alienation of movable property forming part of the **business property** of a PE situated in the other contracting state may be taxed in the PE state. Again, the residence state's right to tax depends on Art 23 OECD Model. The residence state can either tax the capital gain and credit the taxes paid in the PE state or exempt the gain (with progression). The assets covered under Art. 13(2) OECD Model can be determined by reference to Art. 7.

313 Capital gains from the alienation of ships or aircraft operated in international traffic, or of movable property pertaining to the operation of such ships or aircrafts, are covered by Art. 13(3) OECD Model. The state of the enterprise operating such ships and aircraft has the exclusive right to tax. This treatment corresponds to the treatment accorded to business profits of such companies under Art. 8 OECD Model.

Pursuant to Art. 13(4), gains from the **alienation of shares** deriving more than 50% of their value directly or indirectly, at any time during the 365 days preceding the alienation, from immovable property situated in a contracting state may be taxed in that state. The 2017 Update of the OECD Model expanded the article to include alienation of comparable interests, such as interests in a partnership or trust. Whether the residence state can also tax will depend on Art. 23 OECD Model, which provides the applicable method for the elimination of double taxation. 314

Art. 13(5) OECD Model is the **blanket clause**. The alienation of every asset not covered by Art. 13(1) to Art. 13(4) OECD Model falls under Art. 13(5) OECD Model. The right to tax these capital gains is exclusively assigned to the residence state of the recipient. Art. 23 OECD Model is therefore not required. 315

Art. 13(5) OECD Model covers capital gains from the alienation of assets not discussed in the first four allocation rules. Above all, participations not covered by Art. 13(4), receivables, know-how and patents, are covered by this provision, insofar as these assets are not attributable to a PE in a state other than the residence state of the recipient (Art. 13(2) OECD Model). Moreover, this rule covers PE assets if the PE is situated in a third country or in the residence state of the alienator. Finally, the alienation of assets that are not covered by any other allocation rule, and do not serve in the realization of profits, falls under Art. 13(5) OECD Model, pursuant to which the alienator's residence state has the exclusive taxing right. 316

Example 317

A resident of Austria with an apartment in Switzerland owns jewellery. When this person sells the jewellery, the blanket clause of Art. 13(3) Austria–Switzerland DTC provides that the residence state of the alienator has the right to tax. Under Austrian domestic law, the gains may or may not be taxed, depending on how long the person owned the jewellery. If the jewellery is sold during the so called "speculation period", the person must pay income tax in Austria. If, however, the sale takes place outside the "speculation period", the sale is not taxable. Therefore, even though the treaty allocates the taxing right to Austria, it is possible that no tax will be imposed under Austrian domestic law. The treaty does not give rise to an independent right to tax (cf. m.no. 51).

Numerous OECD Member countries have reserved the right to include in their DTCs a provision similar to Art. 13(5) 2001 UN Model. This additional provision provides that capital gains from the **alienation of shares other than those in immovable property companies**, representing a certain percentage of the share in a company, which is a resident of a contracting state, may be taxed in that state. The 2017 update of the UN Model expanded the article to include the alienation of comparable interests, such as interests in a partnership or trust. The intention of this regulation bases on the assumption that such a shareholder can control the dividend policy of the company or entity and is therefore in a position to transform dividends, which are subject to withholding tax in the source state, into capital gains, which, under the OECD Model, are taxable only in the residence state of the alienator. The percentage of the minimum shareholding is to be established 318 through bilateral negotiations. Art. 13(5) UN Model underlines the focus of the UN Model on the special requirements of developing countries, as these countries typically are in the position of the source state.

319 **Example**

Art. 13(5) China–France DTC (Art. 13(5) UN Model) stipulates that gains derived from the alienation of shares, other than those mentioned in Art. 13(4) of that DTC and which represent a participation of 25% in a company that is a resident of a contracting state, may be taxed in that contracting state

9.8. Independent personal services

9.8.1. Independent personal services

320 Until 2000, the OECD Model contained a separate provision for the **income from independent personal services** in Art. 14. The OECD Committee on Fiscal Affairs deleted this allocation rule without replacing it with another. The Committee believed that Art. 14 OECD Model essentially had the same legal consequences as Art. 7 OECD Model and was therefore superfluous. All income previously assigned to the former Art. 14 OECD Model is now covered by Art. 7 OECD Model. Since it will still take some time for Art. 14 OECD Model to disappear from bilateral tax treaties, the former Art. 14 OECD Model is explained below.

321 The concept of services is defined in the former Art. 14(2) OECD Model. In particular, it includes independent scientific, literary, artistic, educational or teaching activities, as well as the independent activities of physicians, lawyers, engineers, architects, dentists and accountants. For an activity to be categorized as other independent services, it must be comparable to the liberal professions.

322 From the list of services set out in the former Art. 14(2) OECD Model, one can identify **two criteria** according to which independent personal services differ from business profits (Art. 7 OECD Model). First, the former Art. 14 OECD Model primarily covers services. Second, the amount of capital expenditure characteristically does not play a decisive role in the field of the former Art. 14 OECD Model (Vogel, *DTC* Art. 14, m.no. 14). However, the legal consequences of the former Art. 14 OECD Model resemble the legal consequences of Art. 7 OECD Model. Therefore, the distinction between Art. 7 OECD Model and the former Art. 14 OECD Model often plays only a minor role in practice.

323 **Example**

A consultant resident in Poland has an office in Norway. The issue is whether the profits can be attributed to the Norwegian office under Art. 7 (business profits) or under Art. 14 (independent personal services) of the Norway–Poland DTC. According to these rules, Norway has the right to tax the profits attributable to a PE (Art. 7 Norway–Poland DTC) and to a fixed base (Art. 14 Norway–Poland DTC). Under both rules, Poland is required to exempt the income from tax; however, the progression clause (Art. 22(1)(c) Norway–Poland DTC) remains applicable.

Nonetheless, the **distinction between Art. 7 OECD Model and the former Art. 14 OECD Model** can sometimes play a role in practice. Some tax treaties, for example, provide for different methods to avoid double taxation depending on which allocation rule applies. 324

Example 325

An interior architect, resident in Austria, derives income from designing houses in Liechtenstein. For the purpose of performing his activities, he has a fixed base in Vaduz (Liechtenstein). Under Art. 14 of the Austria-Liechtenstein DTC, the income shall be taxable in Austria and in Liechtenstein, but in the latter state only as much as is attributable to the fixed base. Under Art. 23(1) of the DTC between Austria and Liechtenstein, Austria has to exempt the income, which may be taxed in Liechtenstein. If the Austria-Liechtenstein DTC would not contain a provision modelled after the former Art. 14 OECD Model, Art. 7 OECD Model would apply. In that case, Art. 23(2) of the DTC would apply and Austria would only have to credit the tax paid in Liechtenstein.

The differentiation of independent personal services from employment **income of Art. 15 OECD Model is more important. The legal consequences set out in Art. 15** OECD Model differ from those in the former Art. 14 OECD Model. In the OECD Model, neither a definition of independence nor an explanation of dependence is found. On the basis of the structure of the allocation rules (cf. m.no. 167), however, these concepts exclude each other. In the literature it is assumed that **"entrepreneurial risk"** and **"relationship of subordination"** are critical to the distinction between these two concepts (in detail Vogel, *DTC* Art. 15). 326

Example 327

An individual working in Canada was found to be a resident of the United States for the purposes of the Canada–US DTC. The tax authorities argued that since he was an employee, the provisions of Art. XV of the DTC allowed Canada to tax the employment income. The taxpayer argued that since he was providing independent personal services, Art. XIV applied instead. In allowing the taxpayer's appeal, the Federal Court of Appeal took the following factors into consideration: the level of control exercised over the taxpayer's activities, the ownership of equipment necessary to perform the work, whether the taxpayer hired his own helpers, and the degree of financial risk and profit that was assumed by the taxpayer (CA, FCA 15 Mar. 2002, Wolf v. Her Majesty the Queen).

9.8.2. Allocation of taxing rights

According to the former Art. 14 OECD Model, income from independent personal services can be taxed only in the **residence state of the recipient**. Under the former Art. 14(1) OECD Model, an exception arises when the recipient has a fixed base regularly available to him in the other contracting state for the purpose of performing his activities. If there is no fixed base in the other state, however, the former Art. 14(1) OECD Model assigns the exclusive right to tax to the residence state of the recipient. In this case, Art. 23 OECD Model does not need to be applied. 328

329 **Example**

A Dutch tax adviser accompanies his client to Belgium and takes part in contract negotiations. As long as a fixed base in Belgium is not constituted, Belgium does not have the right to tax the adviser's income. The sole taxing right under Art. 14 of the Belgium–Netherlands DTC belongs to the Netherlands. The method article does not have to be applied in this case.

330 If the recipient of the income has a fixed base regularly available to him in the other contracting state, the former Art. 14(1) OECD Model provides that the **state of the fixed base** also has the right to tax. This state, however, may only tax the income attributable to the fixed base. The former Art. 14(1) OECD Model does not prevent the residence state from also taxing the income. Art. 23 OECD Model will determine whether the residence state can also tax and credit the taxes paid in the state of the fixed base, or whether the residence state is required to exempt the income (with progression).

331 **Example**

A Bulgarian lawyer has a branch in Ukraine. In addition, he receives interest payments from Ukrainian bank deposits. Art. 11 of the Bulgaria–Ukraine DTC could be applied with respect to these interest payments. Since, however, independent personal services are performed in Ukraine through a fixed base, Art. 11 of that DTC cannot be applied if the interest payments are attributable to the fixed base (Art. 11(4) Bulgaria–Ukraine DTC (PE proviso)). If this is the case, Art. 14 of the Bulgaria–Ukraine DTC is the decisive allocation rule. As long as the profits are attributable to the fixed base, they can be taxed in Ukraine. Bulgaria will exempt the income but has the right to apply the progression clause according to Art. 24 of the Bulgaria–Ukraine DTC (Art. 23 OECD Model).

332 The **concept of the fixed base** is important for the allocation of taxing rights. This concept is not defined in the OECD Model. The OECD Commentary on Art. 7, however, points out the parallels between the former Art. 14 and Art. 7 OECD Model. From those parallels, it can be concluded that the PE definition of Art. 5 OECD Model can be applied for the interpretation of the fixed base concept.

333 **Example**

An Italian lawyer has an office in Brussels. The exclusive purpose of this office is to obtain the latest information from the institutions of the European Commission and to supply this information to the office in Rome (Italy), where it is used for business purposes. According to Art 14(1) of the Belgium–Italy DTC, income derived by a resident of a contracting state in respect of professional services or other activities of an independent character shall be taxable only in that state unless he has a fixed base regularly available to him in the other contracting state for the purpose of performing his activities. Under Art. 5(3)(e) of the Belgium–Italy DTC, a PE is deemed not to include a fixed place of business used solely for the supply of information which has a preparatory or auxiliary character. If the understanding of that concept is transferred to the term "fixed base", Belgium does not have the right to tax the profits attributable to the office in Brussels. These profits can therefore only be taxed in Italy.

The PE concept and the fixed base concept are **similar** but not identical. In the literature, it is pointed out that the PE concept is also shaped by the peculiarities of entrepreneurial activity. In this respect, the definition cannot be carried over to the interpretation of the fixed base concept of the former Art. 14 OECD Model (in detail, cf. Vogel, *DTC* Art. 14, m.no. 21 et seq.; cf. also Baker, *DTC* 14 B.08). This results in a wide range of unresolved questions. 334

Example 335

If a self-employed architect carries out business abroad in the course of construction work during a time period exceeding 12 months, he does not constitute a fixed base (according to Vogel, DTC Art. 14, m.no. 25). Art. 5(3) OECD Model is a special provision for the field of PEs. The provision cannot be transferred to a self-employed person involved in this construction work. In my opinion, however, it is difficult to justify treating a builder, falling under Art. 7 OECD Model, differently from an architect, who often undertakes similar tasks.

In practice, the arm's length principle contained in Art. 7(2) OECD Model applies with respect to the **attribution of profits** to fixed bases. Thus, the income of the fixed base, in principle, should also be determined by means of the direct method. However, this assumes separate accounts of the fixed bases. In practice, the indirect method, i.e. the division of total profits, is therefore of greater importance (Vogel, *DTC* Art. 14, m.no. 27). 336

Contrary to the OECD Model, Art. 14 still forms part of the **UN Model**. When comparing Art. 14(1) of the UN Model with the former Art. 14(1) of the OECD Model, it can be said that under the UN Model, there are more situations leading to taxation in the source state than under the OECD Model. The taxing right of the source state is dependent not only on a fixed base regularly available to the taxpayer but also arises when the taxpayer stays in that state for more than 183 days within a 12-month period (for the 183-day rule, cf. m.no. 344). 337

9.9. Income from employment

9.9.1. Income from employment

Art. 15 OECD Model regulates income from employment. This concept is not defined in Art. 15 OECD Model. Its content, however, can be derived from the distinction drawn between employment income and business profits of Art. 7 OECD Model (cf. m.no. 235 et seq.) or independent personal services of the former Art. 14 OECD Model (cf. m.no. 320 et seq.), respectively. The relationship of subordination and the lack of entrepreneurial risk play a role (Vogel, *DTC* Art. 15). 338

According to Art. 15(1) OECD Model, the allocation rules of Art. 16, Art. 18 and Art. 19 OECD Model take **precedence** over Art. 15 OECD Model. This means that directors' fees (Art. 16 OECD Model), pensions (Art. 18 OECD Model) and income from government service (Art. 19 OECD Model) do not fall within the 339 scope of Art. 15 OECD Model. This also applies with respect to income from the activities of artistes or sportsmen (Art. 17 OECD Model).

340 **Example**

Severance payments that help employees during the transition to another job fall under Art. 15 OECD Model because they are based on employment relationships (Vogel, DTC Art. 15, m.no. 10). If the severance pay is granted in lieu of a pension, however, it should be treated as a pension. Art. 18 OECD Model should then apply, giving the residence state the sole right to tax (GE, BFH 2 Sep. 2009).

9.9.2. Allocation of taxing rights

341 Art. 15 OECD Model attributes the exclusive taxing right to the residence state of the recipient. If, however, the employment is exercised in the other contracting state, the state of activity has a right to tax as well. The rule therefore relies upon the **principle of the place of work**. Whether in these cases the residence state also has the right to tax depends on Art. 23 OECD Model.

342 An essential exception to the principle of the place of work is set out in Art. 15(2) OECD Model. According to this provision, the residence state will have the exclusive right to tax when the employment is exercised in the other contracting state and the following three requirements are met:

- the recipient of the income is not present in the other contracting state for more than **183 days** within a 12-month period;
- the remuneration is paid by an employer or on behalf of an employer who is not resident in the state of activity; and
- the remuneration is not borne by a PE or a fixed base that the employer has in the state of activity. Art. 15(2) OECD Model is only applicable if all three conditions are met. If any of these three conditions is not fulfilled, the state of activity has a right to tax according to the general rule of Art. 15(1) OECD Model.

343 **Example**

An employee of a Pakistani company works at an art exhibition in Turkey for one week. The employee works in Turkey only for this week and during the rest of the year he works in Pakistan. Under Art. 15(2) of the Pakistan–Turkey DTC, only Pakistan has the right to tax the income of the employee during that week. The Pakistani employee is present in Turkey for a period not exceeding 183 days and is paid by a Pakistani company that has no PE in Turkey. If the employee were employed by a Turkish company, Art. 15(2) of the Pakistan–Turkey DTC would be inapplicable. As the state of activity, Turkey would then have the right to tax the employment income of the Pakistani resident.

344 The 183-day period is **calculated** on the basis of days of physical presence. The OECD Commentary on Art. 15 states that holidays are regularly included in the calculation, if they are spent in the state of activity. The 1992 OECD Model specified that the period has to be calculated as the aggregate of 183 days in any 12-month period commencing or ending in the fiscal year concerned. In this

respect, the wording and content of the rule has changed compared to Art. 15(2)(a) OECD Model 1963 and 1977; under the former wording of the OECD Model, the 183-day period was to be calculated separately for every calendar year.

Example 345

A person resident in China works in Greece for a Chinese employer from 5 Jul. X0 to 25 Jun. X1. The Chinese employer does not have a PE in Greece, which could bear the remuneration of the employee. Art. 15(2) of the China–Greece DTC does not apply because the employee is present for more than 183 days within a 12-month period. The state of activity, Greece, and the residence state, China, have taxing rights for that income in the years X0 and X1. The residence state, China, also has the obligation to give relief for double taxation through the credit method based on Art. 23(2) of the China–Greece DTC. If the wording of Art. 15(2) of the China–Greece DTC did not follow the 1992 OECD Model but an earlier version, the taxing rights would have been allocated differently. Since the employee would not have exceeded 183 days of presence in Greece in either calendar year, the exception to the place of work principle would apply: although he would have been active in Greece for nearly one year in total, China would have the sole taxing right.

Art. 15(2) OECD Model is only applicable if the **employer is not resident in the state of activity**. Thus, Art. 15(2) OECD Model also applies if the employer is resident in a third country. 346

Example 347

A taxable person resident in Portugal works for two months for a Spanish company in France. The Spanish employer does not have a PE in France. Art. 16(2) of the France–Portugal DTC (Art. 15(2) OECD Model) is applicable. The residence of the employer in a third state (Spain) does not change the legal situation.

The OECD Model does not contain special rules for **frontier workers**; consequently, these persons are covered by the general provisions of Art. 15 OECD Model. However, a few European DTCs provide for specific provisions for frontier workers. These regulations are not identical but in essence resemble each other: if income from employment is derived by a person who is resident in one state and has his/her place of employment in the other state and returns to that residence state daily, the income is taxable only in the residence state. 348

Example 349

A person is employed by a French bank and is resident in Freiburg (Germany). Every day he commutes from Freiburg to Colmar (France) and returns to Freiburg in the evening. Under Art. 13 of the France–Germany DTC (not corresponding with any article of the OECD Model), income from employment derived by persons who work in the frontier zone of one of the contracting states and have their permanent homes in the frontier zone of the other contracting state, to which they generally return each day, shall be taxable only in that other state. Art. 13(5)(b) France–Germany DTC provides that the frontier zone of each of the contracting states shall include municipalities with territories whose distance is, wholly or partly, not more than 20 km away from the frontier. Therefore, Germany has the right to tax the income from employment and France does not have any taxing right.

9.10. Directors' fees

9.10.1. Directors' fees

350 **Art. 16 OECD Model** covers directors' fees and similar remuneration that a person receives in his/her capacity as a "member of a board of directors". This concept is not defined in the convention but according to prevailing opinion it refers to supervisory activities. Income from management activities is therefore not covered by Art. 16 OECD Model. It needs to be taken into account, that the terms used in the OECD Model ("member of a board of directors" and "membre du conseil d'administration ou de surveillance d'une société") have a broader understanding than the (unofficial) German version of Art. 16 OECD Model ("Aufsichts- und Verwaltungsrat") (cf. Vogel, *DTC* Art. 16, m.no. 6 et seq.).

351 **Example**

A German resident taxpayer is a member of the board of management of a German company and in this regard receives income from employment. In the taxable year in question he is seconded to a Spanish subsidiary for a total of 124 days and he fulfils several tasks: he acts as a member of the subsidiary's supervisory board, as the representative of the group management and he is in charge of the subsidiary's reorganization. Approximately 40% of his total working time is dedicated to the activities conducted for the subsidiary. The taxpayer is remunerated by the parent company for both his activities carried out for the subsidiary and for the parent. In this regard, the German Federal Tax Court held that Art. 16 of the Germany–Spain DTC did not apply because this provision only covers remuneration paid specifically for the participation in one of the bodies mentioned therein (i.e. the "Aufsichtsrat" or the "Verwaltungsrat"). Remuneration that is paid in respect of various activities, however, cannot be split up and attributed proportionately to Art. 16 of the Germany–Spain DTC (GE, BFH 23 Feb. 2005, I R 46/03).

352 **Art. 16 UN Model** deviates from the OECD Model as it has a second paragraph covering remuneration paid to top-level managerial positions. The wording "top-level managerial position" indicates that persons occupied with supervising activities, as well as persons performing management activities, fall within the scope of the provision.

9.10.2. Allocation of taxing rights

353 Under Art. 16 OECD Model, the taxing right is attributed to the **residence state of the company** for which the person receiving the remuneration serves as a member of the board of directors. Whether the residence state of the recipient can also levy taxes is determined by Art. 23 OECD Model. Art. 16 OECD Model, however, applies only if the recipient of the income is resident in one contracting state and the company is resident in the other contracting state. If the company is resident in the recipient's residence state, Art. 16 OECD Model is not applicable. The same holds true for situations in which the company is resident in a third country. In these cases, the residence state has the right to tax according to Art. 21

OECD Model. As regards the allocation of taxing rights, both paragraphs of the UN Model follow the OECD Model.

Example 354

A member of the board of directors of an Indian company is resident in Russia. Under Art. 16 of the India–Russia DTC, since the place of effective management of the company is India, India has the right to tax the board member. The Indian taxes paid have to be credited against Russian taxes (Art. 23(1) and (3) of the India–Russia DTC).

9.11. Entertainers and sportspersons

9.11.1. Entertainers and sportspersons

Art. 17 OECD Model regulates the income of entertainers, such as theatre, motion picture, radio or television artistes and musicians, and of sportspersons The concepts are not defined in the OECD Model. However, it can be concluded from the examples provided that entertainers in terms of Art. 17 OECD Model can only be persons appearing or reciting in public. Consequently, income generated by entertainers not performing in public, such as painters, sculptors, authors or composers, is not covered by Art. 17 OECD Model. The OECD Commentary interprets the concept of sportspersons in a broader sense: Art. 17 OECD Model applies not only to athletes in the classic sense, but also to golfers and jockeys (cf. OECD Commentary on Art. 17, para. 5). Activities from the field of entertainment, such as billiards, chess or bridge, are also regarded as sport activities. For the application of Art. 17, however, an appearance in public is necessary (cf. Vogel, *DTC* Art. 17). 355

Example 356

A Czech tennis player earns income in the United Kingdom from tennis tournaments as well as from giving private lessons. The income from the tournament can be taxed in the United Kingdom pursuant to Art. 17 of the Czech Republic–UK DTC. The income from the tennis lessons is not covered by Art. 17 of that treaty since they are not related to a public performance. The United Kingdom's right to tax this income depends on other allocation rules. If the tennis player is providing independent personal services, the United Kingdom may tax the income if he has a fixed base available to him under the provisions of Art. 14 (Art. 14 of the former OECD Model). If the tennis player is providing these lessons under a contract of employment, Art. 15 of the DTC (Art. 15 OECD Model) applies to determine whether the United Kingdom may tax the income.

9.11.2. Allocation of taxing rights

Under Art. 17(1) OECD Model, the **state of activity** has the right to tax the income. This rule applies regardless of whether the entertainer or the sportsperson performs as an employee or independently. A PE or a fixed base is not required. The residence state's right to tax is governed by Art. 23 OECD Model. 357

358 **Example**

A musician resident in China performs in a concert in India. Under Art. 17 of the China–India DTC, China has the right to tax the income, irrespective of whether the musician performed as an employee or independently. A PE or fixed base is also not required. Art. 23(1)(a) of the China–India DTC (method article) provides that the tax payable in India will be credited against the tax payable in China. However, if the musician's performance is part of a plan of cultural exchange agreed upon by the governments, China will have no taxation right (Art. 17(3) of the China–India DTC).

359 Art. 17(2) stipulates a **"look-through approach"**: if the income does not accrue to the entertainer or the sportsperson himself but to another person, the state of activity of the entertainer can tax the income from an activity personally performed by the entertainer or the sportsperson. If, for example, the entertainer is employed by a company, Art. 7 OECD Model, not Art. 17 OECD Model, would normally apply with respect to the income generated by the company. Under these general rules, the taxation in the state of activity would depend on the existence of a PE to which the income of the entertainer would be attributable. If no such PE existed, the state of activity would have no right to tax. Art. 17(2) OECD Model guarantees the right to tax in these cases. The former version of the OECD Commentary on Art. 17 assumed that this rule should only apply in cases of tax avoidance (in cases of so-called "artiste companies", where an artiste "hires" another person (company) and transfers the right to provide the artiste's services, cf. Baker, *DTC* 17 B.06), but since 1992, the OECD Commentary opines that Art. 17(2) OECD Model should apply independently from the existence of abuse. However, the wording of Art. 17(2) OECD Model has never contained any grounds that would justify restricting the application of this rule to pure cases of abuse.

360 **Example**

An entertainer resident in New Zealand plans to perform in Ireland. For this purpose he establishes a corporation. The entertainer is the only shareholder of that corporation. The New Zealand corporation agrees to provide the services of the entertainer to perform in Ireland and the fee is paid to the corporation. If Art. 9 of the Ireland–New Zealand DTC (Art. 7 OECD Model) is applied, Ireland would only have the right to tax the fee if the corporation had a PE in Ireland. However, Art. 19(1) and (2) of the Ireland–New Zealand DTC (Art. 17(2) OECD Model) guarantee, based on the "look-through approach", that Ireland can tax the entertainer's income.

9.12. Pensions

9.12.1. Pensions

361 Pensions are covered by **Art. 18 OECD Model**. This rule regulates pensions and similar remuneration paid to a person resident in a contracting state with respect to former employment. These payments, which are received during the person's retirement, must primarily serve the maintenance of the person (though not exclusively) (Vogel, *DTC* Art. 18, m.no. 10 with further references). Moreover, the

employment needs to be "past" (cf. Baker, *DTC* 18 B.04). Art. 18 OECD Model consequently only covers pension payments made in consideration of past private employment. If the payments result from a former independent personal service, they do not fall under Art. 18 OECD Model. The rule also contains its own reservation in favour of Art. 19(2) OECD Model: pensions paid for government services do not fall under Art. 18 OECD Model. In addition to pensions, **Art. 18 UN Model** explicitly mentions payments made under a public scheme that forms part of the social security system of a contracting state.

Example 362

An employee resident in Singapore has worked for a Dutch company for nearly 25 years – five years in the Netherlands, the remaining period outside of the Netherlands. During his employment he contributed to the employer's pension plan. When he decides to retire he requests to redeem his pension rights related to his employment outside of the Netherlands. The request is granted and the taxpayer receives a lump sum on which withholding taxes are imposed. The question is whether the Netherlands retains its taxing right under Art. 18 of the Netherlands–Singapore DTC. In this regard, the Dutch Supreme Court ruled that such rights were also covered by the term "other similar remuneration" and, consequently, in the case at hand, Singapore, as the residence state, had the exclusive taxing right (NL, HR 5 Sep. 2003, Case No. 37.657).

9.12.2. Allocation of taxing rights

Under **Art. 18 OECD Model**, the residence state of the recipient has the exclusive right to tax; the state making the pension payment, the former state of activity, cannot tax. There is thus no need to apply Art. 23. 363

Example 364

A managerial employee resident in Hungary was employed by a Hungarian company. After his retirement, he moved to Portugal and now receives a pension in Portugal. Portugal has the exclusive taxation right under Art. 18 of the Hungary–Portugal DTC and, therefore, Hungary cannot tax the pension income.

The **UN Model** offers two alternatives regarding the allocation of taxing rights. Both alternatives have in common that in respect of social security payments, the "state of the fund principle" is applied (cf. also Art. 19(1)(a) OECD/UN Model). Apart from that, Art. 18A UN Model is identical with Art. 18 OECD Model, whereas Art. 18 (2)B UN Model provides for a limited taxation right of the source state if the payments are made by a resident of the source state or a PE situated therein. 365

Policy-wise, Art. 18 often causes problems between two contracting states, especially if a taxpayer was able to deduct his pension contributions from his taxable income in his previous state of residence and then moves to another state. The "new" state of residence will have the exclusive taxing rights, while the other contracting state provided the tax advantage. Depending on the tax system of the 366 respective contracting states, pensions can then either endure double taxation or double non-taxation. If a taxpayer moves from a state where the pension contributions are taxed to a state where the pension payments are taxed, he will endure double taxation. If the situation is reversed, the pension shall remain untaxed altogether. This problematic situation frequently leads to the termination of double tax conventions (Denmark-Spain DTC in 2009 or Denmark-France DTC in 2009), or as a compromise, agreeing on a complex version of Art. 18 (Netherlands-Portugal DTC), deviating from the OECD Model.

9.13. Government service

9.13.1. Government service

367 **Art. 19 OECD Model** regulates salaries, wages and other similar remuneration paid by a contracting state, or by a political subdivision or a local authority thereof, to an individual in respect of services rendered to that state or subdivision or authority. Consequently, the income must be paid by the state itself or by a political subdivision. If the payments are made by other public entities, Art. 19 OECD Model is inapplicable. Furthermore, the words "salaries, wages and other similar remuneration" suggest that these payments would then be categorized as income from employment (cf. Vogel, *DTC* Art. 19).

368 **Example**

An Argentinean consulting firm provides services to the Brazilian government for the recruitment of a highway construction company. The consulting firm works for the Brazilian government on the basis of a service contract. Art. 19 of the Argentina–Brazil DTC cannot be applied. The Argentinian consulting firm's income must be attributed to Art. 7 of the Argentina–Brazil DTC. The Brazilian taxing right depends on the existence of a PE.

369 Art. 19 OECD Model also covers government **pensions** ("pensions and other similar remuneration paid by, or out of funds created by, a Contracting State or a political subdivision or a local authority thereof"). If these pension payments are made to individuals for services performed for the state or its subdivision or authority, they fall under Art. 19(2) OECD Model. This rule consequently takes precedence over Art. 18 OECD Model, which would otherwise be decisive for pensions.

370 Salaries, wages, pensions and other similar remuneration for services rendered in connection with **a business carried on by a contracting state or a political subdivision or a local authority thereof** are not covered by Art. 19 OECD Model. Art. 19(3) OECD Model clarifies that this income is to be taxed according to the rules for employment (Art. 15 OECD Model), directors' fees (Art. 16 OECD Model), artistes and sportsmen (Art. 17 OECD Model) or pensions (Art. 18 OECD Model). The background for this rule is the goal of neutrality with respect to com-

petition: if public authorities provide services that a private company could also provide, the employee should also be taxed as though he had provided his services to a private company. For this reason, the general rules and not the special provisions of Art. 19 OECD Model should be applied.

Example 371

A Spanish resident is employed by a printshop that is operated by a French municipality. The employee works in a PE of this printshop in France and receives his remuneration from the French territorial authority. The France–Spain DTC provides in Art. 19(3) that Art. 19 does not apply because Art. 15 of that DTC applies to remuneration paid in respect of services rendered in connection with a business carried on by a territorial authority of a contracting state. Both states have rights to tax the income. Double taxation is avoided by the application of the method article in Art. 24 of the France–Spain DTC (Art. 23 OECD Model).

9.13.2. Allocation of taxing rights

The basis for Art. 19 OECD Model is the **"state of the fund principle"**. This is clearly expressed in Art. 19(1)(a) OECD Model: the salary, wage or other similar remuneration may only be taxed by the state for which or for whose subdivisions or authorities the services are provided. One contracting state is thereby prevented from indirectly taxing the other contracting state. Under Art. 19(1)(a) OECD Model, the state of activity has no right to tax and Art. 23 OECD Model is not required. 372

Under certain conditions, however, Art. 19(1)(b) OECD Model allocates the exclusive right to tax to the **state of activity**. This is the case when the recipient of the income is resident in the state of activity. In addition, the recipient of the income must either be a national of this state or in any case must not have become a resident of this state exclusively in order to perform services there. This exception overrules the state of the fund principle and grants the state of activity the exclusive right to tax. 373

Example 374

The Saudi Arabian foreign ministry engages a citizen of Pakistan who resides in Pakistan. The employee's job is carried out in Pakistan. Saudi Arabia is the "state of the fund". Under Art. 19(1)(b) of the Pakistan–Saudi Arabia DTC, however, Pakistan has the exclusive taxing right because the recipient of the income is resident in Pakistan, renders his services in Pakistan and is a national of Pakistan. Therefore, Saudi Arabia cannot tax the income.

The state of the fund principle also applies to **pensions**. Pursuant to Art. 19(2)(a) OECD Model, the contracting state making pension payments to a former employee has the exclusive right to tax these payments. The state of the fund principle is overruled if the recipient of the income is both resident in the other contracting state and a national of the other state. 375

376 **Example**

A university professor at an Algerian state-run university is resident in Algeria and has both Algerian and Spanish nationality. After his retirement, he gives up his Algerian residence and moves to Spain. The retirement pension that he receives from Algeria is only subject to tax in Spain since he is resident only in Spain and has the required Spanish nationality (Art. 18(2)(b) of the Algeria–Spain DTC, corresponding to Art. 19(2)(b) OECD Model).

9.14. Students

9.14.1. Payments to students and business apprentices for their maintenance, education or training

377 **Art. 20 OECD Model** covers payments that a student or business apprentice receives for maintenance, education or training. It applies to a student or business apprentice who is or was, immediately before visiting a contracting state, a resident of the other contracting state and who is present in the first-mentioned state solely for the purpose of his or her education or training.

378 The category of persons to which this provision applies is not defined; however, the main **purpose** of the person's presence in the host state must be education or training. In addition, the student or business apprentice might also perform other employment activities on the condition that the main purpose of the stay still remains education or training. Art. 20 OECD Model exclusively deals with payments for these purposes. These payments can also be employment income.

9.14.2. Allocation of taxing rights

379 Art. 20 OECD Model does not allocate taxing rights to the source state but rather **prevents the host state from taxation** (cf. also Baker, *DTC* 20 B.01 and Lang, in Baker/Bobbett, *Tax Polymath*, 257ff.). It is required that the person is present in the host country. The legal consequences therefore come into effect independently from the residence of the person even though Art. 1 OECD Model implies for the application of the convention that the person must be resident in either of the two contracting states. According to the wording of Art. 20, the student or business apprentice does not need to be resident in either one of the two contracting states. It is possible that the recipient of the payments remains resident in the other contracting state or that he or she becomes resident in the host country during the studies, provided he or she was resident in the first-mentioned state directly before the entry. Moreover, if a person changes residence to a third country at the time of starting the training or education in the host country, Art. 20 OECD Model is applicable even though the other allocation rules are not. Furthermore, even students who have previously changed their primary residence to a third country but maintained another residence in their former state of residence are covered by Art. 20. Only payments from sources outside the host country are covered. Payments from sources within the host country can be taxed there (cf. Vogel, *DTC* Art. 20, m.no. 15).

According to some DTCs (Art. 20A UK–US DTC; Art. 20 Italy–Netherlands DTC), this rule also applies to **professors, researchers and teachers**, provided they are only temporarily present in the host country and that such persons are, or immediately before their stay were, resident in the other contracting state (cf. Csoklich/Günther, Intertax 2011, 578 ff.). 380

Example 381

An Italian university professor is a guest professor at a Dutch university. For this teaching activity, Art. 20 of the Italy–Netherlands DTC provides that he is not taxable in the Netherlands, provided that he is present in the Netherlands solely for the purpose of teaching and that he does not stay in the Netherlands for a period exceeding 2 years. In addition, he must either remain an Italian resident or must have been resident in Italy before he started to work as a guest professor in the Netherlands. If the university professor ceases to be a resident of Italy, he must become a Dutch resident to be covered by the Italy–Netherlands DTC. Otherwise, Art. 1 and therefore Art. 20 of the Italy–Netherlands DTC are inapplicable.

9.15. Other Income

9.15.1. The concept of "other income"

The term "other income" is not defined in the OECD Model. **Art. 21 OECD Model** does not set out an exhaustive list of types of income but rather provides a general rule relating to income not dealt with in the foregoing articles (blanket clause). As long as the DTC covers the person and the respective taxes, the income must be categorized according to one of the allocation rules (cf. m.no. 161 et seq.). If no other allocation rule is applicable, Art. 21 OECD Model should be consulted (for a detailed discussion on Art. 21 OECD Model, cf. Rust, in Lang/Pistone/Schuch/Staringer (eds.), *Source versus Residence*, 359 et seq.). 382

Example 383

The beneficiary of a private trust is resident in a DTC state. Since there are no shares in a private trust, no dividends are distributed and the income is not covered by Art. 10 OECD Model. Accordingly, only Art. 21 OECD Model is applicable (cf. more detailed m.no. 271 et seq.).

Art. 21 OECD Model not only covers those sources of income that do not fall under one of the allocation rules of the OECD Model but also applies to income that would normally be covered by another allocation rule that is, however, inapplicable because the conditions are not fulfilled, e.g. income arising in third states. 384

Example 385

An individual resident in Spain pays interest to another individual that has a permanent home available to him both in Algeria and in Spain. The recipient of the interest has his centre of vital interest in Spain. Based on Art. 4(2) of the Algeria–Spain DTC the recipient is a tax resident in Spain. Since both the recipient of the interest and the payer are residents in Spain, Art. 11(1) of the Algeria–Spain DTC does not apply. Thus, Art. 20 of the Algeria–Spain DTC applies to the interest payments and Spain has the sole right to tax the interest income.

9.15.2. Allocation of taxing rights

386 Under Art. 21(1) OECD Model, the **residence state** has the exclusive right to tax. Since the provisions of this article prevent the other contracting state from taxing, the method article does not need to be applied. Art. 21(2) OECD Model contains a PE proviso stating that income, other than income from immovable property, effectively connected with a PE in the source state is governed by Art. 7 OECD Model.

387 **Art 21 UN Model** contains a third paragraph, which stipulates that income originating from the source state not explicitly dealt with in the earlier articles of the treaty, can also be taxed in the source state. Art. 23 UN Model then determines how the residence state has to avoid double taxation. Nevertheless, income that is not attributable to the earlier articles of the treaty and which is derived from the residence state or third states, shall be taxable only in the residence state.

9.16. Taxation of capital

9.16.1. Capital

388 There is only one allocation rule for **taxes on capital**. Art. 22 OECD Model, however, contains several paragraphs. These paragraphs contain sub-allocation rules. The structure of the article is similar to that of Art. 13 OECD Model (capital gains), except for the fact that Art. 13 OECD Model has an additional paragraph (cf. m.no. 314).

389 On the contrary, concerning the **UN Model**, the Group of Experts decided to leave it to bilateral negotiations whether an article on the taxation of capital should be included in a DTC.

390 **Art. 22 OECD Model** is connected to Art. 2 OECD Model. This latter rule specifies that the OECD Model applies to all capital taxes. When the scope of the OECD Model is fulfilled, the taxed capital is to be assigned to one of the sub-allocation rules of Art. 22 OECD Model. Like Art. 13(5) OECD Model (capital gains) and Art. 21 OECD Model (for income taxes in general), Art. 22 OECD Model contains a **blanket clause**. It can be found in Art. 22(4) OECD Model. Capital that cannot be classified under an allocation rule of Art. 22 OECD Model is to be assigned to Art. 22(4) OECD Model.

391 **Example**

A person resident in State A owns land in State B. Both countries levy capital taxes in respect of the property. Under Art. 22(2) OECD Model, the situs principle applies and the country where the property is situated has the taxing right. The residence state has to allow for a credit for the taxes paid in the source state or exempt the capital from the tax base.

9.16.2. Allocation of taxing rights

Immovable property is covered by Art. 22(1) OECD Model. The provision refers to Art. 6 OECD Model. It is always applicable if a person is resident in one contracting state and the immovable property is situated in the other contracting state. In this case, the situs state has the right to tax. Whether the residence state can also tax depends on the method article. The residence state will credit the taxes paid in the situs state if it is entitled to levy taxes. Otherwise, it must exempt the capital (with progression). **392**

Movable property forming part of the **business property** of a PE is governed by Art. 22(2) OECD Model. This allocation rule uses the concepts contained in Art. 7 OECD Model. Consequently, the rules of Art. 7 OECD Model must be taken into account for interpreting the rules in Art. 22(2) OECD Model. That provision applies if the property is business property of a PE and the PE is situated in a state other than the residence state of the property's owner. The PE state has the right to tax. The method article regulates whether the residence state is entitled to tax and credit the taxes of the PE state, or whether the residence state must exempt the capital (with progression). **393**

Art. 22(3) OECD Model applies to **ships and aircraft** operated in international traffic, as well as to movable property pertaining to the operation of such ships and aircraft. There is a clear connection with Art. 8 OECD Model. Capital of an enterprise of a contracting state that operates such ships and aircrafts shall be taxable only in that state. The other contracting state's taxing right is thereby excluded and the method article does not need to be applied. **394**

Art. 22(4) OECD Model is the **blanket clause**. All property not covered by Art. 22(1), (2) or (3) OECD Model falls under this rule. For example, it applies to immovable property situated in the residence state or in a third country. It also applies to business property not attributable to a PE in the other contracting state, such as business property of a PE situated in the residence state or in a third country. Above all, however, Art. 22(4) OECD Model covers private capital, which is otherwise not covered by Art. 22 OECD Model. Under Art. 22(4) OECD Model, the owner's residence state has the exclusive right to tax. Once again, the method article does not need to be applied. **395**

Example **396**

An individual is resident for domestic tax law purposes both in Norway and in Switzerland. The tiebreaker rule of Art. 4(2) Norway–Switzerland DTC leads to Norway being the residence state for treaty purposes. The person holds shares in a Norwegian company – as private property. Norway levies a net wealth tax on this type of capital and a cantonal capital tax is also levied in Switzerland. Consequently, double taxation arises, which is countered by Art. 22(4) of the treaty; Norway, being the residence state, is allocated the exclusive right to tax.

10. Methods for elimination of double taxation

10.1. The importance of the method article

10.1.1. Relation to the allocation rules

397 The methods for elimination of double taxation are set out as rules in **Arts. 23A and/or 23B** of the DTCs patterned after the OECD Model. Under the allocation rules, the residence state's taxing rights are rarely excluded and the source state often keeps its taxing rights as well. The method articles address the residence state. When the residence state's taxing rights are not excluded and a certain item of income may be taxed in the source state, the provision obliges the residence state to either exempt the income or credit the tax paid in the source state.

398 **Example**

A German resident company carries on its activity in part through a PE situated in Spain. Under Art. 7 of the Germany–Spain DTC, profits that are attributable to that PE may be taxed by Spain. Germany's taxing rights with respect to those profits are not excluded by Art. 7 Germany–Spain DTC. Those profits may not be taxed, however, in Germany, according to Art. 22 of the Germany–Spain DTC (equivalent to Art. 23 of the OECD Model), since the exemption method applies with respect to that item of income.

399 The application of the method articles is not always necessary. In some cases, double taxation is avoided by the **allocation rules** themselves, namely when the allocation rules assign exclusive taxing rights to one state.

400 **Example**

The profits derived by the above German resident company are profits from the operation of ships or aircraft in international traffic. The place of effective management of the company is situated in Germany. Under Art. 8 of the Germany–Spain DTC, profits from the operation of ships or aircraft in international traffic shall be taxable only in Germany, notwithstanding the fact that a PE exists in Spain. Spain's taxing rights are therefore excluded by Art. 8 of the Germany–Spain DTC. The application of Art. 22 of that DTC (equivalent to Art. 23 of the OECD Model) is thus unnecessary.

10.1.2. Credit and exemption method

401 Art. 23 OECD Model offers contracting states a choice between two methods for the elimination of double taxation: the **exemption method** and the **credit method**. During the negotiations of a DTC, the contracting states agree upon the method they will apply.

402 **Commonwealth states, as well as certain African and Asian states tend to** prefer the **credit method** (cf. m.no. 175 and 430 et seq.). In **continental European**

countries, the **exemption method** (cf. m.no. 173 and 412 et seq.) is widespread, though the **credit method** is usually applied with respect to **dividends, interest payments and royalties**.

Under some DTCs, **different methods** apply depending on the residence state, i.e. on whether the person is a resident of one or of the other state. For example, under some DTCs, the credit method is applicable as far as residents of one contracting state are concerned, while the exemption method is applicable with respect to residents of the other contracting state. 403

Example 404

Under Art. 23 of the Australia–Austria DTC, different methods to avoid double taxation apply depending on whether the taxpayer is resident in Australia or in Austria. As a general rule, Australia, under the provision of Art. 23(1) of this DTC, shall grant a credit in respect of Austrian tax payable, whereas Art. 23(3) regulates that in Austria for the majority of sources of income the exemption method applies and for specific sources of income the credit method is used.

10.1.3. Switch-over clauses

Some states include **switch-over clauses** in their DTCs to allow a change from the exemption to the credit method in certain circumstances. The aim of these clauses is essentially to avoid double non-taxation, which can arise when the exemption method applies. These clauses can also apply in cases of abuse. Under the switch-over clauses, the residence state retains the right to apply the credit method instead of the exemption method, provided that certain conditions are fulfilled. This change of method can apply, for example, in cases of negative conflicts of qualification, i.e. circumstances in which double non-taxation arises as a consequence of the application of different provisions of the DTC to the same fact pattern by the two contracting states (cf. also m.no. 125). 405

Example 406

Under Sec. 6(c) of the Protocol to the Germany–India DTC, Germany shall avoid double taxation through the credit method and not through the exemption method where "income is placed under differing provisions ... or attributed to different persons", this conflict cannot be resolved by means of a mutual agreement procedure and this placement or attribution would either result in double taxation or in non-taxation, or inappropriately low taxation in India.

Art. 23A(4), added to the OECD Model in 2000, should generally have an effect similar to switch-over clauses as far as negative conflicts of qualification are concerned, i.e. to give the residence state the right to switch from the exemption method to the credit method where different interpretations of the DTC lead to double non-taxation or to the imposition of low taxes because of Art. 10(2) or Art. 11(2) OECD Model on dividends and interest. It is worth noting that the OECD Committee on Fiscal Affairs maintains that cases of negative conflicts of 407 qualification are partially covered by paragraph 1 of Art. 23A (and of 23B) OECD Model. In particular, according to the OECD Committee, Art. 23A(1) allows a state to address negative conflicts of qualification which arise due to differences in the domestic law between the source state and the residence state, and Art. 23A(4) only covers negative conflicts of qualification that arise as a result of disagreements between the residence state and the source state on the facts of a case or on the interpretation of the provisions of the DTC. This approach is questionable, however, from a legal perspective (cf. m.no. 125 et seq.).

10.1.4. No effect of the method articles

408 The rules regarding the methods for the elimination of double taxation do not apply if, under the domestic law of the two contracting states of a certain DTC, the income is attributed to two different taxable persons, each of whom is a resident of a contracting state. DTCs do not provide any autonomous rules with respect to the **attribution of income** but rather follow the classification of the contracting states. Cases of double taxation have thus to be accepted if two states attribute the income to different persons.

409 **Example**

In the case UK, SCITD 19 Nov. 2008, Bayfine UK Products v. Revenue and Customs Commissioners (cf. m.no. 12) the income of a UK unlimited company was taxable both in the United Kingdom in the hands of the UK unlimited company itself and in the United States in the hands of the parent company of the UK unlimited company, since the UK unlimited company was classified as a disregarded entity for US income tax purposes. The income of the UK unlimited company was thus attributed to different persons by the two states. The United Kingdom stated that double taxation relief is not to be granted to the UK unlimited company under the UK–US DTC. The OECD Partnership Report (Example 18) proposes that in such a case, the United States is obliged to give credit for the taxes that are levied in the United Kingdom. However, in my opinion, the OECD Model does not grant an indirect tax credit and there is no systematic argument to ignore the treaty principles in this situation (cf. Lang, Partnerships, 95 et seq.).

410 Cases of double taxation may also arise when two contracting states **impose tax on the same person but with regard to different situations**. This can lead to double taxation that is not always prevented by DTCs.

411 **Example**

In 2009, a resident of State A bought shares in the amount of EUR 100 in a company that does not own immovable property. The person moved from State A to State B in 2017, when the shares had a value of EUR 1,000. The difference of EUR 900 was subject to an exit tax in State A, i.e. it was subject to tax in State A because the person lost her status as a resident of that state. State A claimed its right to tax according to Art. 21 OECD Model since it was the residence state at the time of the transfer of residence. If the person sells the shares in 2019 at EUR 1,000, State B has the exclusive right to tax according to Art. 13(5) of the State A–State B DTC patterned after the OECD Model. State B may therefore tax the gain, i.e. EUR 900.

10.2. Exemption method

10.2.1. Effects

The exemption method has effects on the **taxable base** in the residence state. The foreign income in respect of which a resident must be granted the exemption under the relevant DTC, is excluded from the taxable base. The applicable tax rate is not affected. The residence state may therefore consider the "exempt" foreign income when determining the applicable tax rates in order to safeguard the progression of the taxation. 412

The exemption method guarantees that an entrepreneur investing abroad is subject to the same tax burden as a competitor resident in the country in which the investment is made ("capital import neutrality"). No taxation accrues in the residence state (although the exempt income may be considered to safeguard the progression of the taxation; cf. m.no. 422 et seq.). The **tax rate of the source state** is therefore decisive. 413

Example 414

In the residence state the tax rate is 40%. In the source state the tax rate is 30%. If the exemption method applies and the taxing rights of the source state are not limited by any allocation rule, the income from a capital investment is subject to a 30% tax burden in the source state and is not subject to any taxation in the residence state. The residence state, however, may consider that income to determine the applicable tax rate. In contrast to the credit method, the overall tax rate on the income from the capital investment is not increased to 40%.

The exemption method applies irrespective of whether the other contracting state actually levies a tax on the income in question. The exemption method can therefore lead to double non-taxation when the source state has taxing rights under the DTC but does not levy any tax under its domestic law, and the residence state has no taxing rights (apart from the progression safeguard) since it must grant the exemption under Art. 23(1) OECD Model. The OECD Partnership Report, however, has led to an amendment of the OECD Commentary on Art. 23 with respect to cases where double non-taxation arises because of **conflicts of qualification**, which result from different domestic laws of the two contracting states, i.e. cases where the domestic laws of the two contracting states lead to different characterizations of a certain income and, in turn, to the application of different allocation rules by the two states. According to the amended OECD Commentary on Art. 23, in those cases, the residence state is not required to exempt the income pursuant to Art. 23A(1) OECD Model. The possibility for the residence state not to grant the exemption is, according to that statement, the consequence of the fact that the source state legitimately does not allocate the income to the same allocation rule as the residence state. It is not convincing, however, to infer this interpretation from DTCs patterned after the OECD Model (cf. m.no. 125 et seq.) 415

416 If the DTC contains a **"subject-to-tax clause"**, the exemption will depend on whether taxes are levied in the source state. The OECD Model does not contain such a rule. Subject-to-tax clauses, however, are often found in DTCs. They are usually applicable to particular fact patterns but can also be of a general nature.

417 **Example**

On 17 Oct. 2007 the German Federal Tax Court issued its decision in a case regarding the subject-to-tax clause contained in the DTC between Germany and Italy (GE, BFH 17 Oct. 2007, I R 96/06). Subject to certain exceptions, Art. 24(3) of that DTC (Art. 23A OECD Model) provides for an exemption of the income that a German resident derives from Italy and that may be taxed in Italy under the DTC. However, Sec. 16(d) of the Protocol to the DTC reads as follows: "For the purposes of Article 24(3) income of a resident of a Contracting State is deemed to be derived from the other Contracting State, if it is effectively taxed in the other Contracting State in accordance with the treaty." In the case at issue, a capital gain which might be taxed in Italy was not effectively taxed in Italy. The German Federal Tax Court ruled that Sec. 16(d) of the Protocol to the DTC had to be interpreted as a subject-to-tax clause and, consequently, the gain was not to be exempt from German tax under Art. 24(3) of the DTC.

10.2.2. Exemption from tax base

418 One debated issue is whether the exemption method applies with respect to both positive and negative items (**profits and losses**) or whether it applies only with respect to positive items (i.e. **to profits only**). In this regard, the courts of many states (e.g. Austria, Belgium, the Netherlands and Spain) have stated that the exemption only applies with regard to positive items, while the courts of other states (e.g. Germany, Greece and France) have instead maintained that it also applies with regard to negative items.

419 **Example**

An individual entrepreneur is a resident of Germany and carries on his activity in part through a place of business in Poland. The German profits of the individual entrepreneur amount to EUR 10 million. Through the place of business in Poland, however, the entrepreneur suffers losses of EUR 1 million. His worldwide income consequently amounts to EUR 9 million. According to the interpretation of the German courts, the Polish losses are "exempt" from tax in Germany, i.e. they are excluded from the German resident's taxable base. Thus, the amount of income on which the tax is levied in Germany is EUR 10 million. Under the approach adopted by the courts of other states, the Polish losses should not be "exempt" from tax in Germany, so that the resident's taxable base would be EUR 9 million.

420 Related to the question of the exemption of losses is the question of the **deductibility of the expenses** paid in order to obtain certain income that is exempt under the applicable DTC. Controversy often arises in relation to the allocation rule to which expenses should be assigned, since frequently a connection with several allocation rules exists. For example, certain expenses can be connected to either dividends (Art. 10 OECD Model) or capital gains (Art. 13 OECD Model). Expenses

that can be assigned to more than one allocation rule are related to both items of income covered by those rules and no criterion exists to split those expenses between the two items of income. It thus makes sense to consider that these expenses are covered by Art. 7 or Art. 21 OECD Model. Since these allocation rules grant exclusive taxing rights to the residence state, the expenses are not exempt in the residence state under treaty law and therefore may reduce the resident's taxable base.

Example 421

Under Art. 11(3)(a) of the Bangladesh–Turkey DTC, interest from Turkish bonds paid to the Bangladesh Bank shall be exempt from Turkish withholding tax (10%). However, capital gains from the sale of those bonds shall be taxable only in the state of which the alienator is a resident according to Art. 13(4) of the Bangladesh–Turkey DTC. If the purchase of the bonds is financed through borrowing, the question is whether the outbound financing costs should be added to the interest on the bonds (which is exempt from Turkish withholding tax) or to the capital gain from the sale of the bonds (which is taxable only in Bangladesh). Assigning those expenses to one or the other allocation rule affects the availability of a deduction from the Bangladesh resident's taxable base.

10.2.3. Progression

Arts. 23A(3) and 23B(2) OECD Model contain a rule concerning progression 422
(known as "proviso safeguarding progression"). According to this proviso, where, in accordance with any provision of the DTC, income derived or capital owned by a resident of a contracting state is exempt from tax in that state, that state may nevertheless, in calculating the amount of tax on the remaining income or capital of such resident, take into account the exempted income or capital. This rule does **not provide a legal basis** for the application of progression **in itself**. It merely clarifies that domestic rules on the determination of the applicable tax rate which aim to safeguard the progression of taxation are unaffected by Art. 23 OECD Model (cf. Vogel, *DTC* Art. 23, m.no. 71 et seq. and 208 et seq.).

According to the OECD Model, the proviso safeguarding progression is **addressed** 423
to the residence state. It can therefore be inferred that only the residence state can claim the progression. Implicitly, therefore, the application of progression rules by a contracting state that is not the residence state is arguably excluded (cf. Djanani/Hartmann, *IStR* 2000, 321 et seq.). However, there are also court decisions in some countries, e.g. Germany, which state that the proviso safeguarding progression also addresses the source state because the provision only clarifies that it can be applied by the contracting states (cf. GE, BFH 19 Dec. 2001, I R 63/00; GE, BFH 15 May 2002, I R 40/01; GE, BFH 17 Dec. 2003, I R 14/02; GE, BFH 4 Apr. 2007, I R 110/05; partly discussed in Mössner, *IStR* 2002, 242; Kippenberg, *IStR* 2002, 243; Wassermeyer, *IStR* 2002, 289 et seq.; cf. also Vogel, *DBA* Art. 23, m.no. 46, 209 et seq.).

424 **Example**

Mr X was a German resident and moved to the Netherlands during the calendar year. He gave up his German home and therefore his status as resident taxpayer in Germany and became a Dutch resident. According to the treaty Germany was not entitled to levy taxes on the income he received from Dutch sources after he left Germany. However, the German Federal Tax Court held that Germany may include that income when calculating the tax rate which was applicable on his German income. According to the Court it is not necessary that the treaty entitles a state to include the foreign income for that person. It is only relevant that the treaty does not forbid it (BFH 15 May 2002, I R 40/01). At the end this means that the proviso safeguarding the progression clause in Art. 23A OECD Model becomes meaningless if not only the resident state but also the other state may calculate the tax rate that way. However, from a systematic point of view it makes sense that both states include the income generated in the other state for calculating the tax rate because otherwise the treaty application would go beyond mere avoidance of double taxation.

425 The **effect of the proviso safeguarding progression** is that income that is exempt under the DTC may be included in the resident's taxable base for the purposes of determining the tax rate. The calculation of the tax rate is regulated by domestic law. Normally, the average tax rate applicable is determined with respect to the resident's entire income. This average tax rate is then applied to the resident's taxable base, as reduced after the deduction of the income that is exempt under the DTC. Accordingly, the exemption with progression method does not cause the additional effect that the reduction of the resident's taxable base also reduces the tax rate applicable to the resident's residual income.

426 **Example**

The worldwide income of a resident of State A amounts to EUR 1 million, of which 400,000 is derived from residence State A and the remaining 600,000 from the source State B. Under the State A–State B DTC, State A applies the exemption with progression method towards the income derived in other states. Assume that in State A the rate of tax on income of up to 500,000 is 20% and on income above 500,000 40%. In this case, the tax rate applicable to the worldwide income of the resident taxpayer in the amount of EUR 1 million would be 40%. However, due to the application of the exemption with progression method, this rate will only be applicable to the income derived in residence State A. Hence, the tax due in State A will be calculated as follows: 400,000 × 40% = 160,000.

427 The average tax rate may not be applied, however, to that part of income that is subject to a reduced or increased flat tax rate under a specific domestic provision in the residence state. These peculiarities have to be taken into account when **determining the taxable base** in respect of which the average tax rate has to be applied. In addition, deductible items have to be taken into account in calculating the taxable base in connection with those items of income for which these expenses are paid or incurred. If the deductible items are paid in connection with exempt income, they cannot decrease the residual domestic taxable base. It is different if the deductible items are clearly connected with items of income that form part of the residual domestic taxable base (cf. m.no. 418 et seq.).

Example 428

A resident of Austria receives income from employment exercised in Austria and derives business profits through a PE situated in Germany. In so far as certain income from employment is subject to a 6% flat tax rate, it must be excluded from the taxable base to which the average tax rate determined according to the progression clause is applied. In other words, the average tax rate determined by including income that is exempt under the Austria-Germany DTC (business profits derived through a PE situated in Germany) should be applied to income from employment. Yet that income has to be excluded from the taxable base to which the average tax rate has to be applied. Therefore, income from employment remains subject to a 6% flat tax rate.

Progression does not usually play any role with regard to the **corporate income** 429 **tax** since the tax rate is usually flat. The average tax rate always remains the same. This also holds true in the case of negative progression. However, if the amount of foreign losses corresponds to the amount of domestic source income at such a rate that the worldwide income is zero, one could argue that the average corporate tax rate is 0%. This statement, however, is questionable from a legal standpoint (cf. Vogel, *DTC* Art. 23).

10.3. Credit method

10.3.1. Effects

When the credit method is applied, the residence state first determines the tax 430 due under domestic law on the resident's worldwide income in the absence of the DTC. This tax is then reduced by the foreign tax paid. The credit method has therefore no effect on the taxable base in the residence state. Positive and negative foreign items are ordinarily taken into account in the calculation of the taxable base. Double taxation is avoided only with respect to the amount of tax levied. If the tax rate is higher in the residence state than in the source state, the total tax burden will be equivalent to the **higher rate found in the residence state**. This phenomenon is known as "capital export neutrality".

Example 431

In the source state profits are taxed at an average tax rate of 20%. Thus, if the source state income is EUR 100, the tax burden in the source state is EUR 20. If, however, the average tax rate is 50% in the residence state, taxes in the amount of EUR 50 arise. These taxes are reduced by EUR 20, representing the taxes paid in the source state, and thus equal EUR 30. The overall tax burden, however, amounts to EUR 50.

If the source state has a higher tax rate than the residence state, the **higher tax** 432 **burden of the source state** remains when the ordinary credit method applies. The taxable base is determined in the residence state under domestic law, the tax is then calculated and the foreign taxes are deducted from that amount of tax. If, however, the tax burden is higher in the source state, the tax paid in the source state is not entirely credited. The overall tax burden corresponds in this case to the tax burden in the source state.

433 **Example**

In the source state the tax rate is 50% whereas the tax rate is only 20% in the residence state. In the source state income in the amount of EUR 100 will be subject to a tax burden of EUR 50. When the credit method is applied, the income is also subject to tax in the residence state. On the basis of the tax rate in this contracting state, the tax burden is EUR 20. Foreign taxes in the amount of EUR 20 can be credited on the taxes of EUR 20, so that there is no actual tax burden in the residence state. However, the total tax burden, given the taxation in the source state, is EUR 50.

434 The credit method applies only with respect to foreign taxes paid by the same taxable person. A credit for the taxes paid by a different taxable person, such as the "underlying tax credit" (also known as **"indirect tax credit"**), is not granted unless the particular DTC or the domestic law provides otherwise.

435 **Example**

Company U is a resident of the United Kingdom and controls 50% of the voting power in Company A, a resident of Argentina. According to UK domestic law and to Art. 23(1)(b) Argentina–UK DTC, in cases in which at least 10% of the voting power is controlled, a tax credit shall be granted by the United Kingdom with regard to dividends, not only with respect to Argentinean tax levied in Argentina on Company U with regard to such dividends but also with respect to Argentinean tax paid by Company A with respect to the profits out of which such dividends are paid ("underlying tax").

436 Similar problems arise when, under the domestic legal systems of the two contracting states, a certain item of **income** is regarded as **belonging to two different taxable persons**. In these cases, in my view, there is no legal basis under the DTC for claiming a credit, since the tax is levied in the source state on a different taxable person than that on which the tax is levied in the residence state.

437 **Example**

An Austrian corporation holds a participation in a Slovak entity, which is regarded as a taxable entity under Slovak law and as transparent under Austrian tax law. For Austrian tax purposes the entity is treated as a partnership and the income is taxed in Austria at the level of the Austrian corporation. In the Slovak Republic the profits are taxed in the hands of the entity. The DTC provides for the credit method. The OECD takes in its Partnership Report the view that in such a situation the Slovak tax may be credited against the tax levied at the level of the Austrian corporation (Partnership Report, m.no 139). In my view this goes too far: I do not see a legal basis to grant a credit for a tax which was paid by a different taxpayer.

10.3.2. Amount of allowable tax

438 The credit method provides for the taxes paid in the source state to **offset the taxes** to be paid in the residence state. However, only the amount of tax that is legally due in the source state is covered. Taxes erroneously paid to the source state are not required to be credited. Furthermore, taxes raised in the source state in excess of the limits set forth in the DTC do not have to be credited. If the

source state does not refund the taxes erroneously paid, the taxpayer suffers the consequences.

Example 439

In 2007, an Italian resident company rendered services in Kazakhstan for a 7-month period. A withholding tax was levied in Kazakhstan on the payments to the Italian company. The Italian resident company asked the Italian tax authorities to issue a ruling to state that a tax credit was to be granted with respect to the taxes levied in Kazakhstan. The Italian tax authorities, however, denied the right for the Italian resident company to the tax credit (cf. IT, AE 3 Jul. 2008, Risoluzione N.277/E). They analysed the Italy–Kazakhstan DTC and found that business profits of Italian resident companies may be taxed in Kazakhstan to the extent they are attributable to a PE situated therein. They also found that for a PE to exist under the Italy–Kazakhstan DTC, services have to be rendered for a period of at least 12 months. The Italian tax authorities therefore concluded that no PE existed in Kazakhstan according to the relevant DTC and, accordingly, tax could not be levied in Kazakhstan on business profits of the Italian resident company. Consequently, they stated that no tax credit was to be granted to the Italian resident company, which should instead ask Kazakhstan for a refund of the tax paid therein.

The creditable taxes are limited to those which are **effectively levied**. If the source 440
state levies an amount of tax that is lower than the maximum amount allowed under the DTC, the credit to be granted by the residence state is limited to the amount of tax effectively levied in the source state.

Example 441

A Spanish resident company holds a 5% participation in an Italian resident corporation. In 2009, dividends were paid by the Italian corporation. The Spanish company was the beneficial owner of those dividends. Under Art. 10(2) of the Italy–Spain DTC, a maximum of 15% withholding tax may be levied in Italy. However, only a 1.375% withholding tax was actually levied in Italy. According to Art. 22 of the Italy–Spain DTC, the credit method applies. Since the creditable taxes are limited to those which are effectively levied, Spain was obliged to grant a credit amounting to 1.375% of the dividends, even though the maximum withholding tax that may be levied in Italy was higher.

Some DTCs include exceptions to the above principle. In particular, a **"matching** 442
credit" is sometimes granted under DTCs concluded with developing countries. Under this kind of credit method, a notional amount of foreign taxes established in the relevant allocation rule or in the method article is deemed to be levied at source and is credited by the residence state even if the tax is not actually levied in the source state or a lower amount of tax is levied. This provision is intended to stimulate capital investments in the developing country. The matching credit prevents the residence state from benefiting, in place of the investor, from the non-taxation or reduced taxation by the source state: in the absence of a matching credit mechanism, the residence state would simply credit less foreign tax and would therefore frustrate the non-taxation or reduced taxation by the source state. Under the matching credit, the benefit goes to the investor, since the residence

state grants a credit on a notional basis irrespective of the amount of taxes paid in the source state. The investor obtains the advantage.

443 **Example**

A French company derives interest arising in Brazil. Under the Brazil–France DTC, this interest may be taxed in Brazil. According to Art. XXII(2)(c) of the Brazil–France DTC, with regard to interest which has borne Brazilian tax in accordance with the provisions of the DTC, France shall allow its residents receiving such income a tax credit corresponding to the amount of Brazilian tax that has been paid, within the limits which the French tax establishes in such income. Under Art. XXII(2)(d) of the Brazil–France DTC, with regard to interest, the Brazilian tax shall be considered to have been levied at a minimum rate of 20%. The French company deriving interest arising in Brazil is thus entitled to a tax credit corresponding to at least 20% of the interest, irrespective of whether lower tax is actually levied in Brazil.

444 Some DTCs provide for another kind of credit method based on notional amounts, which is known as a **"tax sparing credit"**. Under the tax sparing credit, when an exemption or reduction is granted in the source state, the residence state grants a credit on the basis of the (fictitious) amount of foreign taxes, which the source state would levy if no exemption or reduction were granted.

445 **Example**

A Belgian company derives interest arising in India. This interest may be taxed in India under the Belgium–India DTC. According to Art. 23(3)(b)(i) of the Belgium–India DTC, when a resident of Belgium derives interest taxable in India in accordance with Art. 11(2) or (6), the Indian tax levied on that income shall be allowed as a credit against Belgian tax related to such income in accordance with Belgian provisions of law. Art. 23(3)(e) of the Belgium–India DTC also provides that: "For the purposes of sub-paragraph (b)(i) the term 'Indian tax levied' shall be deemed to include any amount which would have been payable as Indian tax under the laws of India and in accordance with the provisions of the Agreement for any year …", except for some exemptions or reductions listed in that provision of the DTC. Based on the above, the Belgian company deriving interest from India is entitled to a tax credit for the amount of taxes that would have been payable as Indian tax, even if no taxes are actually levied in India (unless the non-taxation in India is grounded on those exemptions or reductions that are listed in the Belgium–India DTC).

10.3.3. Maximum credit

446 DTCs generally set forth a **maximum credit** that must be granted. The amount of tax which must be credited may not exceed the tax that the resident would pay in the residence state on the same (foreign) item of income. This is known as "ordinary credit". This means that in order for a credit to be granted, a tax on the same (foreign) item of income must first of all be due in the residence state. If no tax is due in the residence state in the same tax period, the tax paid in the source state is not credited. According to the OECD Commentary on Art. 23A and 23B (at para. 32.8), the residence state must nonetheless grant the credit when the lack of tax due in the residence state is the consequence of a timing mismatch.

Example 447

An Argentinean corporation derives business profits from a PE in Russia and receives royalties arising in Russia. The royalties amount to RUB 5 million. However, the PE suffers losses amounting to RUB 5 million as well. Under the Argentina–Russia DTC, the ordinary credit method applies. The taxable base in Argentina on the Russian-sourced income is 0, since the losses suffered through the PE offset the royalties. Therefore, in this fiscal year no tax is due in Argentina on Russian-sourced income. Any tax at source which may be raised in Russia in respect of the royalties can, according to the treaty, consequently not be credited against any Argentinean tax.

The maximum credit limitation is usually applied according to one of the following approaches: the "overall limitation" and the "per-country limitation". Under the **"overall limitation"**, the aggregate amount of taxes paid in all source states may be credited up to the amount of tax due in the residence state on the aggregate amount of items of creditable income from all source states. Under the **"per-country limitation"**, the tax paid in a certain source state may be credited up to the amount of tax due in the residence state as determined on the aggregate amount of items of income derived from the former state; items of income derived from other contracting states are thus disregarded. Sometimes a **"per-item limitation"** is implemented in addition to one of the above limitations (the "overall limitation" or the "per-country limitation"). Under the "per-item limitation", the tax paid per a certain category of income may be credited up to the amount of tax due in the residence state as determined on the aggregate amount of tax paid for a certain category of income. 448

Example 449

Company A is a resident of State A and has a PE in State A and a PE in State B. Company A also derives income from interest arising in State C. In the fiscal year concerned, no profits are derived through the PE in State A; profits amounting to EUR 1 million are derived through the PE in State B, in respect of which a tax of EUR 250,000 is levied (25%); interest amounting to EUR 500,000 arises in State C, in respect of which a tax of EUR 50,000 is levied (10%). Company A's worldwide income amounts to EUR 1.5 million and the tax due in State A on this income amounts to EUR 300,000 (20%). If State A followed the "per-country limitation", the tax credit would be determined as follows. With regard to the tax levied in State B: a tax credit amounting to EUR 200,000 would be granted since the tax due in State A in respect of the profits derived in State B is EUR 200,000 (1 million x (300,000/1.5 million)). With regard to the tax levied in State C: a tax credit amounting to EUR 50,000 would be granted. The total tax credit granted would amount to EUR 250,000, notwithstanding the overall taxes levied abroad amount to EUR 300,000. Hence, taxes amounting to EUR 50,000 would be paid in State A [300,000 (tax due in State A) – 250,000 (tax credit)]. If State A instead followed the "overall limitation", the tax credit would be determined as follows: items of income and foreign taxes would be aggregated. The tax due in State A in respect of all foreign items of income is EUR 300,000. The taxes paid abroad on those items of income amount to EUR 300,000 (250,000 + 50,000). The foreign taxes may thus entirely be credited; hence no tax would have to be paid in State A.

450 The ordinary credit can create difficulties in practice when high **expenses are linked** to the foreign items of income and the residence state considers the maximum credit to be determined with respect to the amount of the foreign items of income as reduced by those expenses ("net amount"). The tax due in the residence state in respect of the net amount can likely be very low, so that the foreign taxes may largely not be credited. This problem could be resolved by calling the connection of expenses into question.

451 **Example**

An Austrian corporation has a total income of EUR 1 million. Part of this income is interest arising in Italy amounting to EUR 100,000. The Italian loans, from which the interest derives, are financed through borrowing. The capital costs that are connected with this interest amount to EUR 90,000. The net amount of interest arising in Italy is thus, according to the opinion of the tax administration, EUR 10,000. The tax due in Austria in respect of that net amount is EUR 2,500 (25%). However, under the Austria–Italy DTC, Italy may levy a tax on that interest that does not exceed 10% of its gross amount. The Italian tax at source on the interest therefore amounts to EUR 10,000. It may be credited only up to EUR 2,500; hence EUR 7,500 may not be credited.

11. The implementation of treaty benefits in both contracting states

11.1. Source state

DTCs frequently **limit or eliminate the source state's taxing rights**. When the DTC rules are applied, they are equivalent to domestic law. Eliminations or reductions of the taxing rights thus have the same consequences as they do in domestic law: the rules have to be taken into consideration by the taxpayer and the administrative authorities when domestic law is applied. Eliminations or reductions of the taxing rights provided for by a DTC must therefore be applied from the beginning, as if no taxing rights existed. 452

> **Example** 453
>
> A Polish corporation pays royalties to a corporation resident in Lebanon. The Lebanese company is the beneficial owner. Under Polish domestic law, royalties paid to non-resident companies are liable to a 20% final withholding tax. According to Art. 12(2) of the Lebanon–Poland DTC, however, Poland's right to tax those royalties is limited to 5%. Consequently, only 5% withholding tax is levied.

Occasionally, a tax limitation contained in a DTC is **not applied**. For example, the full amount of withholding tax is levied in the source state although the relevant DTC eliminates or reduces the source state's taxing rights. This is not a mistake by the taxpayer. Source states often levy the full amount of withholding tax to reduce the risk that, in the event the DTC requirements are not fulfilled, no tax will be withheld. These states grant the taxpayer the possibility of applying for a refund once the DTC requirements have been fulfilled. 454

> **Example** 455
>
> In the above example, if in Poland a 20% withholding tax was (by mistake) withheld with regard to the royalties, the Lebanese company would have to apply for a refund of the withholding tax exceeding the 5% stipulated in the DTC.

The ECJ developed its case law on the **principles of equivalence and effectiveness** and therefore requires that these principles are followed by the domestic legislators and administrative authorities. Due to the fact that EC law and tax treaty law are to a certain extent comparable, one can argue that the phrase "irrespective of the remedies provided by the domestic law of those State" in Art. 25(1) OECD Model, seems to apply that **"remedies provided by domestic law"** exist and that they are relevant for the application of tax treaties. One cannot assume that the drafters of the OECD Model had remedies in mind that are not effective. Secondly, one can also argue that the true legal basis for the application of the principles of equivalence and effectiveness in the context of tax treaties is the OECD Model itself and the DTCs following the OECD Model as a whole (cf. Lang, *Intertax* 2007, 146 et seq.). 456

457 Under the law of some states, specific provisions set forth that the reduction of the withholding tax may be granted **directly at source** rather than through a tax refund procedure. As a rule, such provisions are not part of the DTC. They are instead part of domestic law. In fact, domestic law normally regulates when an immediate tax reduction at source is allowed or when that reduction may only be obtained through a tax refund procedure carried out by the taxpayer.

458 In some cases, the tax authorities of the source state request **evidence of taxation** by the residence state if the taxpayer is seeking a tax exemption on the basis of a DTC. However, this evidence is not necessary in cases in which the DTC grants exclusive taxing rights to the residence state. The effective taxation by the residence state is irrelevant as long as the relevant DTC does not contain a subject-to-tax clause.

11.2. Residence state

459 In residence states the DTC rules are often **equivalent to domestic law**. An exemption of foreign income as well as a deduction of foreign taxes has to be executed ex officio. No specific request by the taxpayer is necessary, unless the DTC provides otherwise.

460 If, in the residence state, the measures for the avoidance of double taxation are not part of the assessment of the taxpayer, the DTC rules may be applied by the taxpayer or third parties. In particular, a DTC **could be applied directly** if a withholding tax is levied at source and the obligation to credit foreign taxes or to exempt foreign income exists on the basis of the DTC.

461 **Example**

The current Austrian corporate tax rate is 25%. Under Art. 22(1)(e) of the Austria–Turkey DTC, the amount of credit that has to be granted by Austria to its residents in respect of royalty arising in Turkey is (at least) 10% of that royalty (matching credit, cf. m.no. 442 et seq.). Assume an Austrian resident corporation derives royalty arising in Turkey. If the DTC could be applied directly, the tax actually levied in Austria on that royalty would amount to 15%. An immediate advantage for the Austrian corporation would thus ensue.

11.3. The importance of the evidence of taxation in the other contracting state

462 The tax authorities of many countries tend to make the application of a tax limitation in a DTC dependent on whether the taxable person provides **evidence that taxes have been levied in the other contracting state, or that the taxable person is resident of the other contracting state which implicitly refers to prospective tax liability therein**. This way they can test that the relevant DTC is interpreted uniformly compared to the other contracting state and that the same DTC provision

is applied. However, there is no legal basis for such a requirement: neither the actual imposition of taxes nor an identical interpretation by the tax authorities is a precondition for the application of OECD-patterned DTCs. Even if this were relevant, the tax authorities would still have the possibility of obtaining information by themselves through an exchange of information (cf. m.no. 516 et seq.), so that no increased obligation to cooperate can be imposed upon the taxable person. Thus, the existence of evidence of taxation is not a precondition for the application of a DTC.

Example 463

In order to apply for beneficial treatment as "beneficial owner" under articles regarding dividend, interest and royalty under DTCs, the Chinese tax authority requires taxpayers to provide evidence of tax residence identity issued by tax authorities in the other contracting state, proving that the present taxpayer is tax resident of that other contracting state in the tax year or in the previous year when the Chinese-sourced income is derived (Guo Shui Han [2009] No.601 SAT).

12. The arm's length principle of Art. 9 OECD Model

464 Multinational enterprises with affiliates in different tax jurisdictions face the challenge of determining a price for transactions effectuated within their groups of companies, which is called the **transfer price**. Transfer price does not result from supply and demand in an open market and is established by the group. The determination of transfer price influences the assessment of the single entities' profitability and related accounting issues as well as the taxable profit of each company in the respective jurisdiction. Particularly, by over- or underpricing intercompany transactions, the group can shift profits to low-tax jurisdictions and thereby minimize the overall tax burden of the group. Therefore, a specific set of tax rules (i.e. transfer pricing rules) exist in many countries to determine transfer prices in a proper way. Such rules apply to all intra-group transactions. For multinational enterprises as well as for tax authorities, the issue of transfer pricing is of utmost importance, especially in light of global tax planning.

465 **Art. 9(1) OECD Model** is the basis for DTC provisions relating to transfer pricing, providing that "[w]here an enterprise of a Contracting State participates directly or indirectly in the management, control or capital of an enterprise of the other Contracting State, or the same persons participate directly or indirectly in the management, control or capital of an enterprise of a Contracting State and an enterprise of the other Contracting State, and in either case conditions are made or imposed between the two enterprises in their commercial or financial relations which differ from those which would be made between independent enterprises, then any profits which would, but for those conditions, have accrued to one of the enterprises, but, by reason of those conditions, have not so accrued, may be included in the profits of that enterprise and taxed accordingly."

466 This provision is placed in between the allocation rules. However, Art. 9 OECD Model is not an allocation rule but has a special role. Although this rule has a confining effect similar to that of the allocation rules, it addresses cases of economic double taxation arising from affiliated enterprises. Accordingly, domestic rules that provide for profit adjustments between affiliated companies are limited by the arm's length principle.

467 DTC rules patterned after Art. 9 OECD Model are not an independent legal basis for the adjustment of profits between affiliated companies. Like every other DTC provision, these rules do not create tax liability. The legal basis can therefore only be found in domestic law. If there is no domestic law allowing for the **adjustment of profits**, there can be no profit adjustment pursuant to Art. 9 OECD Model.

Example 468

A Romanian company delivers single components of cars to its parent company, which is resident in Spain, and receives compensation amounting to EUR 100 for each component. If the subsidiary had sold these goods to a third party, a price of EUR 200 for each component could have been realized (arm's length price). Domestic law will determine whether or not the Romanian tax authorities may adjust the profits of the subsidiary. If a profit adjustment takes place, Art. 9(1) of the Spain–Romania DTC provides that the transfer price must be set in accordance with the arm's length principle. It is now assumed that Romania adjusts the profit of the subsidiary in accordance with the arm's length principle and adds EUR 100 per component to the profits. This will lead to economic double taxation because the part of the profit that does not meet the arm's length price is also taxed in Spain – at the level of the parent company. In order to avoid this, Art. 9(2) of the Spain–Romania DTC provides for an adjustment in Spain as well, as long as Spain agrees with Romania's adjustment.

Art. 9(2) is designated to relieve economic double taxation (2017 OECD Commentary on Art. 9 at para. 5). It provides that if one contracting state (State A) makes an upward adjustment in the profit of an enterprise in State A pursuant to Art. 9(1), the other contracting state (State B) should make a corresponding adjustment with respect to the profit that has already been taxed in the hands of the associated enterprise in State B. However, State B is only obliged to make such corresponding adjustment if it agrees that the adjusted amount in State A is in line with the arm's length principle. It also provides that if the two contracting states have disputes over the amount and character of the appropriate adjustment, they could initiate a mutual agreement procedure (MAP) under Art. 25 OECD Model (2017 OECD Commentary on Art. 9 at para. 11). 469

Since 2001, unlike the OECD Model, the **UN Model** contains a third paragraph in Art. 9. It addresses circumstances under which Art. 9(2) UN Model ("corresponding adjustment") shall not apply. Therefore, a contracting state is not required to conduct a corresponding adjustment where judicial, administrative or other legal proceedings have resulted in a final ruling that, by actions giving rise to an adjustment of profits under Art. 9(1) UN Model (identical with Art. 9(1) OECD Model), one of the enterprises is liable to penalty with respect to fraud, gross negligence or wilful default. This provision resembles Art. 8(1) of the EU Arbitration Convention and the necessity of its inclusion can be discussed controversially (in detail Kosters, *Asia-Pacific Tax Bulletin* 2004, 7 et seq.). 470

The OECD has published **Transfer Pricing Guidelines (OECD TPGs)**. These reports are extremely important in practice since they provide an interpretation of the arm's length principle as well as several methods for establishing the arm's length price. However, since the OECD TPGs are recommendations, they are not legally binding principles. If they were available at the time of the conclusion of a particular DTC that is based on the OECD Model, they can be used for the interpretation of that DTC. The OECD TPGs are not, however, an independent legal 471 basis for the adjustment of profits between affiliated companies. As stated above, there must be domestic rules providing for a profit adjustment.

472 The OECD TPGs present several **methods** for establishing the arm's length price. The selection of one method is not easy and may vary from company to company, but, generally, an appropriate method can be found to estimate the arm's length price in the best possible way. One can distinguish the traditional transaction methods (**traditional transaction methods**) and transactional profit methods (transactional **profit methods**). There is no "best method rule"; the company does not have to test all methods in order to find the best transfer price. However, according to the OECD, the "most appropriate method to the circumstances of the case" should be used in order to calculate the arm's length price.

473 The three **traditional transaction methods** are the comparable uncontrolled price (CUP) method, the resale price (RP) method and the cost-plus (CP) method. They all have in common the fact that they are based on the price. The CUP compares the transaction with "real-life" uncontrolled transactions to calculate the arm's length price. This is the most direct and precise method but is in most cases inapplicable due to the lack of comparability. The RP method takes into account the price of the product when it is resold on the next supply chain level to a third party and deducts a gross margin in order to calculate the arm's length price. Finally, the CP method is very similar to the RP method but proceeds the other way around, i.e. the arm's length price is calculated by adding a mark-up to the company's costs.

474 The transactional **profit methods** are the transactional net margin method (TNMM) and the transactional profit split method (TPSM), both of which assess the profit level of the controlled enterprises. While the TNMM establishes the transfer price by reference to profits earned by other similar unrelated enterprises, the TPSM evaluates the combined profits earned by the controlled enterprises and splits the combined profits between controlled enterprises as if they were independent enterprises.

475 Establishing the arm's length principle is largely based on the **comparability** of controlled and uncontrolled situations. According to the OECD TPGs, being "comparable means that none of the differences between the situations being compared could materially affect the condition being examined in the methodology or that reasonably accurate adjustments can be made to eliminate the effect of any such differences" (OECD TPGs, para. 3.47). The OECD TPGs (paras. 1.36, 1.42–1.118) identify **five comparability factors** determining the comparability: (1) the contractual terms; (2) the functional analysis; (3) the characteristics of property or services; (4) the economic circumstances; and (5) the business strategies. The contractual terms of transactions generally define (explicitly or implicitly) how the responsibilities, risks and benefits are to be divided between enterprises

in arm's length dealings. It always and merely serves as a starting point of a transfer pricing analysis and the real conduct of controlled parties prevails if it is different from the contractual terms. Besides, the difference in the characteristics of property and services, such as in respect of the transfer of tangible property, the physical features of the property, the quality and reliability, and the availability and volume of supply, often leads to differences in their value. Moreover, the functional analysis of the parties is important because in dealings between independent enterprises the compensation reflects the functions performed, risks assumed and assets used by each enterprise. The arm's length price varies across different markets and it is therefore important to identify the relevant markets and achieve comparability. Some economic circumstances, which determine market comparability, are geographic location, the size of the markets and availability of substitute goods and services. In addition, business strategies are also relevant to determine the comparability for transfer pricing purposes. Examples include innovation, new product development, degree of diversification, risk aversion, assessment of political changes, and input of existing and planned labour laws.

13. Non-discrimination

13.1. Scope of application of non-discrimination rules

476 DTCs also contain non-discrimination rules. Art. 24 is the relevant rule in the OECD Model. It provides certain specific grounds that cannot be relied on by a state to discriminate for purposes of taxation. In relation to nationals of the treaty partner state, **Art. 24 OECD Model** prohibits discrimination by reason of nationality (para. 1) and contains similar protection for stateless persons (para. 2). In relation to residents of the other contracting state, Art. 24 OECD Model prohibits discrimination against PEs belonging to (para. 3), against deductions of certain payments and debts to (para. 4), and against enterprises owned by residents of the other contracting state (para. 5).

477 Art. 24 OECD Model prohibits only overt discrimination which meets the specific criteria of the non-discrimination provisions. If domestic law contravenes a non-discrimination rule, the domestic law is ousted when the DTC is applied. The DTC provisions regarding non-discrimination rules have priority.

478 Under Art. 24(6) OECD Model, the non-discrimination rules are **not limited by Art. 2** OECD Model. Consequently, the non-discrimination rules also apply to taxes that are not covered by the scope of the DTC. The non-discrimination rules therefore impact the entire domestic tax law.

13.2. Non-discrimination on the grounds of nationality

479 Under Art. 24(1) OECD Model, **nationals** of a contracting state shall not be subjected in the other contracting state to any taxation or any requirement connected therewith which is other or more burdensome than the taxation and connected requirements to which nationals of that other contracting state in the same circumstances (in particular with respect to residence) are or may be subjected. This provision also applies to persons who are not resident in either contracting state.

480 Nationals of one contracting state must therefore be treated like nationals of the other contracting state, provided they are in a **comparable situation**. The rule does not provide grounds upon which discrimination can be justified. However, special reasons can cause the situation of the taxpayer to be incomparable to that of nationals of a contracting state, in which case the non-discrimination rules will not apply.

481 **Example**

A Slovakian employer (the taxpayer) posted employees to his PE in the Czech Republic. However, this employer neither declared the income nor paid any wage tax in the Czech Republic. After a tax audit, the Czech tax authorities imposed the wages tax due. In this assessment, the authorities included the travel reimbursements paid to the employees, although these reimbursements do not represent taxable income under the Czech Income Tax Act (ITA). The Supreme Administrative Court held for the taxpayer. The Court observed that the travel reimbursements do not present any income to the employee as they only cover the expenses incurred by the employee on a business trip. The Court then considered the non-discrimination provisions of Art. 24(1) of the Czech Republic–Slovakia tax treaty, which were not invoked in the earlier instances of this case. The Court held that under this treaty provision the tax treatment of Slovakian and Czech employees has to be equal. Therefore, if the conditions of the Czech law are met, Slovakian employees should have the same rights to exclude the reimbursed travel expenses from their tax base (Case 2 Afs 77/2007-62, 17 April 2008).

Art. 24(2) OECD Model enables national treatment to be accorded to **stateless persons**, which means individuals who are not considered to be nationals of any state under the operation of its law. This non-discrimination provision is rarely agreed upon in international tax treaty practice because a very similar rule can be found in the Convention relating to the Status of Stateless Persons concluded in New York in 1954. **482**

13.3. Non-discrimination on the grounds of the PE of an enterprise

Under Art. 24(3) OECD Model, the taxation of a **PE** that an enterprise of a contracting state has in the other contracting state shall not be less favourable in that other contracting state than the taxation levied on enterprises of that other contracting state carrying on the same activities (discrimination based on the situs of the enterprise). Art. 24(3) OECD Model expressly states that this provision shall not be construed as obliging a contracting state to grant to residents of the other contracting state any personal allowances, reliefs and reductions for taxation purposes on account of civil status or family responsibilities that it grants to its own residents. **483**

This non-discrimination rule is, in practice, the most important provision of Art. 24 OECD Model. PEs of persons that are residents in the other contracting state must be **treated like companies that are residents in the PE state**. If the situation is comparable, there can be no discrimination of the PE. **484**

Example **485**

Saderat was a bank established in Iran with a branch in France. In tax year 2009, the French branch of Saderat realized profits on which a source tax was withheld, after deduction of the French corporate income tax due by the branch, pursuant to Art. 115 quinquies of the General Tax Code (Code général des impôts, CGI) by reason of the deemed distribution of the branch's profits to non-resident shareholders. Afterwards, in 2014, Saderat requested the reimbursement of the tax withheld, arguing that it had been withheld unduly. The French tax authorities rejected the reimbursement and the Administrative Tribunal rejected Saderat's action for annulment of this decision. Saderat appealed to the Administrative Court of Appeal of Paris, arguing that, as the withholding tax did not constitute a tax on profits but on profit distributions, the levying of the tax was contrary to Art. 24 of the France–Iran Tax Treaty. The Administrative Court of Appeal then observed that the levying of the tax was also not contrary to Art. 24(1) of the treaty. Saderat argued that its branch was taxed less favourable than a French enterprise exercising the same activities because it had to pay the withholding tax on top of the corporate income tax. The Court held that the withholding tax was justified because the company's profits were deemed to have been distributed abroad. A French enterprise performing the same activities that would distribute profits abroad would also suffer a withholding tax on top of the corporate tax levied on its profits (Case 16PA03777, 30 November 2017).

486 For the application of Art. 24(3) OECD Model the definition of a PE in Art. 5 OECD Model is relevant. However, that does not necessarily mean that the application of Art. 24(3) OECD Model is limited to cases which are covered by Art. 7 OECD Model.

487 **Example**

The OECD PE Report specified that the determination of the existence of a PE is independent from the kind of income derived from the PE. For example, a rental office may constitute a PE regardless if the income derived through that office qualifies as income from immovable property (under Art. 6 OECD Model). In the same way, the existence of a PE would remain relevant for the application of other articles, such as Art. 24(3) OECD Model.

13.4. Non-discrimination according to Art. 24(4) OECD Model

488 Under Art. 24(4) OECD Model, **interest, royalties and other disbursements** that are paid by an enterprise of a contracting state to a resident of the other contracting state, shall, for the purpose of determining the taxable profits of such enterprise, be deductible under the same conditions as if they had been paid to a resident of the first-mentioned state. The provisions of Arts. 9(1), 11(6) and 12(4) OECD Model have priority over the rule in Art. 24(4) OECD Model. This non-discrimination rule is also applicable in the area of capital taxes.

489 The provision prohibits discrimination on the basis of **the recipient of the payment**: payments made to persons resident in the other contracting state must have the same effect on the domestic tax basis as they would when made to persons that are resident in the state of residence of the creditor. If payments to residents decrease the tax basis of the creditor, payments to non-residents must also decrease the creditor's tax basis.

490 **Example**

The taxpayer company was tax resident of India. It was engaged in the business of high-end software products. During the relevant tax year, the taxpayer company had made certain payments to one of its group companies that was tax resident of the Netherlands. As per the taxpayer company, the payments were not subject to withholding tax.

Accordingly, the taxpayer company did not withhold tax while making the payments to the Netherlands' company. The tax authorities, however, concluded that the payments were in the nature of fees for technical services that were subject to withholding tax. On that basis, the tax authorities denied deduction to the taxpayer company (since the taxpayer company did not withhold tax). The ITAT held that the payments were not subject to withholding tax, in view of Art. 24(4) of the treaty because a similar payment to a resident payee (in India) was not subject to withholding tax (ITA No. 1595/Mum./2009, 18 May 2012).

13.5. Non-discrimination in connection with the shareholders/partners of a company

Under Art. 24(5) OECD Model, an enterprise of a contracting state, the capital of which is **wholly or partly owned or controlled, directly or indirectly**, by one or more residents of the other contracting state, shall not be subjected in the first-mentioned state to any taxation or any requirement connected therewith that is other or more burdensome than the taxation and connected requirements to which other similar enterprises of the first-mentioned state are, or may be, subjected. This provision prohibits discrimination on the basis of the residence of a shareholder or partner in the other contracting state. 491

Example 492

The taxpayer was a company resident in Russia. In 2007 and 2008 the taxpayer had debts to foreign affiliated companies, one registered in Switzerland and which owned more than 20% of the Russian company's shares. Prior to this, the taxpayer was a subsidiary of a Cyprus company. The taxpayer also had loans from other affiliated companies. Under the relevant provisions of the Tax Code of the Russian Federation, the thin capitalization rules (a ratio of 3 to 1 debt to equity) apply if a Russian company has a debt to a non-resident company which directly or indirectly holds or controls more than 20% of its share capital, or if a Russian company has a debt to another Russian company which is an affiliate of a non-resident company. The thin capitalization rules do not apply if a Russian company is wholly owned by other Russian entities or individuals. The tax authorities took the position that the terms of the taxpayer's loans significantly diverged from the arm's length standards and that the general principle of non-discrimination does not affect arrangements that are not at arm's length. The Supreme Arbitration Court held in favour of the tax authorities stating that in general tax treaties do not preclude the application of domestic anti-avoidance rules, in particular, in respect of the recharacterization of loan into equity contributions. On this ground the Supreme Arbitration Court concluded that the anti-avoidance provisions in Russian domestic law in respect of thin capitalization rules are not discriminatory or in conflict with Russia's obligations under its tax treaties (Case 8654/11, 15 November 2011). This result, however, is questionable.

14. Mutual agreement procedure

14.1. Mutual agreement procedure

493 DTCs also contain rules dealing with the **legal protection of the taxpayer**. In DTC law, the competent authorities in the two contracting states are responsible for the application of the DTC rules. In practice, it is possible for the authorities of the two contracting states to come up with different conclusions. Even if in both states the assessments are appealed, it is possible that the different interpretations of the same rule will remain since the courts of appeal of the two contracting states can also interpret situations differently. There is a lack of a superior authority.

494 The rules of the mutual agreement procedure try to cure this deficiency. **Art. 25 OECD Model** contains the mutual agreement procedure. It can be initiated by any resident person who considers that the actions of one or both of the contracting states result or will result for him/her in taxation not in accordance with the provisions of the DTC. The condition is therefore not double taxation but rather taxation not in line with the DTC. Often, mutual agreement procedures are initiated on the basis of economic double taxation (Art. 9 OECD Model).

495 **Example**

A taxable person, resident in the United Arab Emirates, receives capital gains from the alienation of shares in a company resident in Malta. The capital gains are not subject to taxation under United Arab Emirates domestic law. Under Art. 13(5) of the Malta–United Arab Emirates DTC, Malta does not have the right to tax. If the Maltese tax authorities nevertheless want to tax these earnings because the administration does not consider Art. 13(5) of the Malta–United Arab Emirates DTC to be applicable, the taxable person may present his case to the competent authority of his state of residence. Under Art. 24 of the treaty (Art. 25 OECD Model), the taxpayer may initiate a mutual agreement procedure even though the actions of the Maltese tax authorities would not lead to double taxation but only to the imposition of taxes in Malta.

496 For the initiation of the mutual agreement procedure, it is sufficient that the intended **taxation be not in accordance with the DTC**. The taxation does not have to have been already imposed. The taxable person must only be able to assume that taxes will be imposed on his/her income or capital contrary to the DTC.

497 **Example**

On the basis of written communications between the taxpayer and the tax authorities, the taxpayer knows that the tax authorities want to tax income that, in his opinion, is exempt on the basis of the applicable DTC. The taxpayer does not need to wait for an assessment by the tax administration in order to present his case to the tax authorities of either contracting state.

The taxable person can present his/her case to either competent authority irrespective of the **remedies provided by domestic law**. A waiver of the legal remedy is not a condition for a mutual agreement procedure. Thus, the taxpayer has the option of using different remedies side by side. The case must be presented within three years from the first notification of the action resulting in taxation not in accordance with the provisions of the DTC. 498

The taxpayer must present the case to the **competent authority of either contracting state.** The OECD Model differs from the UN Model in this aspect. In the UN Model, the taxpayer presents the request to initiate a **MAP** only to the competent authority of the residence state. The DTC defines the competent authorities of the contracting states. A MAP can be initiated in either contracting state. 499

Under Art. 25(2) OECD Model, the competent authority shall **"endeavour"** to resolve the case by mutual agreement with the competent authority of the other contracting state, with a view to the avoidance of taxation that is not in accordance with the DTC. The objection must appear to the competent authorities to be justified and the competent authority must not itself be able to arrive at a satisfactory solution. 500

Whether the competent authority is **obliged to initiate a mutual agreement procedure** is controversial. However, the representatives are obligated to negotiate and use their best endeavours to resolve the problem. Apart from the taxpayer's right to present objections, the OECD Model does not include provisions that refer to the taxpayer's position in the mutual agreement procedure. According to the OECD Commentary on Art. 25, however, it is the duty of the contracting states to give the taxpayers "certain essential guarantees". "The proper approach is to give the taxpayer the right to a hearing and the possibility to obtain information on how the mutual agreement is proceeding" (cf. Vogel, *DTC* Art. 25, m.no. 83). 501

The duration of the mutual agreement procedure is unregulated. In practice, it can take a long time. There is **no guarantee** that the mutual agreement procedure will result in an agreement being reached between the competent authorities of the two contracting states. Furthermore, the mutual agreement procedure can be discontinued without a solution having been reached. Even if an agreement between the competent authorities is reached, there is no guarantee that the result of the agreement procedure will correspond to the wishes of the taxpayer. One of the key objectives of the OECD is to improve the timeliness of processing and completing MAP cases. Therefore, the OECD publishes on its website annual statistics on the MAP caseloads of all its Member countries and of non-OECD countries that agreed to provide such statistics (cf. https://www.oecd.org/tax/dispute/mutual-agreement-procedure-statistics.htm; accessed on 27 August 2020). 502

503 **Example**

A person resident in Chile earns income that is taxed in both Chile and Ecuador. The taxpayer presents his case to the Chilean competent authority in accordance with Art. 25(1) of the Chile–Ecuador DTC. The competent authorities reach an agreement under the mutual agreement procedure to the effect that the income is taxable only in Chile. Double taxation is thereby avoided. The taxpayer, however, may have been of the view that only Ecuador should tax the income. The agreement does not, however, have to accord with the taxpayer's wishes.

504 The **result of a mutual agreement procedure shall be implemented** notwithstanding any time limits in the domestic law of the contracting states.

14.2. Consultation procedure

505 Under the first sentence of Art. 25(3) OECD Model, the competent authorities of the contracting states shall endeavour to resolve by mutual agreement any difficulties or doubts arising as to the interpretation or application of the DTC. This means that the competent authorities can resolve any interpretation problem **irrespective of a case put forward** by a taxpayer.

506 However, in many jurisdictions the competent authorities are bound by the DTC; they cannot come to a conclusion that overrides the DTC. Art. 25 OECD Model contains **no legal basis** for a treaty override by the competent authorities. In this respect, the relevance of this rule is limited (cf. especially also m.no. 112 et seq.).

507 In addition, according to the second sentence of Art. 25(3) OECD Model, the competent authorities can discuss the resolution of double taxation in cases that are **not in accordance with the DTC**. This rule is not an independent legal basis to resolve double taxation; it does not authorize the competent authorities to resolve cases of double taxation not covered by the DTC. If the competent authorities reach an agreement, they must utilize the statutory sources of domestic law.

14.3. Arbitration procedure

508 Art. 25(5) OECD Model provides that where the competent authorities, after two years of discussions, have not been able to resolve the case completely, the pending issues preventing them from reaching a full accord can, upon request of the taxpayer, be submitted to the arbitral process. No procedural requirements have been fixed by Art. 25(5) OECD Model; the competent authorities shall settle the mode of application by mutual agreement. A sample mutual agreement setting out a number of procedural rules is attached as an annex to the Commentary on Art. 25 OECD Model as guidance.

Example 509

State A has concluded a DTC with State B in accordance with the OECD Model which contains an arbitration clause similar to Art. 25(5). Company X, resident of State A, has a manufacturing facility in State B from which it buys finished goods to be sold in State A. States A and B disagree on the transfer pricing of the sale of finished goods from the manufacturing facility in State B to Company X in State A and therefore a case of taxation not in accordance with the DTC arises. A MAP is initiated, however, after two years of discussions, the competent authorities of States A and B still are not able to reach an agreement on the case. The taxpayer then requests for an arbitration procedure to be installed under Art. 25(5) of the State A–State B DTC. The procedural rules governing the arbitration procedure will be agreed between States A and B through mutual agreement.

The UN Model, however, differs slightly from the OECD regarding the arbitration procedure. Art. 25(5) Alternative B of the UN Model provides for the following main differences: 510

- If the mutual agreement is not completely resolved within three years (instead of two years under the OECD Model), the competent authority of either contracting state can request the unresolved issues to be taken to arbitration (instead of the taxpayer submitting the request as in the OECD Model).
- The UN Model provides in Art. 25(5) Alternative B that the competent authorities may deviate from the arbitral decision if they can reach an alternative agreement within six months counting from when the arbitral decision was announced (this is not provided in the text of Art. 25(5) of the OECD Model, however, the Commentary suggests that contracting states may allow competent authorities to deviate from the arbitral decision if they can reach an alternative solution within three months from the communication of the arbitral decision).

Apart from the OECD and UN Model Conventions, US tax treaties mostly contain specific arbitration clauses. A typical US arbitration procedure is the so-called "baseball arbitration": the tax authorities of each government involved submit a proposed solution for the case to the arbitrator; afterwards, the arbitrator will choose the solution he finds to be the best one, without modification or reasoning. This procedure speeds up the arbitration process. 511

Example 512

Art. XXVI (6) of the Canada–US DTC contains a mandatory arbitration clause applicable in cases that the competent authorities have been unable to resolve by mutual agreement. In connection with this DTC, the treaty negotiators agreed to an Arbitration Note. This Arbitration Note provides the practices and procedures that the two countries will follow, including the commencement of the arbitration proceedings and the selection of the arbitration board. In particular, the arbitration board has 6 months to reach a decision on the case and the decision must be one of the two solutions proposed by the contracting states. This is known as "baseball arbitration".

513 Another type of arbitration mechanism is the so-called "independent opinion", whereas the arbitrators have the freedom to formulate their own decision without being bound by the opinion of the competent authorities. This type of procedure is longer and more costly than the baseball arbitration; however, it provides for a reasoning for the decision and grants more rights to the taxpayers (e.g. the taxpayer can participate in a hearing). This type of arbitration procedure is more commonly appropriate for cases involving a question on general interpretation of a provision in the law or principle.

514 The OECD Commentary on Art. 25(5) depicts the advantages and disadvantages of each type of arbitration procedure and states that, to a certain extent, the most appropriate type of arbitration will depend on the specificities of the case under analysis. While on the sample agreement annexed to the commentary the "baseball arbitration" or "best final offer" is presented as the default type, with the "independent opinion" arbitration being the optional procedure, contracting states are free to agree on either procedure, a combination of both or other variations as they see fit.

515 Moreover, the MLI presents the arbitration procedure as best practice and not as a minimum standard. The baseball (or "final offer") arbitration is stated in Part VI of the MLI as the default method (if countries opt for arbitration but do not state a different method of application), however, similar to Art. 25(5) OECD Model, countries are free to choose other types of arbitration in their bilateral negotiations or state their preferred method upon signature of the MLI.

15. Exchange of information

15.1. Scope of application of the exchange of information

DTCs also contain rules regarding the exchange of information. The decisive rule is **Art. 26 OECD Model**. The rule provides that the competent authorities of the contracting states shall exchange such information as is foreseeably relevant for carrying out the provisions of the applicable DTC or for the administration or enforcement of the domestic laws concerning taxes of every kind and description imposed on behalf of the contracting states, insofar as the taxation thereunder is not contrary to the DTC. According to this "major information clause", the exchange of information can also include information that relates to domestic law and not only to the DTC itself. 516

Example 517

When applying Art. 15 and Art. 24 of the Australia–Belgium DTC (Art. 15 and Art. 23 OECD Model), Belgium can inform Australia of the amount of employment income exempt from taxation in Belgium when the employment of a Belgian resident is exercised for more than 183 days in Australia. In addition, Belgium can ask Australia what an independent company in Australia paid for goods delivered by a company in Belgium with a view to the correct application of the provisions of its domestic laws.

Since the 2011 Update, **Art. 26 UN Model** basically reproduces Art. 26 OECD Model. There are, however, two deviations worth mentioning. First, Art. 26(1) UN Model emphasizes that information should particularly be exchanged for the purpose of preventing fraud or evasion of taxes. Second, the UN Model contains in Art. 26(6) a provision that is non-existent in the OECD Model. Accordingly, the UN Model stipulates that the competent authorities shall, through consultation, develop appropriate methods and techniques concerning the matters in respect of which exchanges of information shall be made. 518

Under the **"minor information clause"**, the competent authorities can only exchange information that is necessary for carrying out the DTC. Consequently, information that relates only to a tax liability under domestic law cannot be exchanged. However, the current OECD standard provides for the application of the "major information clause" with the broad scope of information rather than the "minor information clause" (Art. 26(1) OECD Model). 519

Example 520

The "minor information clause" also covers the exchange of information in connection with the tax base or with consequences on the qualification of the tax due, for example, in the case of transfer pricing applied between associated enterprises or the adjustment of the profits stated in the accounts of the PE in one state and the head office accounts in the other state (no. 7c OECD Model Comm. on Art. 26). A request for information is related to carrying out the provisions of a DTC because it may affect the application of the arm's length principle, even if the tax belongs to one of the contracting states and information can be used to adjust the tax base serving the domestic interest. Minor information clause is applicable in cases where a DTC restricts domestic law either effectively or potentially (i.e., the information is foreseeably relevant for carrying out the provisions of the DTC) (Dourado, Klaus Vogel on double taxation conventions Art. 26, m.no. 227, m.no. 231).

521 The implementation of a "major information clause" or a "minor information clause" **affects the personal scope** of the exchange of information. If the "major information clause" is part of the DTC, residence in one of the two contracting states is not a condition for the application of the exchange of information article by one of the states. This is the result of Art. 26(1) OECD Model, which states that the exchange of information is not restricted by Art. 1 OECD Model. The residence is neither a condition for enquiry concerning the person who is the subject of the request nor the person for whose assessment the information is required. However, the exchange of information is not permitted for people who are not covered by the DTC if the "minor information clause" applies. In this case, the exchange of information only serves the application of the DTC.

15.2. Types of exchange of information

522 There are different forms of information exchange. It is possible to differentiate between the following forms of information exchange:

- an **exchange upon request**: a request for information is made to the other contracting state, having a special case in mind;
- an **automatic exchange** of information: information about one or various categories of income having their source in one contracting state and received in the other contracting state is transmitted systematically to the other contracting state;
- a **spontaneous** exchange of information: exchange of information without request because one state has acquired, through certain investigations, information that it supposes will be of interest to the other state;
- a **simultaneous tax examination**: an agreement between two or more parties to examine simultaneously, each in its own territory, the tax affairs of one or more taxpayers in which they have a common or related interest, with a view to exchanging any relevant information that they obtain;
- a **tax examination abroad**: representatives of one contracting state are authorized to participate in a tax examination taking place within the territory of the other contracting state;
- an **industry-wide exchange** of information: the exchange of tax information concerning an entire economic sector and not taxpayers in particular; and
- a **group request**: a request relating to a group of taxpayers not individually identified. The requesting state, however, has to provide a detailed description of the group and the specific facts and circumstances that led to the request.

For many years it was rather common to accept an information exchange only upon request. The 1963 OECD Commentary on Art. 26 (at para. 7) held spontaneous information to be inadmissible. The 1977 OECD Commentary on Art. 26, on the contrary, regarded spontaneous information as admissible (at para. 9), although the wording of the OECD Model had not changed in this respect. The current OECD Commentary on Art. 26 (at para. 9) provides for the application of all forms of information exchange mentioned above. The Commentary (at para. 10) even states that the manner in which the exchange of information agreed to in the DTC will be effected can be **decided upon by the competent authorities** of the contracting states. 523

15.3. Limitations on the exchange of information

Art. 26(3) OECD Model contains various restrictions on the exchange of information. The exchange of information article does not oblige the contracting states to carry out administrative measures at variance with the laws and the administrative practice of either contracting state. In addition, information that cannot be obtained under the law or in the ordinary administrative procedure of this or the other contracting state is not required to be exchanged. The principle of reciprocity is a part of the exchange of information since the requesting contracting state (the "other Contracting State") is subject to these limits. Accordingly, the requested contracting state ("this Contracting State") does not need to provide information that the requesting contracting state could not obtain under its own law or administrative practice. Furthermore, the contracting states do not need to release information that discloses a trade, industry or professional secret or business practice or that would be contrary to public order ("ordre public"). 524

Art. 26(5) OECD Model, which was added in 2005, is intended to ensure that those limitations set out by Art. 26(3) OECD Model cannot be used to prevent the exchange of information held by banks, other financial institutions, nominees and agents and fiduciaries, as well as ownership information. According to the Commentary, this insertion only reflected current practice since the vast majority of the OECD Member countries have exchanged such information also under the previous version of Art. 26 OECD Model. 525

15.4. Competence and obligation of secrecy

The competent authorities responsible for the exchange of information are the **supreme tax authorities**, i.e. in most cases the ministry of finance. The competent authorities are obliged to keep information received from the other contracting state **secret**. Under Art. 26(2) OECD Model, any information received by a contracting state shall be treated as secret in the same manner as information obtained under domestic laws of that state. The information shall be disclosed 526 only to persons or authorities concerned with the assessment or collection of, the enforcement or prosecution in respect of the determination of appeals in relation to the taxes referred to in the DTC, or the oversight of the above. Such persons or authorities shall use the information only for these purposes. They may disclose the information in public court proceedings or in judicial decisions. The information may also be used for other purposes when laws of both contracting states allow for such use and the competent authority of the supplying state authorizes such use.

527 **Art. 26(4) OECD Model** was added in 2005 and it deals with the duty to exchange information in situations where the requested information is not needed by the requested state for domestic tax purposes. Prior to the addition of Art. 26(4) OECD Model, this obligation was not expressly stated in the article but was clearly evidenced by the practice followed by OECD Member countries.

16. Assistance in the collection of taxes

In 2002, the OECD Committee on Fiscal Affairs added **Art. 27** to the OECD Model, which provides for assistance in the collection of taxes. The contracting states assist each other in the execution of revenue claims. It remains to be seen if – and how efficiently – Art. 27 OECD Model will be enforced in practice. 528

The administrative assistance covers revenue claims. The term **"revenue claim"** means an amount owed with respect to taxes of every kind and description imposed on behalf of the contracting states or of their political subdivisions or local authorities, including interest, administrative fines, penalties and costs that are linked to the execution or safeguarding of this amount. This is subject to the condition that the taxation is not contrary to the DTC or another agreement concluded between the contracting states. Revenue claims that are enforceable under the laws of a contracting state and are owed by a person who, at that time, cannot, under the laws of that state, prevent its collection, shall, at the request of the competent authority of this state, be accepted for purposes of collection by the competent authority of the other contracting state. These revenue claims shall be collected by that other contracting state in accordance with the provisions of its law applicable to the enforcement and collection of its own taxes as if the revenue claims were revenue claims of that other contracting state. 529

In no case, however, shall the provisions be construed so as to impose on a contracting state the obligation to carry out administrative measures at variance with the laws and administration practice of that or the other contracting state, or to carry out measures which would be contrary to public policy (**"ordre public"**). In addition, administrative assistance is not required to be provided if the other contracting state has not pursued all reasonable measures of collection or conservancy, as the case may be, available under its laws or administrative practice, or in those cases where the administrative burden for that state is clearly dis-proportionate to the benefit to be derived by the other contracting state. 530

Example 531

A citizen of the United States, who owes taxes in the United States, moves to Canada. Under Art. XXVIA of the Canada–US DTC (Art. 27 OECD Model), the United States may request that Canada collects the tax due in the United States. The United States will send the request to Canada, certifying that the revenue claim has been finally determined (the taxpayer's appeals have been exhausted). Provided all the conditions are met, the Canadian tax administration will proceed to collect the tax from the individual in the same way as it would if the tax debt were a debt owing to Canada (formal requests, court proceedings and garnishment). If the individual challenges these actions in court, the court cannot consider the validity or correctness of the claim, since it has to be settled in the United States in the end. It must treat the tax debt as an amount due under the Canadian Income Tax Act, the collection of which is not subject to any restriction. Once these proceedings have been concluded and Canada has collected the tax, it will forward the tax to the US competent authority.

532 With the 2011 Update, a provision as regards assistance in the collection of taxes, has been included in the UN Model as well. Art. 27 UN Model equates to Art. 27 OECD Model. Prior to that Update in 2011, no such provision was found in the UN Model.

17. Inheritance tax treaties

17.1. Structure

In addition to the OECD Model on Income and on Capital (hereafter OECD Income Tax Model), there is an OECD model in the field of estate, inheritance and gift taxes (hereafter **OECD Inheritance Tax Model**). It was published in 1966 and modified in 1982 (cf. m.no. 24). Gift taxes were not included in the substantive scope of the model until 1982. In practice, taxes on income and on capital, on the one hand, and estate, inheritance and gift taxes, on the other hand, are regulated by different DTCs. The conclusion of a common DTC remains an exception (e.g. Germany's DTCs with Denmark and Sweden, and many French DTCs). However, there are academic aspirations to build a unitary system (common approach) of the two existing OECD Model solutions (cf. Szczepański, *Intertax* 2018, 766 et seq.). 533

The structure of the existing OECD Inheritance Tax Model is **similar to that of the OECD Income Tax Model**. When the person and the respective taxes are covered by the DTC, one of the allocation rules definitely applies. The method article (Art. 9A or 9B OECD Inheritance Tax Model) will determine whether double taxation is avoided by the credit or the exemption method. 534

17.2. Scope of the convention

The scope of the OECD Inheritance Tax Model is set out in **Art. 1 and Art. 2**. In contrast to the 1966 version of this model, the 1982 version covers gifts in addition to estates and inheritances. Both the deceased at the time of death and the donor at the time of the gift must be resident in one or both contracting states. Pursuant to Art. 4(1) OECD Inheritance Tax Model, a person is **resident** in a contracting state if the person's estate or gift is liable to tax in that state by reason of the domicile, residence or place of management of that person or any other criterion of a similar nature. The OECD Inheritance Tax Model applies to **taxes** on estates and inheritances, and on gifts (Art. 2(1) OECD Inheritance Tax Model). 535

Example 536

A resident of Belgium owns a summer home in France. When he dies, the house is passed on to his children who live in France. Under the laws of both states, the transfer of property mortis causa is taxable. In Belgium, tax liability arises from the decedent's residency status. In France, tax is levied by reason of the residence of the heirs. Since the decedent was domiciled in Belgium at the time of his death, the Belgium–France Inheritance Tax DTC applies to the inheritance. Art. 1(2) of the treaty covers all taxes imposed by reason of death. Consequently, the heirs can invoke the treaty's allocation rules.

Art. 4(2) and 4(3) OECD Inheritance Tax Model include a **tiebreaker rule** similar to that found in the OECD Income Tax Model (cf. m.no. 209 et seq.). Where a 537 person, at the time of his/her death or of the gift, is a resident of both contracting states, the residence state is determined according to the provisions set forth therein.

538 **Example**

A woman had a permanent home in State A, where she lived with her husband and children. At her death, however, she was staying temporarily in State B to carry out work there. For this purpose she had rented a small apartment. If, under the domestic laws of both states, she is regarded as being domiciled at her death in both states, the tiebreaker rule gives preference to State A because her only permanent home was in that state (cf. OECD Commentary on Art. 4 Inheritance Tax Model, para. 8).

539 In practice, a number of **deviations** from the OECD Inheritance Tax Model can be found. Many existing inheritance tax treaties – primarily those concluded before 1982 – are not applicable to gift taxes. Some treaties limit the scope to citizens of one of the two contracting states or tie it to tax liability. However, since a majority of OECD Member countries impose comprehensive tax liability if the deceased or the donor was domiciled in their countries, Arts. 1 and 2 OECD Inheritance Tax Model were drafted accordingly.

17.3. General definitions

540 **Art. 3** OECD Inheritance Tax Model defines the most relevant term for the model: "property which forms part of the estate of, or of a gift made by, a person domiciled in a Contracting State" includes any property the devolution or transfer of which, under the law of a contracting state, is liable to a tax covered by the Convention. Moreover, Art. 3 includes a definition of the term "competent authority".

541 In addition to the definitions in Art. 3 OECD Inheritance Tax Model, the meanings of other **important terms** are explained in other articles. The term "domicile" is defined in Art. 4 OECD Inheritance Tax Model and the terms "immovable property", "PE" and "nationals" are clarified by the respective provisions (cf. OECD Commentary on Art. 3 Inheritance Tax Model, para. 1).

17.4. Allocation of taxing rights

542 The allocation rules correspond to the allocation rules for the taxation of capital and capital gains in the OECD Income Tax Model. Consequently, there is an independent allocation rule for **immovable property** (Art. 5 OECD Inheritance Tax Model) and for **property of a PE or a fixed base** (Art. 6 OECD Inheritance Tax Model). Art. 7 OECD Inheritance Tax Model is a **blanket clause**.

543 Pursuant to Art. 5 OECD Inheritance Tax Model, **immovable property** can be taxed in the contracting state in which the property is situated. Art. 5(2) OECD Inheritance Tax Model defines immovable property corresponding to Art. 6(2)

OECD Income Tax Model (cf. m.no. 227). The order of precedence set forth in Art. 5(3) OECD Inheritance Tax Model guarantees that Art. 5 OECD Inheritance Tax Model also applies to immovable property of an enterprise and to immovable property used for the performance of professional services or other activities of an independent character. Art. 5 OECD Inheritance Tax Model is dominated by the principle of situs: the situs state also has a taxing right. The method article then determines whether double taxation is avoided by means of the exemption or the credit method.

Art. 6 OECD Inheritance Tax Model regulates the imposition of taxes on **movable** 544
property representing business property of a PE of an enterprise forming part of the estate or gift. The PE state has the right to tax. The method article determines whether the residence state can also tax and then credit the taxes paid in the PE state, or whether it must grant an exemption.

Art. 7 OECD Inheritance Tax Model is a **blanket clause**. According to this rule, 545
all capital not dealt with in Arts. 5 or 6 may only be taxed in the contracting state in which the deceased or the donor was resident at the time of the transaction.

Example 546

An individual primarily domiciled in Switzerland with a secondary residence in Denmark dies. Among the assets he leaves are Danish and Swiss shares. Under Art. 6 of the Denmark–Switzerland Inheritance Tax DTC, the assets not covered by Art. 5 of the treaty are taxable only in the contracting state in which the deceased was resident at the time of death. Since the deceased was domiciled in both contracting states at the time of his death, the tiebreaker rule must be consulted in order to resolve the problem of dual residence. Pursuant to Art. 4(2)(a) of the treaty, the residence state is Switzerland, provided that the deceased's personal and economic relationships were closer to Switzerland than they were to Denmark. Consequently, Switzerland has the exclusive taxing right (all provisions mentioned above correspond to the OECD Inheritance Tax Model).

17.5. Special provisions

Arts. 10 to 16 OECD Inheritance Tax Model contain special provisions similar 547
to the OECD Income Tax Model. There are rules regarding non-discrimination, the mutual agreement procedure, exchange of information, diplomatic agents and consular officers, territorial extension, entry into force and termination.

Annex 1

OECD MODEL CONVENTION WITH RESPECT TO TAXES ON INCOME AND ON CAPITAL 2017 UPDATE

SUMMARY OF THE CONVENTION

Title and Preamble

CHAPTER I
SCOPE OF THE CONVENTION

CHAPTER II
DEFINITIONS

CHAPTER III
TAXATION OF INCOME

TITLE OF THE CONVENTION

Convention between (State A) and (State B)

for the elimination of double taxation with respect to taxes on income and on capital and the prevention of tax evasion and avoidance

PREAMBLE TO THE CONVENTION

(State A) and (State B),

Desiring to further develop their economic relationship and to enhance their co-operation in tax matters,

Intending to conclude a Convention for the elimination of double taxation with respect to taxes on income and on capital without creating opportunities for non-taxation or reduced taxation through tax evasion or avoidance (including through treaty-shopping arrangements aimed at obtaining reliefs provided in this Convention for the indirect benefit of residents of third States),

Have agreed as follows:

CHAPTER I
SCOPE OF THE CONVENTION

ARTICLE 1
PERSONS COVERED

1. This Convention shall apply to persons who are residents of one or both of the Contracting States.

2. For the purposes of this Convention, income derived by or through an entity or arrangement that is treated as wholly or partly fiscally transparent under the tax law of either Contracting State shall be considered to be income of a resident of a Contracting State but only to the extent that the income is treated, for purposes of taxation by that State, as the income of a resident of that State.

3. This Convention shall not affect the taxation, by a Contracting State, of its residents except with respect to the benefits granted under paragraph 3 of Article 7, paragraph 2 of Article 9 and Articles 19, 20, 23 [A] [B], 24, 25 and 28.

ARTICLE 2
TAXES COVERED

1. This Convention shall apply to taxes on income and on capital imposed on behalf of a Contracting State or of its political subdivisions or local authorities, irrespective of the manner in which they are levied.

2. There shall be regarded as taxes on income and on capital all taxes imposed on total income, on total capital, or on elements of income or of capital, including taxes on gains from the alienation of movable or immovable property, taxes on the total amounts of wages or salaries paid by enterprises, as well as taxes on capital appreciation.

3. The existing taxes to which the Convention shall apply are in particular:

a) (in State A): ....

b) (in State B): ....

4. The Convention shall apply also to any identical or substantially similar taxes that are imposed after the date of signature of the Convention in addition to, or in place of, the existing taxes. The competent authorities of the Contracting States shall notify each other of any significant changes that have been made in their taxation laws.

CHAPTER II
DEFINITIONS

ARTICLE 3
GENERAL DEFINITIONS

1. For the purposes of this Convention, unless the context otherwise requires:

a) the term "person" includes an individual, a company and any other body of persons;
b) the term "company" means any body corporate or any entity that is treated as a body corporate for tax purposes;
c) the term "enterprise" applies to the carrying on of any business;

d) the terms "enterprise of a Contracting State" and "enterprise of the other Contracting State" mean respectively an enterprise carried on by a resident of a Contracting State and an enterprise carried on by a resident of the other Contracting State;
e) the term "international traffic" means any transport by a ship or aircraft except when the ship or aircraft is operated solely between places in a Contracting State and the enterprise that operates the ship or aircraft is not an enterprise of that State;
f) the term "competent authority" means:
   (i) (in State A): ....
   (ii) (in State B): ....
g) the term "national", in relation to a Contracting State, means:
   (i) any individual possessing the nationality or citizenship of that Contracting State; and
   (ii) any legal person, partnership or association deriving its status as such from the laws in force in that Contracting State;
h) the term "business" includes the performance of professional services and of other activities of an independent character.
i) the term "recognised pension fund" of a State means an entity or arrangement established in that State that is treated as a separate person under the taxation laws of that State and:
   (i) that is established and operated exclusively or almost exclusively to administer or provide retirement benefits and ancillary or incidental benefits to individuals and that is regulated as such by that State or one of its political subdivisions or local authorities; or
   (ii) that is established and operated exclusively or almost exclusively to invest funds for the benefit of entities or arrangements referred to in subdivision *(i)*.

2. As regards the application of the Convention at any time by a Contracting State, any term not defined therein shall, unless the context otherwise requires or the competent authorities agree to a different meaning pursuant to the provisions of Article 25, have the meaning that it has at that time under the law of that State for the purposes of the taxes to which the Convention applies, any meaning under the applicable tax laws of that State prevailing over a meaning given to the term under other laws of that State.

ARTICLE 4
RESIDENT

1. For the purposes of this Convention, the term "resident of a Contracting State" means any person who, under the laws of that State, is liable to tax therein by reason of his domicile, residence, place of management or any other criterion of a similar nature, and also includes that State and any political subdivision or local authority thereof as well as a recognised pension fund of that State. This term, however, does not include any person who is liable to tax in that State in respect only of income from sources in that State or capital situated therein.

2. Where by reason of the provisions of paragraph 1 an individual is a resident of both Contracting States, then his status shall be determined as follows:

a) he shall be deemed to be a resident only of the State in which he has a permanent home available to him; if he has a permanent home available to him in both States, he shall be deemed to be a resident only of the State with which his personal and economic relations are closer (centre of vital interests);

b) if the State in which he has his centre of vital interests cannot be determined, or if he has not a permanent home available to him in either State, he shall be deemed to be a resident only of the State in which he has an habitual abode;
c) if he has an habitual abode in both States or in neither of them, he shall be deemed to be a resident only of the State of which he is a national;
d) if he is a national of both States or of neither of them, the competent authorities of the Contracting States shall settle the question by mutual agreement.

3. Where by reason of the provisions of paragraph 1 a person other than an individual is a resident of both Contracting States, the competent authorities of the Contracting States shall endeavour to determine by mutual agreement the Contracting State of which such person shall be deemed to be a resident for the purposes of the Convention, having regard to its place of effective management, the place where it is incorporated or otherwise constituted and any other relevant factors. In the absence of such agreement, such person shall not be entitled to any relief or exemption from tax provided by this Convention except to the extent and in such manner as may be agreed upon by the competent authorities of the Contracting States.

ARTICLE 5
PERMANENT ESTABLISHMENT

1. For the purposes of this Convention, the term "permanent establishment" means a fixed place of business through which the business of an enterprise is wholly or partly carried on.

2. The term "permanent establishment" includes especially:

a) a place of management;
b) a branch;
c) an office;
d) a factory;
e) a workshop, and
f) a mine, an oil or gas well, a quarry or any other place of extraction of natural resources.

3. A building site or construction or installation project constitutes a permanent establishment only if it lasts more than twelve months.

4. Notwithstanding the preceding provisions of this Article, the term "permanent establishment" shall be deemed not to include:

a) the use of facilities solely for the purpose of storage, display or delivery of goods or merchandise belonging to the enterprise;
b) the maintenance of a stock of goods or merchandise belonging to the enterprise solely for the purpose of storage, display or delivery;
c) the maintenance of a stock of goods or merchandise belonging to the enterprise solely for the purpose of processing by another enterprise;
d) the maintenance of a fixed place of business solely for the purpose of purchasing goods or merchandise or of collecting information, for the enterprise;
e) the maintenance of a fixed place of business solely for the purpose of carrying on, for the enterprise, any other activity;
f) the maintenance of a fixed place of business solely for any combination of activities mentioned in subparagraphs *a)* to *e)*,

provided that such activity or, in the case of subparagraph f), the overall activity of the fixed place of business, is of a preparatory or auxiliary character.

4.1 Paragraph 4 shall not apply to a fixed place of business that is used or maintained by an enterprise if the same enterprise or a closely related enterprise carries on business activities at the same place or at another place in the same Contracting State

and

a) that place or other place constitutes a permanent establishment for the enterprise or the closely related enterprise under the provisions of this Article, or
b) the overall activity resulting from the combination of the activities carried on by the two enterprises at the same place, or by the same enterprise or closely related enterprises at the two places, is not of a preparatory or auxiliary Character,

provided that the business activities carried on by the two enterprises at the same place, or by the same enterprise or closely related enterprises at the two places, constitute complementary functions that are part of a cohesive business operation.

5. Notwithstanding the provisions of paragraphs 1 and 2 but subject to the provisions of paragraph 6, where a person is acting in a Contracting State on behalf of an enterprise and, in doing so, habitually concludes contracts, or habitually plays the principal role leading to the conclusion of contracts that are routinely concluded without material modification by the enterprise, and these contracts are

a) in the name of the enterprise, or
b) for the transfer of the ownership of, or for the granting of the right to use, property owned by that enterprise or that the enterprise has the right to use, or
c) for the provision of services by that enterprise,

that enterprise shall be deemed to have a permanent establishment in that State in respect of any activities which that person undertakes for the enterprise, unless the activities of such person are limited to those mentioned in paragraph 4 which, if exercised through a fixed place of business (other than a fixed place of business to which paragraph 4.1 would apply), would not make this fixed place of business a permanent establishment under the provisions of that paragraph.

6. Paragraph 5 shall not apply where the person acting in a Contracting State on behalf of an enterprise of the other Contracting State carries on business in the first-mentioned State as an independent agent and acts for the enterprise in the ordinary course of that business. Where, however, a person acts exclusively or almost exclusively on behalf of one or more enterprises to which it is closely related, that person shall not be considered to be an independent agent within the meaning of this paragraph with respect to any such enterprise.

7. The fact that a company which is a resident of a Contracting State controls or is controlled by a company which is a resident of the other Contracting State, or which carries on business in that other State (whether through a permanent establishment or otherwise), shall not of itself constitute either company a permanent establishment of the other.

8. For the purposes of this Article, a person or enterprise is closely related to an enterprise if, based on all the relevant facts and circumstances, one has control of the other or both are under the control of the same persons or enterprises. In any case, a person or enterprise

shall be considered to be closely related to an enterprise if one possesses directly or indirectly more than 50 per cent of the beneficial interest in the other (or, in the case of a company, more than 50 per cent of the aggregate vote and value of the company's shares or of the beneficial equity interest in the company) or if another person or enterprise possesses directly or indirectly more than 50 per cent of the beneficial interest (or, in the case of a company, more than 50 per cent of the aggregate vote and value of the company's shares or of the beneficial equity interest in the company) in the person and the enterprise or in the two enterprises.

CHAPTER III
TAXATION OF INCOME

ARTICLE 6
INCOME FROM IMMOVABLE PROPERTY

1. Income derived by a resident of a Contracting State from immovable property (including income from agriculture or forestry) situated in the other Contracting State may be taxed in that other State.

2. The term "immovable property" shall have the meaning which it has under the law of the Contracting State in which the property in question is situated. The term shall in any case include property accessory to immovable property, livestock and equipment used in agriculture and forestry, rights to which the provisions of general law respecting landed property apply, usufruct of immovable property and rights to variable or fixed payments as consideration for the working of, or the right to work, mineral deposits, sources and other natural resources; ships and aircraft shall not be regarded as immovable property.

3. The provisions of paragraph 1 shall apply to income derived from the direct use, letting, or use in any other form of immovable property.

4. The provisions of paragraphs 1 and 3 shall also apply to the income from immovable property of an enterprise.

ARTICLE 7
BUSINESS PROFITS

1. Profits of an enterprise of a Contracting State shall be taxable only in that State unless the enterprise carries on business in the other Contracting State through a permanent establishment situated therein. If the enterprise carries on business as aforesaid, the profits that are attributable to the permanent establishment in accordance with the provisions of paragraph 2 may be taxed in that other State.

2. For the purposes of this Article and Article [23 A] [23 B], the profits that are attributable in each Contracting State to the permanent establishment referred to in paragraph 1 are the profits it might be expected to make, in particular in its dealings with other parts of the enterprise, if it were a separate and independent enterprise engaged in the same or similar activities under the same or similar conditions, taking into account the functions performed, assets used and risks assumed by the enterprise through the permanent establishment and through the other parts of the enterprise.

3. Where, in accordance with paragraph 2, a Contracting State adjusts the profits that are attributable to a permanent establishment of an enterprise of one of the Contracting States and taxes accordingly profits of the enterprise that have been charged to tax in the other

State, the other State shall, to the extent necessary to eliminate double taxation on these profits, make an appropriate adjustment to the amount of the tax charged on those profits. In determining such adjustment, the competent authorities of the Contracting States shall if necessary consult each other.

4. Where profits include items of income which are dealt with separately in other Articles of this Convention, then the provisions of those Articles shall not be affected by the provisions of this Article.

ARTICLE 8
INTERNATIONAL SHIPPING AND AIR TRANSPORT

1. Profits of an enterprise of a Contracting State from the operation of ships or aircraft in international traffic shall be taxable only in that State.

2. The provisions of paragraph 1 shall also apply to profits from the participation in a pool, a joint business or an international operating agency.

ARTICLE 9
ASSOCIATED ENTERPRISES

1. Where

a) an enterprise of a Contracting State participates directly or indirectly in the management, control or capital of an enterprise of the other Contracting State, or
b) the same persons participate directly or indirectly in the management, control or capital of an enterprise of a Contracting State and an enterprise of the other Contracting State,

and in either case conditions are made or imposed between the two enterprises in their commercial or financial relations which differ from those which would be made between independent enterprises, then any profits which would, but for those conditions, have accrued to one of the enterprises, but, by reason of those conditions, have not so accrued, may be included in the profits of that enterprise and taxed accordingly.

2. Where a Contracting State includes in the profits of an enterprise of that State — and taxes accordingly — profits on which an enterprise of the other Contracting State has been charged to tax in that other State and the profits so included are profits which would have accrued to the enterprise of the first-mentioned State if the conditions made between the two enterprises had been those which would have been made between independent enterprises, then that other State shall make an appropriate adjustment to the amount of the tax charged therein on those profits. In determining such adjustment, due regard shall be had to the other provisions of this Convention and the competent authorities of the Contracting States shall if necessary consult each other.

ARTICLE 10
DIVIDENDS

1. Dividends paid by a company which is a resident of a Contracting State to a resident of the other Contracting State may be taxed in that other State.

2. However, dividends paid by a company which is a resident of a Contracting State may also be taxed in that State according to the laws of that State, but if the beneficial owner of the dividends is a resident of the other Contracting State, the tax so charged shall not exceed:

a) 5 per cent of the gross amount of the dividends if the beneficial owner is a company which holds directly at least 25 per cent of the capital of the company paying the dividends throughout a 365 day period that includes the day of the payment of the dividend (for the purpose of computing that period, no account shall be taken of changes of ownership that would directly result from a corporate reorganisation, such as a merger or divisive reorganisation, of the company that holds the shares or that pays the dividend);
b) 15 per cent of the gross amount of the dividends in all other cases.

The competent authorities of the Contracting States shall by mutual agreement settle the mode of application of these limitations. This paragraph shall not affect the taxation of the company in respect of the profits out of which the dividends are paid.

3. The term “dividends” as used in this Article means income from shares, “jouissance” shares or “jouissance” rights, mining shares, founders’ shares or other rights, not being debt-claims, participating in profits, as well as income from other corporate rights which is subjected to the same taxation treatment as income from shares by the laws of the State of which the company making the distribution is a resident.

4. The provisions of paragraphs 1 and 2 shall not apply if the beneficial owner of the dividends, being a resident of a Contracting State, carries on business in the other Contracting State of which the company paying the dividends is a resident through a permanent establishment situated therein and the holding in respect of which the dividends are paid is effectively connected with such permanent establishment. In such case the provisions of Article 7 shall apply.

5. Where a company which is a resident of a Contracting State derives profits or income from the other Contracting State, that other State may not impose any tax on the dividends paid by the company, except insofar as such dividends are paid to a resident of that other State or insofar as the holding in respect of which the dividends are paid is effectively connected with a permanent establishment situated in that other State, nor subject the company’s undistributed profits to a tax on the company’s undistributed profits, even if the dividends paid or the undistributed profits consist wholly or partly of profits or income arising in such other State.

ARTICLE 11
INTEREST

1. Interest arising in a Contracting State and paid to a resident of the other Contracting State may be taxed in that other State.

2. However, interest arising in a Contracting State may also be taxed in that State according to the laws of that State, but if the beneficial owner of the interest is a resident of the other Contracting State, the tax so charged shall not exceed 10 per cent of the gross amount of the interest. The competent authorities of the Contracting States shall by mutual agreement settle the mode of application of this limitation.

3. The term “interest” as used in this Article means income from debt-claims of every kind, whether or not secured by mortgage and whether or not carrying a right to participate in the debtor’s profits, and in particular, income from government securities and income from bonds or debentures, including premiums and prizes attaching to such securities, bonds or debentures. Penalty charges for late payment shall not be regarded as interest for the purpose of this Article.

4. The provisions of paragraphs 1 and 2 shall not apply if the beneficial owner of the interest, being a resident of a Contracting State, carries on business in the other Contracting State in which the interest arises through a permanent establishment situated therein and the debt-claim in respect of which the interest is paid is effectively connected with such permanent establishment. In such case the provisions of Article 7 shall apply.

5. Interest shall be deemed to arise in a Contracting State when the payer is a resident of that State. Where, however, the person paying the interest, whether he is a resident of a Contracting State or not, has in a Contracting State a permanent establishment in connection with which the indebtedness on which the interest is paid was incurred, and such interest is borne by such permanent establishment, then such interest shall be deemed to arise in the State in which the permanent establishment is situated.

6. Where, by reason of a special relationship between the payer and the beneficial owner or between both of them and some other person, the amount of the interest, having regard to the debt-claim for which it is paid, exceeds the amount which would have been agreed upon by the payer and the beneficial owner in the absence of such relationship, the provisions of this Article shall apply only to the last-mentioned amount. In such case, the excess part of the payments shall remain taxable according to the laws of each Contracting State, due regard being had to the other provisions of this Convention.

ARTICLE 12
ROYALTIES

1. Royalties arising in a Contracting State and beneficially owned by a resident of the other Contracting State shall be taxable only in that other State.

2. The term "royalties" as used in this Article means payments of any kind received as a consideration for the use of, or the right to use, any copyright of literary, artistic or scientific work including cinematograph films, any patent, trade mark, design or model, plan, secret formula or process, or for information concerning industrial, commercial or scientific experience.

3. The provisions of paragraph 1 shall not apply if the beneficial owner of the royalties, being a resident of a Contracting State, carries on business in the other Contracting State in which the royalties arise through a permanent establishment situated therein and the right or property in respect of which the royalties are paid is effectively connected with such permanent establishment. In such case the provisions of Article 7 shall apply.

4. Where, by reason of a special relationship between the payer and the beneficial owner or between both of them and some other person, the amount of the royalties, having regard to the use, right or information for which they are paid, exceeds the amount which would have been agreed upon by the payer and the beneficial owner in the absence of such relationship, the provisions of this Article shall apply only to the last-mentioned amount. In such case, the excess part of the payments shall remain taxable according to the laws of each Contracting State, due regard being had to the other provisions of this Convention.

ARTICLE 13
CAPITAL GAINS

1. Gains derived by a resident of a Contracting State from the alienation of immovable property referred to in Article 6 and situated in the other Contracting State may be taxed in that other State.

2. Gains from the alienation of movable property forming part of the business property of a permanent establishment which an enterprise of a Contracting State has in the other Contracting State, including such gains from the alienation of such a permanent establishment (alone or with the whole enterprise), may be taxed in that other State.

3. Gains that an enterprise of a Contracting State that operates ships or aircraft in international traffic derives from the alienation of such ships or aircraft, or of movable property pertaining to the operation of such ships or aircraft, shall be taxable only in that State.

4. Gains derived by a resident of a Contracting State from the alienation of shares or comparable interests, such as interests in a partnership or trust, may be taxed in the other Contracting State if, at any time during the 365 days preceding the alienation, these shares or comparable interests derived more than 50 per cent of their value directly or indirectly from immovable property, as defined in Article 6, situated in that other State.

5. Gains from the alienation of any property, other than that referred to in paragraphs 1, 2, 3 and 4, shall be taxable only in the Contracting State of which the alienator is a resident.

[ARTICLE 14 – INDEPENDENT PERSONAL SERVICES]

[DELETED]

ARTICLE 15 INCOME FROM EMPLOYMENT

1. Subject to the provisions of Articles 16, 18 and 19, salaries, wages and other similar remuneration derived by a resident of a Contracting State in respect of an employment shall be taxable only in that State unless the employment is exercised in the other Contracting State. If the employment is so exercised, such remuneration as is derived therefrom may be taxed in that other State.

2. Notwithstanding the provisions of paragraph 1, remuneration derived by a resident of a Contracting State in respect of an employment exercised in the other Contracting State shall be taxable only in the first-mentioned State if:

a) the recipient is present in the other State for a period or periods not exceeding in the aggregate 183 days in any twelve month period commencing or ending in the fiscal year concerned, and
b) the remuneration is paid by, or on behalf of, an employer who is not a resident of the other State, and
c) the remuneration is not borne by a permanent establishment which the employer has in the other State.

3. Notwithstanding the preceding provisions of this Article, remuneration derived by a resident of a Contracting State in respect of an employment, as a member of the regular complement of a ship or aircraft, that is exercised aboard a ship or aircraft operated in international traffic, other than aboard a ship or aircraft operated solely within the other Contracting State, shall be taxable only in the first-mentioned State.

ARTICLE 16
DIRECTORS' FEES

Directors' fees and other similar payments derived by a resident of a Contracting State in his capacity as a member of the board of directors of a company which is a resident of the other Contracting State may be taxed in that other State.

ARTICLE 17
ENTERTAINERS AND SPORTSPERSONS

1. Notwithstanding the provisions of Article 15, income derived by a resident of a Contracting State as an entertainer, such as a theatre, motion picture, radio or television artiste, or a musician, or as a sportsperson, from that resident's personal activities as such exercised in the other Contracting State, may be taxed in that other State.

2. Where income in respect of personal activities exercised by an entertainer or a sportsperson acting as such accrues not to the entertainer or sportsperson but to another person, that income may, notwithstanding the provisions of Article 15, be taxed in the Contracting State in which the activities of the entertainer or sportsperson are exercised.

ARTICLE 18
PENSIONS

Subject to the provisions of paragraph 2 of Article 19, pensions and other similar remuneration paid to a resident of a Contracting State in consideration of past employment shall be taxable only in that State.

ARTICLE 19
GOVERNMENT SERVICE

1.

a) Salaries, wages and other similar remuneration paid by a Contracting State or a political subdivision or a local authority thereof to an individual in respect of services rendered to that State or subdivision or authority shall be taxable only in that State.
b) However, such salaries, wages and other similar remuneration shall be taxable only in the other Contracting State if the services are rendered in that State and the individual is a resident of that State who:
   (i) is a national of that State; or
   (ii) did not become a resident of that State solely for the purpose of rendering the services.

2.

a) Notwithstanding the provisions of paragraph 1, pensions and other similar remuneration paid by, or out of funds created by, a Contracting State or a political subdivision or a local authority thereof to an individual in respect of services rendered to that State or subdivision or authority shall be taxable only in that State.
b) However, such pensions and other similar remuneration shall be taxable only in the other Contracting State if the individual is a resident of, and a national of, that State.

3. The provisions of Articles 15, 16, 17, and 18 shall apply to salaries, wages, pensions, and other similar remuneration in respect of services rendered in connection with a business carried on by a Contracting State or a political subdivision or a local authority thereof.

ARTICLE 20
STUDENTS

Payments which a student or business apprentice who is or was immediately before visiting a Contracting State a resident of the other Contracting State and who is present in the first-mentioned State solely for the purpose of his education or training receives for the purpose of his maintenance, education or training shall not be taxed in that State, provided that such payments arise from sources outside that State.

ARTICLE 21
OTHER INCOME

1. Items of income of a resident of a Contracting State, wherever arising, not dealt with in the foregoing Articles of this Convention shall be taxable only in that State.

2. The provisions of paragraph 1 shall not apply to income, other than income from immovable property as defined in paragraph 2 of Article 6, if the recipient of such income, being a resident of a Contracting State, carries on business in the other Contracting State through a permanent establishment situated therein and the right or property in respect of which the income is paid is effectively connected with such permanent establishment. In such case the provisions of Article 7 shall apply.

CHAPTER IV
TAXATION OF CAPITAL

ARTICLE 22
CAPITAL

1. Capital represented by immovable property referred to in Article 6, owned by a resident of a Contracting State and situated in the other Contracting State, may be taxed in that other State.

2. Capital represented by movable property forming part of the business property of a permanent establishment which an enterprise of a Contracting State has in the other Contracting State may be taxed in that other State.

3. Capital of an enterprise of a Contracting State that operates ships or aircraft in international traffic represented by such ships or aircraft, and by movable property pertaining to the operation of such ships or aircraft, shall be taxable only in that State.

4. All other elements of capital of a resident of a Contracting State shall be taxable only in that State.

CHAPTER V
METHODS FOR ELIMINATION OF DOUBLE TAXATION

ARTICLE 23 A
EXEMPTION METHOD

1. Where a resident of a Contracting State derives income or owns capital which may be taxed in the other Contracting State in accordance with the provisions of this Convention (except to the extent that these provisions allow taxation by that other State solely because the income is also income derived by a resident of that State or because the capital is also capital owned by a resident of that State), the first- mentioned State shall, subject to the provisions of paragraphs 2 and 3, exempt such income or capital from tax.

2. Where a resident of a Contracting State derives items of income which may be taxed in the other Contracting State in accordance with the provisions of Articles 10 and 11 (except to the extent that these provisions allow taxation by that other State solely because the income is also income derived by a resident of that State), the first- mentioned State shall allow as a deduction from the tax on the income of that resident an amount equal to the tax paid in that other State. Such deduction shall not, however, exceed that part of the tax, as computed before the deduction is given, which is attributable to such items of income derived from that other State.

3. Where in accordance with any provision of the Convention income derived or capital owned by a resident of a Contracting State is exempt from tax in that State, such State may nevertheless, in calculating the amount of tax on the remaining income or capital of such resident, take into account the exempted income or capital.

4. The provisions of paragraph 1 shall not apply to income derived or capital owned by a resident of a Contracting State where the other Contracting State applies the provisions of this Convention to exempt such income or capital from tax or applies the provisions of paragraph 2 of Article 10 or 11 to such income.

ARTICLE 23 B
CREDIT METHOD

1. Where a resident of a Contracting State derives income or owns capital which may be taxed in the other Contracting State in accordance with the provisions of this Convention (except to the extent that these provisions allow taxation by that other State solely because the income is also income derived by a resident of that State or because the capital is also capital owned by a resident of that State), the first- mentioned State shall allow:

a) as a deduction from the tax on the income of that resident, an amount equal to the income tax paid in that other State;
b) as a deduction from the tax on the capital of that resident, an amount equal to the capital tax paid in that other State.

Such deduction in either case shall not, however, exceed that part of the income tax or capital tax, as computed before the deduction is given, which is attributable, as the case may be, to the income or the capital which may be taxed in that other State.

2. Where in accordance with any provision of the Convention income derived or capital owned by a resident of a Contracting State is exempt from tax in that State, such State may nevertheless, in calculating the amount of tax on the remaining income or capital of such resident, take into account the exempted income or capital.

CHAPTER VI
SPECIAL PROVISIONS

ARTICLE 24
NON-DISCRIMINATION

1. Nationals of a Contracting State shall not be subjected in the other Contracting State to any taxation or any requirement connected therewith, which is other or more burdensome than the taxation and connected requirements to which nationals of that other State in the same circumstances, in particular with respect to residence, are or may be subjected. This

provision shall, notwithstanding the provisions of Article 1, also apply to persons who are not residents of one or both of the Contracting States.

2. Stateless persons who are residents of a Contracting State shall not be subjected in either Contracting State to any taxation or any requirement connected therewith, which is other or more burdensome than the taxation and connected requirements to which nationals of the State concerned in the same circumstances, in particular with respect to residence, are or may be subjected.

3. The taxation on a permanent establishment which an enterprise of a Contracting State has in the other Contracting State shall not be less favourably levied in that other State than the taxation levied on enterprises of that other State carrying on the same activities. This provision shall not be construed as obliging a Contracting State to grant to residents of the other Contracting State any personal allowances, reliefs and reductions for taxation purposes on account of civil status or family responsibilities which it grants to its own residents.

4. Except where the provisions of paragraph 1 of Article 9, paragraph 6 of Article 11, or paragraph 4 of Article 12, apply, interest, royalties and other disbursements paid by an enterprise of a Contracting State to a resident of the other Contracting State shall, for the purpose of determining the taxable profits of such enterprise, be deductible under the same conditions as if they had been paid to a resident of the first-mentioned State. Similarly, any debts of an enterprise of a Contracting State to a resident of the other Contracting State shall, for the purpose of determining the taxable capital of such enterprise, be deductible under the same conditions as if they had been contracted to a resident of the first-mentioned State.

5. Enterprises of a Contracting State, the capital of which is wholly or partly owned or controlled, directly or indirectly, by one or more residents of the other Contracting State, shall not be subjected in the first-mentioned State to any taxation or any requirement connected therewith which is other or more burdensome than the taxation and connected requirements to which other similar enterprises of the first- mentioned State are or may be subjected.

6. The provisions of this Article shall, notwithstanding the provisions of Article 2, apply to taxes of every kind and description.

ARTICLE 25
MUTUAL AGREEMENT PROCEDURE

1. Where a person considers that the actions of one or both of the Contracting States result or will result for him in taxation not in accordance with the provisions of this Convention, he may, irrespective of the remedies provided by the domestic law of those States, present his case to the competent authority of either Contracting State. The case must be presented within three years from the first notification of the action resulting in taxation not in accordance with the provisions of the Convention.

2. The competent authority shall endeavour, if the objection appears to it to be justified and if it is not itself able to arrive at a satisfactory solution, to resolve the case by mutual agreement with the competent authority of the other Contracting State, with a view to the avoidance of taxation which is not in accordance with the Convention. Any agreement

reached shall be implemented notwithstanding any time limits in the domestic law of the Contracting States.

3. The competent authorities of the Contracting States shall endeavour to resolve by mutual agreement any difficulties or doubts arising as to the interpretation or application of the Convention. They may also consult together for the elimination of double taxation in cases not provided for in the Convention.

4. The competent authorities of the Contracting States may communicate with each other directly, including through a joint commission consisting of themselves or their representatives, for the purpose of reaching an agreement in the sense of the preceding paragraphs.

5. Where,

a) under paragraph 1, a person has presented a case to the competent authority of a Contracting State on the basis that the actions of one or both of the Contracting States have resulted for that person in taxation not in accordance with the provisions of this Convention, and
b) the competent authorities are unable to reach an agreement to resolve that case pursuant to paragraph 2 within two years from the date when all the information required by the competent authorities in order to address the case has been provided to both competent authorities,

any unresolved issues arising from the case shall be submitted to arbitration if the person so requests in writing. These unresolved issues shall not, however, be submitted to arbitration if a decision on these issues has already been rendered by a court or administrative tribunal of either State. Unless a person directly affected by the case does not accept the mutual agreement that implements the arbitration decision, that decision shall be binding on both Contracting States and shall be implemented notwithstanding any time limits in the domestic laws of these States. The competent authorities of the Contracting States shall by mutual agreement settle the mode of application of this paragraph.

ARTICLE 26
EXCHANGE OF INFORMATION

1. The competent authorities of the Contracting States shall exchange such information as is foreseeably relevant for carrying out the provisions of this Convention or to the administration or enforcement of the domestic laws concerning taxes of every kind and description imposed on behalf of the Contracting States, or of their political subdivisions or local authorities, insofar as the taxation thereunder is not contrary to the Convention. The exchange of information is not restricted by Articles 1 and 2.

2. Any information received under paragraph 1 by a Contracting State shall be treated as secret in the same manner as information obtained under the domestic laws of that State and shall be disclosed only to persons or authorities (including courts and administrative bodies) concerned with the assessment or collection of, the enforcement or prosecution in respect of, the determination of appeals in relation to the taxes referred to in paragraph 1, or the oversight of the above. Such persons or authorities shall use the information only for such purposes. They may disclose the information in public court proceedings or in judicial decisions. Notwithstanding the foregoing, information received by a Contracting State may be used for other purposes when such information may be used for such other

purposes under the laws of both States and the competent authority of the supplying State authorises such use.

3. In no case shall the provisions of paragraphs 1 and 2 be construed so as to impose on a Contracting State the obligation:

a) to carry out administrative measures at variance with the laws and administrative practice of that or of the other Contracting State;
b) to supply information which is not obtainable under the laws or in the normal course of the administration of that or of the other Contracting State;
c) to supply information which would disclose any trade, business, industrial, commercial or professional secret or trade process, or information the disclosure of which would be contrary to public policy (ordre public).

4. If information is requested by a Contracting State in accordance with this Article, the other Contracting State shall use its information gathering measures to obtain the requested information, even though that other State may not need such information for its own tax purposes. The obligation contained in the preceding sentence is subject to the limitations of paragraph 3 but in no case shall such limitations be construed to permit a Contracting State to decline to supply information solely because it has no domestic interest in such information.

5. In no case shall the provisions of paragraph 3 be construed to permit a Contracting State to decline to supply information solely because the information is held by a bank, other financial institution, nominee or person acting in an agency or a fiduciary capacity or because it relates to ownership interests in a person.

ARTICLE 27
ASSISTANCE IN THE COLLECTION OF TAXES[1]

1. The Contracting States shall lend assistance to each other in the collection of revenue claims. This assistance is not restricted by Articles 1 and 2. The competent authorities of the Contracting States may by mutual agreement settle the mode of application of this Article.

2. The term "revenue claim" as used in this Article means an amount owed in respect of taxes of every kind and description imposed on behalf of the Contracting States, or of their political subdivisions or local authorities, insofar as the taxation thereunder is not contrary to this Convention or any other instrument to which the Contracting States are parties, as well as interest, administrative penalties and costs of collection or conservancy related to such amount.

3. When a revenue claim of a Contracting State is enforceable under the laws of that State and is owed by a person who, at that time, cannot, under the laws of that State, prevent its collection, that revenue claim shall, at the request of the competent authority of that State, be accepted for purposes of collection by the competent authority of the other Contracting

1 In some countries, national law, policy or administrative considerations may not allow or justify the type of assistance envisaged under this Article or may require that this type of assistance be restricted, e.g. to countries that have similar tax systems or tax administrations or as to the taxes covered. For that reason, the Article should only be included in the Convention where each State concludes that, based on the factors described in paragraph 1 of the Commentary on the Article, they can agree to provide assistance in the collection of taxes levied by the other State.

State. That revenue claim shall be collected by that other State in accordance with the provisions of its laws applicable to the enforcement and collection of its own taxes as if the revenue claim were a revenue claim of that other State.

4. When a revenue claim of a Contracting State is a claim in respect of which that State may, under its law, take measures of conservancy with a view to ensure its collection, that revenue claim shall, at the request of the competent authority of that State, be accepted for purposes of taking measures of conservancy by the competent authority of the other Contracting State. That other State shall take measures of conservancy in respect of that revenue claim in accordance with the provisions of its laws as if the revenue claim were a revenue claim of that other State even if, at the time when such measures are applied, the revenue claim is not enforceable in the first-mentioned State or is owed by a person who has a right to prevent its collection.

5. Notwithstanding the provisions of paragraphs 3 and 4, a revenue claim accepted by a Contracting State for purposes of paragraph 3 or 4 shall not, in that State, be subject to the time limits or accorded any priority applicable to a revenue claim under the laws of that State by reason of its nature as such. In addition, a revenue claim accepted by a Contracting State for the purposes of paragraph 3 or 4 shall not, in that State, have any priority applicable to that revenue claim under the laws of the other Contracting State.

6. Proceedings with respect to the existence, validity or the amount of a revenue claim of a Contracting State shall not be brought before the courts or administrative bodies of the other Contracting State.

7. Where, at any time after a request has been made by a Contracting State under paragraph 3 or 4 and before the other Contracting State has collected and remitted the relevant revenue claim to the first-mentioned State, the relevant revenue claim ceases to be

a) in the case of a request under paragraph 3, a revenue claim of the first-mentioned State that is enforceable under the laws of that State and is owed by a person who, at that time, cannot, under the laws of that State, prevent its collection, or
b) in the case of a request under paragraph 4, a revenue claim of the first-mentioned State in respect of which that State may, under its laws, take measures of conservancy with a view to ensure its collection

the competent authority of the first-mentioned State shall promptly notify the competent authority of the other State of that fact and, at the option of the other State, the first-mentioned State shall either suspend or withdraw its request.

8. In no case shall the provisions of this Article be construed so as to impose on a Contracting State the obligation:

a) to carry out administrative measures at variance with the laws and administrative practice of that or of the other Contracting State;
b) to carry out measures which would be contrary to public policy (*ordre public*);
c) to provide assistance if the other Contracting State has not pursued all reasonable measures of collection or conservancy, as the case may be, available under its laws or administrative practice;
d) to provide assistance in those cases where the administrative burden for that State is clearly disproportionate to the benefit to be derived by the other Contracting State.

ARTICLE 28
MEMBERS OF DIPLOMATIC MISSIONS AND CONSULAR POSTS

Nothing in this Convention shall affect the fiscal privileges of members of diplomatic missions or consular posts under the general rules of international law or under the provisions of special agreements.

ARTICLE 29
ENTITLEMENT TO BENEFITS[2]

1. [Provision that, subject to paragraphs 3 to 5, restricts treaty benefits to a resident of a Contracting State who is a "qualified person" as defined in paragraph 2].

2. [Definition of situations where a resident is a qualified person, which covers

- an individual;
- a Contracting State, its political subdivisions and their agencies and instrumentalities;
- certain publicly-traded companies and entities;
- certain affiliates of publicly-listed companies and entities;
- certain non-profit organisations and recognised pension funds;
- other entities that meet certain ownership and base erosion requirements;
- certain collective investment vehicles.]

3. [Provision that provides treaty benefits to certain income derived by a person that is not a qualified person if the person is engaged in the active conduct of a business in its State of residence and the income emanates from, or is incidental to, that business].

4. [Provision that provides treaty benefits to a person that is not a qualified person if at least more than an agreed proportion of that entity is owned by certain persons entitled to equivalent benefits].

5. [Provision that provides treaty benefits to a person that qualifies as a "headquarters company"].

6. [Provision that allows the competent authority of a Contracting State to grant certain treaty benefits to a person where benefits would otherwise be denied under paragraph 1].

7. [Definitions applicable for the purposes of paragraphs 1 to 7].

8.

a) Where
   (i) an enterprise of a Contracting State derives income from the other Contracting State and the first-mentioned State treats such income as attributable to a permanent establishment of the enterprise situated in a third jurisdiction, and
   (ii) the profits attributable to that permanent establishment are exempt from tax in the first-mentioned State,

2 The drafting of this Article will depend on how the Contracting States decide to implement their common intention, reflected in the preamble of the Convention and incorporated in the minimum standard agreed to as part of the OECD/G20 Base Erosion and Profit Shifting Project, to eliminate double taxation without creating opportunities for non-taxation or reduced taxation through tax evasion or avoidance, including through treaty-shopping arrangements. This may be done either through the adoption of paragraph 9 only, through the adoption of the detailed version of paragraphs 1 to 7 that is described in the Commentary on Article 29 together with the implementation of an anti-conduit mechanism as described in paragraph 187 of that Commentary, or through the adoption of paragraph 9 together with any variation of paragraphs 1 to 7 described in the Commentary on Article 29.

the benefits of this Convention shall not apply to any item of income on which the tax in the third jurisdiction is less than the lower of [rate to be determined bilaterally] of the amount of that item of income and 60 per cent of the tax that would be imposed in the first-mentioned State on that item of income if that permanent establishment were situated in the first-mentioned State. In such a case any income to which the provisions of this paragraph apply shall remain taxable according to the domestic law of the other State, notwithstanding any other provisions of the Convention.

b) The preceding provisions of this paragraph shall not apply if the income derived from the other State emanates from, or is incidental to, the active conduct of a business carried on through the permanent establishment (other than the business of making, managing or simply holding investments for the enterprise's own account, unless these activities are banking, insurance or securities activities carried on by a bank, insurance enterprise or registered securities dealer, respectively).

c) If benefits under this Convention are denied pursuant to the preceding provisions of this paragraph with respect to an item of income derived by a resident of a Contracting State, the competent authority of the other Contracting State may, nevertheless, grant these benefits with respect to that item of income if, in response to a request by such resident, such competent authority determines that granting such benefits is justified in light of the reasons such resident did not satisfy the requirements of this paragraph (such as the existence of losses). The competent authority of the Contracting State to which a request has been made under the preceding sentence shall consult with the competent authority of the other Contracting State before either granting or denying the request

9. Notwithstanding the other provisions of this Convention, a benefit under this Convention shall not be granted in respect of an item of income or capital if it is reasonable to conclude, having regard to all relevant facts and circumstances, that obtaining that benefit was one of the principal purposes of any arrangement or transaction that resulted directly or indirectly in that benefit, unless it is established that granting that benefit in these circumstances would be in accordance with the object and purpose of the relevant provisions of this Convention.

ARTICLE 30
TERRITORIAL EXTENSION[3]

1. This Convention may be extended, either in its entirety or with any necessary modifications [to any part of the territory of (State A) or of (State B) which is specifically excluded from the application of the Convention or], to any State or territory for whose international relations (State A) or (State B) is responsible, which imposes taxes substantially similar in character to those to which the Convention applies. Any such extension shall take effect from such date and subject to such modifications and conditions, including conditions as to termination, as may be specified and agreed between the Contracting States in notes to be exchanged through diplomatic channels or in any other manner in accordance with their constitutional procedures.

2. Unless otherwise agreed by both Contracting States, the termination of the Convention by one of them under Article 32 shall also terminate, in the manner provided for in that Article, the application of the Convention [to any part of the territory of (State A) or of (State B) or] to any State or territory to which it has been extended under this Article.

3 The words between brackets are of relevance when, by special provision, a part of the territory of a Contracting State is excluded from the application of the Convention.

CHAPTER VII
FINAL PROVISIONS

ARTICLE 31
ENTRY INTO FORCE

1. This Convention shall be ratified and the instruments of ratification shall be exchanged at … as soon as possible.

2. The Convention shall enter into force upon the exchange of instruments of ratification and its provisions shall have effect:

a) (in State A): ....

b) (in State B): ....

ARTICLE 32
TERMINATION

This Convention shall remain in force until terminated by a Contracting State. Either Contracting State may terminate the Convention, through diplomatic channels, by giving notice of termination at least six months before the end of any calendar year after the year In such event, the Convention shall cease to have effect:

a) (in State A): ....

b) (in State B): ....

TERMINAL CLAUSE[4]

4 The terminal clause concerning the signing shall be drafted in accordance with the constitutional procedure of both Contracting States.

Annex 2

UNITED NATIONS MODEL DOUBLE TAXATION CONVENTION BETWEEN DEVELOPED AND DEVELOPING COUNTRIES 2017 UPDATE

SUMMARY OF THE CONVENTION

CHAPTER IV
Taxation of capital

CHAPTER V
Methods for elimination of double taxation

CHAPTER VI
Special provisions

CHAPTER VII
Final provisions

TITLE OF THE CONVENTION

Convention between (State A) and (State B) for the elimination of double taxation with respect to taxes on income and capital and the prevention of tax avoidance and evasion

PREAMBLE OF THE CONVENTION[1]

(State A) and (State B),

Desiring to further develop their economic relationship and to enhance their cooperation in tax matters,

Intending to conclude a Convention for the elimination of double taxation with respect to taxes on income and on capital without creating opportunities for non-taxation or reduced taxation through tax avoidance or evasion (including through treaty-shopping arrangements aimed at obtaining reliefs provided in this Convention for the indirect benefit of residents of third States)

Have agreed as follows:

1 The Preamble of the Convention shall be drafted in accordance with the constitutional procedures of the Contracting States.

Chapter I
SCOPE OF THE CONVENTION

Article 1
Persons covered

1. This Convention shall apply to persons who are residents of one or both of the Contracting States.

2. For the purposes of this Convention, income derived by or through an entity or arrangement that is treated as wholly or partly fiscally transparent under the tax law of either Contracting State shall be considered to be income of a resident of a Contracting State but only to the extent that the income is treated, for purposes of taxation by that State, as the income of a resident of that State.

3. This Convention shall not affect the taxation, by a Contracting State, of its residents except with respect to the benefits granted under [paragraph 3 of Article 7], paragraph 2 of Article 9 and Articles 19, 20, 23 A [23 B], 24 and 25 A [25 B] and 28.

Article 2
Taxes covered

1. This Convention shall apply to taxes on income and on capital imposed on behalf of a Contracting State or of its political subdivisions or local authorities, irrespective of the manner in which they are levied.

2. There shall be regarded as taxes on income and on capital all taxes imposed on total income, on total capital, or on elements of income or of capital, including taxes on gains from the alienation of movable or immovable property, taxes on the total amounts of wages or salaries paid by enterprises, as well as taxes on capital appreciation.

3. The existing taxes to which the Convention shall apply are in particular:

a) (in State A): ....

b) (in State B): ....

4. The Convention shall apply also to any identical or substantially similar taxes which are imposed after the date of signature of the Convention in addition to, or in place of, the existing taxes. The competent authorities of the Contracting States shall notify each other of significant changes made to their tax law.

Chapter II
DEFINITIONS

Article 3
General definitions

1. For the purposes of this Convention, unless the context otherwise requires:

(a) The term "person" includes an individual, a company and any other body of persons;
(b) The term "company" means any body corporate or any entity that is treated as a body corporate for tax purposes;
(c) The terms "enterprise of a Contracting State" and "enterprise of the other Contracting State" mean respectively an enterprise carried on by a resident of a Contracting State and an enterprise carried on by a resident of the other Contracting State;

(d) The term "international traffic" means any transport by a ship or aircraft, except when the ship or aircraft is operated solely between places in a Contracting State and the enterprise that operates the ship or aircraft is not an enterprise of that State;
(e) The term "competent authority" means:
  (i) (in State A): ....
  (ii) (in State B): ....
(f) The term "national" means:
  (i) any individual possessing the nationality of a Contracting State
  (ii) any legal person, partnership or association deriving its status as such from the laws in force in a Contracting State.

2. As regards the application of the Convention at any time by a Contracting State, any term not defined therein shall, unless the context otherwise requires, have the meaning that it has at that time under the law of that State for the purposes of the taxes to which the Convention applies, any meaning under the applicable tax laws of that State prevailing over a meaning given to the term under other laws of that State.

Article 4
Resident

1. For the purposes of this Convention, the term "resident of a Contracting State" means any person who, under the laws of that State, is liable to tax therein by reason of his domicile, residence, place of incorporation, place of management or any other criterion of a similar nature, and also includes that State and any political subdivision or local authority thereof. This term, however, does not include any person who is liable to tax in that State in respect only of income from sources in that State or capital situated therein.

2. Where by reason of the provisions of paragraph 1 an individual is a resident of both Contracting States, then his status shall be deter- mined as follows:

(a) He shall be deemed to be a resident only of the State in which he has a permanent home available to him; if he has a permanent home available to him in both States, he shall be deemed to be a resident only of the State with which his personal and economic relations are closer (centre of vital interests);
(b) If the State in which he has his centre of vital interests cannot be determined, or if he has not a permanent home available to him in either State, he shall be deemed to be a resident only of the State in which he has an habitual abode;
(c) If he has an habitual abode in both States or in neither of them, he shall be deemed to be a resident only of the State of which he is a national;
(d) If he is a national of both States or of neither of them, the competent authorities of the Contracting States shall settle the question by mutual agreement.

3. Where by reason of the provisions of paragraph 1 a person other than an individual is a resident of both Contracting States, the competent authorities of the Contracting States shall endeavour to determine by mutual agreement the Contracting State of which such person shall be deemed to be a resident for the purposes of the Convention, having regard to its place of effective management, the place where it is incorporated or otherwise constituted and any other relevant factors. In the absence of such agreement, such person shall not be entitled to any relief or exemption from tax provided by this Convention except to

the extent and in such manner as may be agreed upon by the competent authorities of the Contracting States.

Article 5
Permanent Establishment

1. For the purposes of this Convention, the term "permanent establishment" means a fixed place of business through which the business of an enterprise is wholly or partly carried on.

2. The term "permanent establishment" includes especially:

(a) A place of management;
(b) A branch;
(c) An office;
(d) A factory;
(e) A workshop;
(f) A mine, an oil or gas well, a quarry or any other place of extraction of natural resources.

3. The term "permanent establishment" also encompasses:

(a) A building site, a construction, assembly or installation project or supervisory activities in connection therewith, but only if such site, project or activities last more than six months;
(b) The furnishing of services, including consultancy services, by an enterprise through employees or other personnel engaged by the enterprise for such purpose, but only if activities of that nature continue within a Contracting State for a period or periods aggregating more than 183 days in any 12-month period commencing or ending in the fiscal year concerned.

4. Notwithstanding the preceding provisions of this Article, the term "permanent establishment" shall be deemed not to include:

(a) The use of facilities solely for the purpose of storage or display of goods or merchandise belonging to the enterprise;
(b) The maintenance of a stock of goods or merchandise belonging to the enterprise solely for the purpose of storage or display;
(c) The maintenance of a stock of goods or merchandise belonging to the enterprise solely for the purpose of processing by another enterprise;
(d) The maintenance of a fixed place of business solely for the purpose of purchasing goods or merchandise or of collecting information, for the enterprise;
(e) The maintenance of a fixed place of business solely for the purpose of carrying on, for the enterprise, any other activity;
(f) The maintenance of a fixed place of business solely for any combination of activities mentioned in subparagraphs *(a)* to *(e)*,

provided that such activity or, in the case of subparagraph *(f)*, the overall activity of the fixed place of business, is of a preparatory or auxiliary character.

4.1 Paragraph 4 shall not apply to a fixed place of business that is used or maintained by an enterprise if the same enterprise or a closely related enterprise carries on business activities at the same place or at another place in the same Contracting State and:

(a) that place or other place constitutes a permanent establishment for the enterprise or the closely related enterprise under the provisions of this Article, or
(b) the overall activity resulting from the combination of the activities carried on by the two enterprises at the same place, or by the same enterprise or closely related enterprises at the two places, is not of a preparatory or auxiliary character,

provided that the business activities carried on by the two enterprises at the same place, or by the same enterprise or closely related enterprises at the two places, constitute complementary functions that are part of a cohesive business operation.

5. Notwithstanding the provisions of paragraphs 1 and 2 but subject to the provisions of paragraph 7, where a person is acting in a Contracting State on behalf of an enterprise, that enterprise shall be deemed to have a permanent establishment in that State in respect of any activities which that person undertakes for the enterprise, if such a person:

(a) habitually concludes contracts, or habitually plays the principal role leading to the conclusion of contracts that are routinely concluded without material modification by the enterprise, and these contracts are
   (i) in the name of the enterprise, or
   (ii) for the transfer of the ownership of, or for the granting of the right to use, property owned by that enterprise or that the enterprise has the right to use, or
   (iii) for the provision of services by that enterprise,

   unless the activities of such person are limited to those mentioned in paragraph 4 which, if exercised through a fixed place of business (other than a fixed place of business to which paragraph 4.1 would apply), would not make this fixed place of business a permanent establishment under the provisions of that paragraph; or
(b) the person does not habitually conclude contracts nor plays the principal role leading to the conclusion of such contracts, but habitually maintains in that State a stock of goods or merchandise from which that person regularly delivers goods or merchandise on behalf of the enterprise.

6. Notwithstanding the preceding provisions of this Article but subject to the provisions of paragraph 7, an insurance enterprise of a Contracting State shall, except in regard to reinsurance, be deemed to have a permanent establishment in the other Contracting State if it collects premiums in the territory of that other State or insures risks situated therein through a person.

7. Paragraphs 5 and 6 shall not apply where the person acting in a Contracting State on behalf of an enterprise of the other Contracting State carries on business in the first-mentioned State as an independent agent and acts for the enterprise in the ordinary course of that business. Where, however, a person acts exclusively or almost exclusively on behalf of one or more enterprises to which it is closely related, that person shall not be considered to be an independent agent within the meaning of this paragraph with respect to any such enterprise.

8. The fact that a company which is a resident of a Contracting State controls or is controlled by a company which is a resident of the other Contracting State, or which carries on business in that other State (whether through a permanent establishment or otherwise), shall not of itself constitute either company a permanent establishment of the other.

9. For the purposes of this Article, a person or enterprise is closely related to an enterprise if, based on all the relevant facts and circumstances, one has control of the other or both are under the control of the same persons or enterprises. In any case, a person or enterprise shall be considered to be closely related to an enterprise if one possesses directly or indirectly more than 50 per cent of the beneficial interest in the other (or, in the case of a company, more than 50 per cent of the aggregate vote and value of the company's shares or of the beneficial equity interest in the company) or if another person or enterprise possesses directly or indirectly more than 50 per cent of the beneficial interest (or, in the case of a company, more than 50 per cent of the aggregate vote and value of the company's shares or of the beneficial equity interest in the company) in the person and the enterprise or in the two enterprises.

Chapter III
TAXATION OF INCOME

Article 6
Income from immovable property

1. Income derived by a resident of a Contracting State from immovable property (including income from agriculture or forestry) situated in the other Contracting State may be taxed in that other State.

2. The term "immovable property" shall have the meaning which it has under the law of the Contracting State in which the property in question is situated. The term shall in any case include property accessory to immovable property, livestock and equipment used in agriculture and forestry, rights to which the provisions of general law respecting landed property apply, usufruct of immovable property and rights to variable or fixed payments as consideration for the working of, or the right to work, mineral deposits, sources and other natural resources; ships and aircraft shall not be regarded as immovable property.

3. The provisions of paragraph 1 shall also apply to income derived from the direct use, letting or use in any other form of immovable property.

4. The provisions of paragraphs 1 and 3 shall also apply to the income from immovable property of an enterprise and to income from immovable property used for the performance of independent personal services.

Article 7
Business profits

1. The profits of an enterprise of a Contracting State shall be tax- able only in that State unless the enterprise carries on business in the other Contracting State through a permanent establishment situated therein. If the enterprise carries on business as aforesaid, the profits of the enterprise may be taxed in the other State but only so much of them as is attributable to (a) that permanent establishment; (b) sales in that other State of goods or merchandise of the same or similar kind as those sold through that permanent establishment; or (c) other business activities carried on in that other State of the same or similar kind as those effected through that permanent establishment.

2. Subject to the provisions of paragraph 3, where an enterprise of a Contracting State carries on business in the other Contracting State through a permanent establishment situated

therein, there shall in each Contracting State be attributed to that permanent establishment the profits which it might be expected to make if it were a distinct and separate enterprise engaged in the same or similar activities under the same or similar conditions and dealing wholly independently with the enterprise of which it is a permanent establishment.

3. In the determination of the profits of a permanent establishment, there shall be allowed as deductions expenses which are incurred for the purposes of the business of the permanent establishment including executive and general administrative expenses so incurred, whether in the State in which the permanent establishment is situated or elsewhere. However, no such deduction shall be allowed in respect of amounts, if any, paid (otherwise than towards reimbursement of actual expenses) by the permanent establishment to the head office of the enterprise or any of its other offices, by way of royalties, fees or other similar payments in return for the use of patents or other rights, or by way of commission, for specific services performed or for management, or, except in the case of a banking enterprise, by way of interest on moneys lent to the permanent establishment. Likewise, no account shall be taken, in the determination of the profits of a permanent establishment, for amounts charged (otherwise than towards reimbursement of actual expenses), by the permanent establishment to the head office of the enterprise or any of its other offices, by way of royalties, fees or other similar payments in return for the use of patents or other rights, or by way of commission for specific services performed or for management, or, except in the case of a banking enterprise, by way of interest on moneys lent to the head office of the enterprise or any of its other offices.

4. In so far as it has been customary in a Contracting State to determine the profits to be attributed to a permanent establishment on the basis of an apportionment of the total profits of the enterprise to its various parts, nothing in paragraph 2 shall preclude that Contracting State from determining the profits to be taxed by such an apportionment as may be customary; the method of apportionment adopted shall, however, be such that the result shall be in accordance with the principles contained in this Article.

5. For the purposes of the preceding paragraphs, the profits to be attributed to the permanent establishment shall be determined by the same method year by year unless there is good and sufficient reason to the contrary.

6. Where profits include items of income which are dealt with separately in other Articles of this Convention, then the provisions of those Articles shall not be affected by the provisions of this Article.

(NOTE: The question of whether profits should be attributed to a permanent establishment by reason of the mere purchase by that permanent establishment of goods and merchandise for the enterprise was not resolved. It should therefore be settled in bilateral negotiations.)

Article 8
International shipping and air transport

Article 8 (alternative A)

1. Profits of an enterprise of a Contracting State from the operation of ships or aircraft in international traffic shall be taxable only in that State.

2. The provisions of paragraph 1 shall also apply to profits from the participation in a pool, a joint business or an international operating agency.

Article 8 (alternative B)

1. Profits of an enterprise of a Contracting State from the operation of aircraft in international traffic shall be taxable only in that State.

2. Profits of an enterprise of a Contracting State from the operation of ships in international traffic shall be taxable only in that State unless the shipping activities arising from such operation in the other Contracting State are more than casual. If such activities are more than casual, such profits may be taxed in that other State. The profits to be taxed in that other State shall be determined on the basis of an appropriate allocation of the overall net profits derived by the enterprise from its shipping operations. The tax computed in accordance with such allocation shall then be reduced by ... per cent. (The percentage is to be established through bilateral negotiations.)

3. The provisions of paragraphs 1 and 2 shall also apply to profits from the participation in a pool, a joint business or an international operating agency.

Article 9
Associated enterprises

1. Where:

(a) an enterprise of a Contracting State participates directly or indirectly in the management, control or capital of an enterprise of the other Contracting State, or
(b) the same persons participate directly or indirectly in the management, control or capital of an enterprise of a Contracting State and an enterprise of the other Contracting State,

and in either case conditions are made or imposed between the two enterprises in their commercial or financial relations which differ from those which would be made between independent enterprises, then any profits which would, but for those conditions, have accrued to one of the enterprises, but, by reason of those conditions, have not so accrued, may be included in the profits of that enterprise and taxed accordingly.

2. Where a Contracting State includes in the profits of an enterprise of that State — and taxes accordingly — profits on which an enterprise of the other Contracting State has been charged to tax in that other State and the profits so included are profits which would have accrued to the enterprise of the first-mentioned State if the conditions made between the two enterprises had been those which would have been made between independent enterprises, then that other State shall make an appropriate adjustment to the amount of the tax charged therein on those profits. In determining such adjustment, due regard shall be had to the other provisions of the 3. Convention and the competent authorities of the Contracting States shall, if necessary, consult each other.

The provisions of paragraph 2 shall not apply where judicial, administrative or other legal proceedings have resulted in a final ruling that by actions giving rise to an adjustment of profits under paragraph 1, one of the enterprises concerned is liable to penalty with respect to fraud, gross negligence or wilful default.

Article 10
Dividends

1. Dividends paid by a company which is a resident of a Contracting State to a resident of the other Contracting State may be taxed in that other State.

2. However, such dividends may also be taxed in the Contracting State of which the company paying the dividends is a resident and according to the laws of that State, but if the beneficial owner of the dividends is a resident of the other Contracting State, the tax so charged shall not exceed:

(a) per cent (the percentage is to be established through bilateral negotiations) of the gross amount of the dividends if the beneficial owner is a company (other than a partnership) which holds directly at least 25 per cent of the capital of the company paying the dividends throughout a 365 day period that includes the day of the payment of the dividend (for the purpose of computing that period, no account shall be taken of change of ownership that would directly result from a corporate reorganisation, such as a merger or divisive reorganisation, of the company that holds the shares or that pays the dividend);
(b) per cent (the percentage is to be established through bilateral negotiations) of the gross amount of the dividends in all other cases.

The competent authorities of the Contracting States shall by mutual agreement settle the mode of application of these limitations. This paragraph shall not affect the taxation of the company in respect of the profits out of which the dividends are paid.

3. The term "dividends" as used in this Article means income from shares, "jouissance" shares or "jouissance" rights, mining shares, founders' shares or other rights, not being debt claims, participating in profits, as well as income from other corporate rights which is subjected to the same taxation treatment as income from shares by the laws of the State of which the company making the distribution is a resident.

4. The provisions of paragraphs 1 and 2 shall not apply if the beneficial owner of the dividends, being a resident of a Contracting State, carries on business in the other Contracting State of which the company paying the dividends is a resident, through a permanent establishment situated therein, or performs in that other State independent personal services from a fixed base situated therein, and the holding in respect of which the dividends are paid is effectively connected with such permanent establishment or fixed base. In such case the provisions of Article 7 or Article 14, as the case may be, shall apply.

5. Where a company which is a resident of a Contracting State derives profits or income from the other Contracting State, that other State may not impose any tax on the dividends paid by the company, except in so far as such dividends are paid to a resident of that other State or in so far as the holding in respect of which the dividends are paid is effectively connected with a permanent establishment or a fixed base situated in that other State, nor subject the company's undistributed profits to a tax on the company's undistributed profits, even if the dividends paid or the undistributed profits consist wholly or partly of profits or income arising in such other State.

Article 11
Interest

1. Interest arising in a Contracting State and paid to a resident of the other Contracting State may be taxed in that other State.

2. However, such interest may also be taxed in the Contracting State in which it arises and according to the laws of that State, but if the beneficial owner of the interest is a resident of the other Contracting State, the tax so charged shall not exceed … per cent (the percentage

is to be established through bilateral negotiations) of the gross amount of the interest. The competent authorities of the Contracting States shall by mutual agreement settle the mode of application of this limitation.

3. The term “interest” as used in this Article means income from debt claims of every kind, whether or not secured by mortgage and whether or not carrying a right to participate in the debtor’s profits, and in particular, income from government securities and income from bonds or debentures, including premiums and prizes attaching to such securities, bonds or debentures. Penalty charges for late payment shall not be regarded as interest for the purpose of this Article.

4. The provisions of paragraphs 1 and 2 shall not apply if the beneficial owner of the interest, being a resident of a Contracting State, carries on business in the other Contracting State in which the interest arises, through a permanent establishment situated therein, or per- forms in that other State independent personal services from a fixed base situated therein, and the debt claim in respect of which the interest is paid is effectively connected with (a) such permanent establishment or fixed base, or with (b) business activities referred to in (c) of paragraph 1 of Article 7. In such cases the provisions of Article 7 or Article 14, as the case may be, shall apply.

5. Interest shall be deemed to arise in a Contracting State when the payer is a resident of that State. Where, however, the person paying the interest, whether he is a resident of a Contracting State or not, has in a Contracting State a permanent establishment or a fixed base in connection with which the indebtedness on which the interest is paid was incurred, and such interest is borne by such permanent establishment or fixed base, then such interest shall be deemed to arise in the State in which the permanent establishment or fixed base is situated.

6. Where, by reason of a special relationship between the payer and the beneficial owner or between both of them and some other person, the amount of the interest, having regard to the debt claim for which it is paid, exceeds the amount which would have been agreed upon by the payer and the beneficial owner in the absence of such relationship, the provisions of this Article shall apply only to the last-mentioned amount. In such case, the excess part of the payments shall remain taxable according to the laws of each Contracting State, due regard being had to the other provisions of this Convention.

Article 12
Royalties

1. Royalties arising in a Contracting State and paid to a resident of the other Contracting State may be taxed in that other State.

2. However, such royalties may also be taxed in the Contracting State in which they arise and according to the laws of that State, but if the beneficial owner of the royalties is a resident of the other Contracting State, the tax so charged shall not exceed ... per cent (the percentage is to be established through bilateral negotiations) of the gross amount of the royalties. The competent authorities of the Contracting States shall by mutual agreement settle the mode of application of this limitation.

3. The term “royalties” as used in this Article means payments of any kind received as a consideration for the use of, or the right to use, any copyright of literary, artistic or scientific work including cinematograph films, or films or tapes used for radio or television broad-

casting, any patent, trademark, design or model, plan, secret formula or process, or for the use of, or the right to use, industrial, commercial or scientific equipment or for information concerning industrial, commercial or scientific experience.

4. The provisions of paragraphs 1 and 2 shall not apply if the beneficial owner of the royalties, being a resident of a Contracting State, carries on business in the other Contracting State in which the royalties arise, through a permanent establishment situated therein, or performs in that other State independent personal services from a fixed base situated therein, and the right or property in respect of which the royalties are paid is effectively connected with (a) such permanent establishment or fixed base, or with (b) business activities referred to in (c) of paragraph 1 of Article 7. In such cases the provisions of Article 7 or Article 14, as the case may be, shall apply.

5. Royalties shall be deemed to arise in a Contracting State when the payer is a resident of that State. Where, however, the person paying the royalties, whether he is a resident of a Contracting State or not, has in a Contracting State a permanent establishment or a fixed base in connection with which the liability to pay the royalties was incurred, and such royalties are borne by such permanent establishment or fixed base, then such royalties shall be deemed to arise in the State in which the permanent establishment or fixed base is situated.

6. Where by reason of a special relationship between the payer and the beneficial owner or between both of them and some other person, the amount of the royalties, having regard to the use, right or information for which they are paid, exceeds the amount which would have been agreed upon by the payer and the beneficial owner in the absence of such relationship, the provisions of this Article shall apply only to the last-mentioned amount. In such case, the excess part of the payments shall remain taxable according to the laws of each Contracting State, due regard being had to the other provisions of this Convention.

Article 12A
Fees for technical services

1. Fees for technical services arising in a Contracting State and paid to a resident of the other Contracting State may be taxed in that other State.

2. However, notwithstanding the provisions of Article 14 and subject to the provisions of Articles 8, 16 and 17, fees for technical services arising in a Contracting State may also be taxed in the Contracting State in which they arise and according to the laws of that State, but if the beneficial owner of the fees is a resident of the other Contracting State, the tax so charged shall not exceed ... percent of the gross amount of the fees [the percentage to be established through bilateral negotiations].

3. The term "fees for technical services" as used in this Article means any payment in consideration for any service of a managerial, technical or consultancy nature, unless the payment is made:

(a) to an employee of the person making the payment;
(b) for teaching in an educational institution or for teaching by an educational institution; or
(c) by an individual for services for the personal use of an individual.

3. The provisions of paragraphs 1 and 2 shall not apply if the beneficial owner of fees for technical services, being a resident of a Contracting State, carries on business in the other Contracting State in which the fees for technical services arise through a permanent estab-

lishment situated in that other State, or performs in the other Contracting State independent personal services from a fixed base situated in that other State, and the fees for technical services are effectively connected with:

(a) such permanent establishment or fixed base, or
(b) business activities referred to in (c) of paragraph 1 of Article 7.

In such cases the provisions of Article 7 or Article 14, as the case may be, shall apply.

5. For the purposes of this Article, subject to paragraph 6, fees for technical services shall be deemed to arise in a Contracting State if the payer is a resident of that State or if the person paying the fees, whether that person is a resident of a Contracting State or not, has in a Contracting State a permanent establishment or a fixed base in connection with which the obligation to pay the fees was incurred, and such fees are borne by the permanent establishment or fixed base.

6. For the purposes of this Article, fees for technical services shall be deemed not to arise in a Contracting State if the payer is a resident of that State and carries on business in the other Contracting State through a permanent establishment situated in that other State or performs independent personal services through a fixed base situated in that other State and such fees are borne by that permanent establishment or fixed base.

7. Where, by reason of a special relationship between the payer and the beneficial owner of the fees for technical services or between both of them and some other person, the amount of the fees, having regard to the services for which they are paid, exceeds the amount which would have been agreed upon by the payer and the beneficial owner in the absence of such relationship, the provisions of this Article shall apply only to the last-mentioned amount. In such case, the excess part of the fees shall remain taxable according to the laws of each Contracting State, due regard being had to the other provisions of this Convention.

Article 13
Capital gains

1. Gains derived by a resident of a Contracting State from the alienation of immovable property referred to in Article 6 and situated in the other Contracting State may be taxed in that other State.

2. Gains from the alienation of movable property forming part of the business property of a permanent establishment which an enterprise of a Contracting State has in the other Contracting State or of movable property pertaining to a fixed base available to a resident of a Contracting State in the other Contracting State for the purpose of performing independent personal services, including such gains from the alienation of such a permanent establishment (alone or with the whole enterprise) or of such fixed base, may be taxed in that other State.

3. Gains that an enterprise of a Contracting State that operates ships or aircraft in international traffic derives from the alienation of such ships or aircraft, or of movable property pertaining to the operation of such ships or aircraft, shall be taxable only in that State.

4. Gains derived by a resident of a Contracting State from the alienation of shares or comparable interests, such as interests in a partnership or trust, may be taxed in the other Contracting State if, at any time during the 365 days preceding the alienation, these shares or

comparable interests derived more than 50 per cent of their value directly or indirectly from immovable property, as defined in Article 6, situated in that other State.

5. Gains, other than those to which paragraph 4 applies, derived by a resident of a Contracting State from the alienation of shares of a company, or comparable interests, such as interests in a partnership or trust, which is a resident of the other Contracting State, may be taxed in that other State if the alienator, at any time during the 365 days preceding such alienation, held directly or indirectly at least … per cent (the percentage is to be established through bilateral negotiations) of the capital of that company or entity.

6. Gains from the alienation of any property other than that referred to in paragraphs 1, 2, 3, 4 and 5 shall be taxable only in the Contracting State of which the alienator is a resident.

Article 14
Independent personal services

1. Income derived by a resident of a Contracting State in respect of professional services or other activities of an independent character shall be taxable only in that State except in the following circumstances, when such income may also be taxed in the other Contracting State:

(a) If he has a fixed base regularly available to him in the other Contracting State for the purpose of performing his activities; in that case, only so much of the income as is attributable to that fixed base may be taxed in that other Contracting State; or
(b) If his stay in the other Contracting State is for a period or periods amounting to or exceeding in the aggregate 183 days in any twelve-month period commencing or ending in the fiscal year concerned; in that case, only so much of the income as is derived from his activities performed in that other State may be taxed in that other State.

2. The term "professional services" includes especially independent scientific, literary, artistic, educational or teaching activities as well as the independent activities of physicians, lawyers, engineers, architects, dentists and accountants.

Article 15
Dependent personal services

1. Subject to the provisions of Articles 16, 18 and 19, salaries, wages and other similar remuneration derived by a resident of a Contracting State in respect of an employment shall be taxable only in that State unless the employment is exercised in the other Contracting State. If the employment is so exercised, such remuneration as is derived therefrom may be taxed in that other State.

2. Notwithstanding the provisions of paragraph 1, remuneration derived by a resident of a Contracting State in respect of an employment exercised in the other Contracting State shall be taxable only in the first-mentioned State if:

(a) The recipient is present in the other State for a period or periods not exceeding in the aggregate 183 days in any twelve-month period commencing or ending in the fiscal year concerned; and
(b) The remuneration is paid by, or on behalf of, an employer who is not a resident of the other State; and
(c) The remuneration is not borne by a permanent establishment or a fixed base which the employer has in the other State.

3. Notwithstanding the preceding provisions of this Article, remuneration derived by a resident of a Contracting State in respect of an employment, as a member of the regular complement of a ship or aircraft, that is exercised aboard a ship or aircraft operated in international traffic, other than aboard a ship or aircraft operated solely within the other Contracting State, shall be taxable only in the first-mentioned State.

Article 16
Directors' fees and remuneration of top-level managerial officials

1. Directors' fees and other similar payments derived by a resident of a Contracting State in his capacity as a member of the Board of Directors of a company which is a resident of the other Contracting State may be taxed in that other State.

2. Salaries, wages and other similar remuneration derived by a resident of a Contracting State in his capacity as an official in a top-level managerial position of a company which is a resident of the other Contracting State may be taxed in that other State.

Article 17
Artistes and sportspersons

1. Notwithstanding the provisions of Articles 14 and 15, income derived by a resident of a Contracting State as an entertainer, such as a theatre, motion picture, radio or television artiste, or a musician, or as a sportsperson, from his personal activities as such exercised in the other Contracting State, may be taxed in that other State.

2. Where income in respect of personal activities exercised by an entertainer or a sportsperson in his capacity as such accrues not to the entertainer or sportsperson himself but to another person, that income may, notwithstanding the provisions of Articles 7, 14 and 15, be taxed in the Contracting State in which the activities of the entertainer or sportsperson are exercised.

Article 18
Pensions and social security payments

Article 18 (alternative A)

1. Subject to the provisions of paragraph 2 of Article 19, pensions and other similar remuneration paid to a resident of a Contracting State in consideration of past employment shall be taxable only in that State.

2. Notwithstanding the provisions of paragraph 1, pensions paid and other payments made under a public scheme which is part of the social security system of a Contracting State or a political subdivision or a local authority thereof shall be taxable only in that State.

Article 18 (alternative B)

1. Subject to the provisions of paragraph 2 of Article 19, pensions and other similar remuneration paid to a resident of a Contracting State in consideration of past employment may be taxed in that State.

2. However, such pensions and other similar remuneration may also be taxed in the other Contracting State if the payment is made by a resident of that other State or a permanent establishment situated therein.

3. Notwithstanding the provisions of paragraphs 1 and 2, pensions paid and other payments made under a public scheme which is part of the social security system of a Contracting State or a political subdivision or a local authority thereof shall be taxable only in that State.

Article 19
Government service

1.

(a) Salaries, wages and other similar remuneration paid by a Contracting State or a political subdivision or a local authority thereof to an individual in respect of services rendered to that State or subdivision or authority shall be taxable only in that State.
(b) However, such salaries, wages and other similar remuneration shall be taxable only in the other Contracting State if the services are rendered in that other State and the individual is a resident of that State who:
   (i) is a national of that State; or
   (ii) did not become a resident of that State solely for the purpose of rendering the services.

2.

(a) Notwithstanding the provisions of paragraph 1, pensions and other similar remuneration paid by, or out of funds created by, a Contracting State or a political subdivision or a local authority thereof to an individual in respect of services rendered to that State or subdivision or authority shall be taxable only in that State.
(b) However, such pensions and other similar remuneration shall be taxable only in the other Contracting State if the individual is a resident of, and a national of, that other State.

3. The provisions of Articles 15, 16, 17 and 18 shall apply to salaries, wages, pensions, and other similar remuneration in respect of services rendered in connection with a business carried on by a Contracting State or a political subdivision or a local authority thereof.

Article 20
Students

Payments which a student or business trainee or apprentice who is or was immediately before visiting a Contracting State a resident of the other Contracting State and who is present in the first-mentioned State solely for the purpose of his education or training receives for the purpose of his maintenance, education or training shall not be taxed in that State, provided that such payments arise from sources outside that State.

Article 21
Other Income

1. Items of income of a resident of a Contracting State, wherever arising, not dealt with in the foregoing Articles of this Convention shall be taxable only in that State.

2. The provisions of paragraph 1 shall not apply to income, other than income from immovable property as defined in paragraph 2 of Article 6, if the recipient of such income, being a resident of a Contracting State, carries on business in the other Contracting State through a permanent establishment situated therein, or performs in that other State independent personal services from a fixed base situated therein, and the right or property in respect of which the income is paid is effectively connected with such permanent establishment

or fixed base. In such case the provisions of Article 7 or Article 14, as the case may be, shall apply.

3. Notwithstanding the provisions of paragraphs 1 and 2, items of income of a resident of a Contracting State not dealt with in the fore- going Articles of this Convention and arising in the other Contracting State may also be taxed in that other State.

Chapter IV
TAXATION OF CAPITAL

Article 22
Capital

1. Capital represented by immovable property referred to in Article 6, owned by a resident of a Contracting State and situated in the other Contracting State, may be taxed in that other State.

2. Capital represented by movable property forming part of the business property of a permanent establishment which an enterprise of a Contracting State has in the other Contracting State or by movable property pertaining to a fixed base available to a resident of a Contracting State in the other Contracting State for the purpose of performing independent personal services may be taxed in that other State.

3. Capital of an enterprise of a Contracting State that operates ships or aircraft in international traffic represented by such ships or aircraft, and by movable property pertaining to the operation of such ships or aircraft, shall be taxable only in that State.

[4. All other elements of capital of a resident of a Contracting State shall be taxable only in that State.]

(The question of the taxation of all other elements of capital of a resident of a Contracting State is left to bilateral negotiations. Should the negotiating parties decide to include in the Convention an article on the taxation of capital, they will have to determine whether to use the wording of paragraph 4 as shown or wording that leaves taxation to the State in which the capital is located.)

Chapter V
METHODS FOR THE ELIMINATION OF DOUBLE TAXATION

Article 23 A
Exemption Method

1. Where a resident of a Contracting State derives income or owns capital which may be taxed in the other Contracting State, in accordance with the provisions of this Convention (except to the extent that these provisions allow taxation by that other State solely because the income is also income derived by a resident of that State or because the capital is also capital owned by a resident of that State), the first-mentioned State shall, subject to the provisions of paragraphs 2 and 3, exempt such income or capital from tax.

2. Where a resident of a Contracting State derives items of income which, in accordance with the provisions of Articles 10, 11, 12, and 12A may be taxed in the other Contracting State, the first-mentioned State shall allow as a deduction from the tax on the income of that resident an amount equal to the tax paid in that other State. Such deduction shall not,

however, exceed that part of the tax, as computed before the deduction is given, which is attributable to such items of income which may be taxed in that other State.

3. Where in accordance with any provision of this Convention income derived or capital owned by a resident of a Contracting State is exempt from tax in that State, such State may nevertheless, in calculating the amount of tax on the remaining income or capital of such resident, take into account the exempted income or capital.

4. The provisions of paragraph 1 shall not apply to income derived or capital owned by a resident of a Contracting State where the other Contracting State applies the provisions of this Convention to exempt such income or capital from tax or applies the provisions of paragraph 2 of Article 10, 11, 12 or 12A to such income; in the latter case, the first-mentioned State shall allow the deduction of tax provided for by paragraph 2.

Article 23 B
Credit Method

1. Where a resident of a Contracting State derives income or owns capital which may be taxed in the other Contracting State, in accordance with the provisions of this Convention (except to the extent that these provisions allow taxation by that other State solely because the income is also income derived by a resident of that State or because the capital is also capital owned by a resident of that State), the first-mentioned State shall allow:

(a) as a deduction from the tax on the income of that resident an amount equal to the income tax paid in that other State;
(b) as a deduction from the tax on the capital of that resident, an amount equal to the capital tax paid in that other State.

Such deduction in either case shall not, however, exceed that part of the income tax or capital tax, as computed before the deduction is given, which is attributable, as the case may be, to the income or the capital which may be taxed in that other State.

2. Where, in accordance with any provision of this Convention, income derived or capital owned by a resident of a Contracting State is exempt from tax in that State, such State may nevertheless, in calculating the amount of tax on the remaining income or capital of such resident, take into account the exempted income or capital.

Chapter VI
SPECIAL PROVISIONS

Article 24
Non-Discrimination

1. Nationals of a Contracting State shall not be subjected in the other Contracting State to any taxation or any requirement connected therewith which is other or more burdensome than the taxation and connected requirements to which nationals of that other State in the same circumstances, in particular with respect to residence, are or may be subjected. This provision shall, notwithstanding the provisions of Article 1, also apply to persons who are not residents of one or both of the Contracting States.

2. Stateless persons who are residents of a Contracting State shall not be subjected in either Contracting State to any taxation or any requirement connected therewith which is other

or more burdensome than the taxation and connected requirements to which nationals of the State concerned in the same circumstances, in particular with respect to residence, are or may be subjected.

3. The taxation on a permanent establishment which an enterprise of a Contracting State has in the other Contracting State shall not be less favourably levied in that other State than the taxation levied on enterprises of that other State carrying on the same activities. This provision shall not be construed as obliging a Contracting State to grant to residents of the other Contracting State any personal allowances, reliefs and reductions for taxation purposes on account of civil status or family responsibilities which it grants to its own residents.

4. Except where the provisions of paragraph 1 of Article 9, paragraph 6 of Article 11, paragraph 6 of Article 12, or paragraph 6 of Article 12A apply, interest, royalties, fees for technical services, and other disbursements paid by an enterprise of a Contracting State to a resident of the other Contracting State shall, for the purpose of determining the taxable profits of such enterprise, be deductible under the same conditions as if they had been paid to a resident of the first-mentioned State. Similarly, any debts of an enterprise of a Contracting State to a resident of the other Contracting State shall, for the purpose of determining the taxable capital of such enterprise, be deductible under the same conditions as if they had been contracted to a resident of the first-mentioned State.

5. Enterprises of a Contracting State, the capital of which is wholly or partly owned or controlled, directly or indirectly, by one or more residents of the other Contracting State, shall not be subjected in the first-mentioned State to any taxation or any requirement connected therewith which is other or more burdensome than the taxation and connected requirements to which other similar enterprises of the first-mentioned State are or may be subjected.

6. The provisions of this Article shall, notwithstanding the provisions of Article 2, apply to taxes of every kind and description.

Article 25
Mutual Agreement Procedure

Article 25 (alternative A)

1. Where a person considers that the actions of one or both of the Contracting States result or will result for him in taxation not in accordance with the provisions of this Convention, he may, irrespective of the remedies provided by the domestic law of those States, present his case to the competent authority of the Contracting State of which he is a resident or, if his case comes under paragraph 1 of Article 24, to that of the Contracting State of which he is a national. The case must be presented within three years from the first notification of the action resulting in taxation not in accordance with the provisions of the Convention.

2. The competent authority shall endeavour, if the objection appears to it to be justified and if it is not itself able to arrive at a satisfactory solution, to resolve the case by mutual agreement with the competent authority of the other Contracting State, with a view to the avoidance of taxation which is not in accordance with this Convention. Any agreement reached shall be implemented notwithstanding any time limits in the domestic law of the Contracting States.

3. The competent authorities of the Contracting States shall endeavour to resolve by mutual agreement any difficulties or doubts arising as to the interpretation or application of the Convention. They may also consult together for the elimination of double taxation in cases not provided for in the Convention.

4. The competent authorities of the Contracting States may communicate with each other directly, including through a joint commission consisting of themselves or their representatives, for the purpose of reaching an agreement in the sense of the preceding paragraphs. The competent authorities, through consultations, may develop appropriate bilateral procedures, conditions, methods and techniques for the implementation of the mutual agreement procedure provided for in this Article.

Article 25 (alternative B)

1. Where a person considers that the actions of one or both of the Contracting States result or will result for him in taxation not in accordance with the provisions of this Convention, he may, irrespective of the remedies provided by the domestic law of those States, present his case to the competent authority of the Contracting State of which he is a resident or, if his case comes under paragraph 1 of Article 24, to that of the Contracting State of which he is a national. The case must be presented within three years from the first notification of the action resulting in taxation not in accordance with the provisions of the Convention.

2. The competent authority shall endeavour, if the objection appears to it to be justified and if it is not itself able to arrive at a satisfactory solution, to resolve the case by mutual agreement with the competent authority of the other Contracting State, with a view to the avoidance of taxation which is not in accordance with this Convention. Any agreement reached shall be implemented notwithstanding any time limits in the domestic law of the Contracting States.

3. The competent authorities of the Contracting States shall endeavour to resolve by mutual agreement any difficulties or doubts arising as to the interpretation or application of the Convention. They may also consult together for the elimination of double taxation in cases not provided for in the Convention.

4. The competent authorities of the Contracting States may communicate with each other directly, including through a joint commission consisting of themselves or their representatives, for the purpose of reaching an agreement in the sense of the preceding paragraphs. The competent authorities, through consultations, may develop appropriate bilateral procedures, conditions, methods and techniques for the implementation of the mutual agreement procedure provided for in this Article.

5. Where,

(a) under paragraph 1, a person has presented a case to the competent authority of a Contracting State on the basis that the actions of one or both of the Contracting States have resulted for that person in taxation not in accordance with the provisions of this Convention, and
(b) the competent authorities are unable to reach an agreement to resolve that case pursuant to paragraph 2 within three years from the presentation of the case to the competent authority of the other Contracting State,

any unresolved issues arising from the case shall be submitted to arbitration if either competent authority so requests. The person who has presented the case shall be notified of the request. These unresolved issues shall not, however, be submitted to arbitration if a decision on these issues has already been rendered by a court or administrative tribunal of either State. The arbitration decision shall be binding on both States and shall be implemented notwithstanding any time limits in the domestic laws of these States unless both competent authorities agree on a different solution within six months after the decision has been communicated to them or unless a person directly affected by the case does not accept the mutual agreement that implements the arbitration decision. The competent authorities of the Contracting States shall by mutual agreement settle the mode of application of this paragraph.

Article 26
Exchange of information

1. The competent authorities of the Contracting States shall exchange such information as is foreseeably relevant for carrying out the provisions of this Convention or to the administration or enforcement of the domestic laws of the Contracting States concerning taxes of every kind and description imposed on behalf of the Contracting States, or of their political subdivisions or local authorities, insofar as the taxation thereunder is not contrary to the Convention. In particular, information shall be exchanged that would be helpful to a Contracting State in preventing avoidance or evasion of such taxes. The exchange of information is not restricted by Articles 1 and 2.

2. Any information received under paragraph 1 by a Contracting State shall be treated as secret in the same manner as information obtained under the domestic laws of that State and it shall be disclosed only to persons or authorities (including courts and administrative bodies) concerned with the assessment or collection of, the enforcement or prosecution in respect of, or the determination of appeals in relation to, the taxes referred to in paragraph 1, or the oversight of the above. Such persons or authorities shall use the information only for such purposes. They may disclose the information in public court proceedings or in judicial decisions. Notwithstanding the foregoing, information received by a Contracting State may be used for other purposes when such information may be used for such other purposes under the laws of both States and the competent authority of the supplying State authorizes such use.

3. In no case shall the provisions of paragraphs 1 and 2 be construed so as to impose on a Contracting State the obligation:

(a) To carry out administrative measures at variance with the laws and administrative practice of that or of the other Contracting State;
(b) To supply information which is not obtainable under the laws or in the normal course of the administration of that or of the other Contracting State;
(c) To supply information which would disclose any trade, business, industrial, commercial or professional secret or trade process, or information, the disclosure of which would be contrary to public policy (ordre public).

4. If information is requested by a Contracting State in accordance with this Article, the other Contracting State shall use its information gathering measures to obtain the requested information, even though that other State may not need such information for its own tax purposes. The obligation contained in the preceding sentence is subject to the limitations of paragraph 3 but in no case shall such limitations be construed to permit a Contracting State to decline to supply information solely because it has no domestic interest in such information.

5. In no case shall the provisions of paragraph 3 be construed to permit a Contracting State to decline to supply information solely because the information is held by a bank, other financial institution, nominee or person acting in an agency or a fiduciary capacity or because it relates to ownership interests in a person.

6. The competent authorities shall, through consultation, develop appropriate methods and techniques concerning the matters in respect of which exchanges of information under paragraph 1 shall be made.

Article 27
Assistance in the collection of taxes[2]

1. The Contracting States shall lend assistance to each other in the collection of revenue claims. This assistance is not restricted by Articles 1 and 2. The competent authorities of the Contracting States may by mutual agreement settle the mode of application of this Article.

2. The term "revenue claim" as used in this Article means an amount owed in respect of taxes of every kind and description imposed on behalf of the Contracting States, or of their political subdivisions or local authorities, insofar as the taxation thereunder is not contrary to this Convention or any other instrument to which the Contracting States are parties, as well as interest, administrative penalties and costs of collection or conservancy related to such amount.

3. When a revenue claim of a Contracting State is enforceable under the laws of that State and is owed by a person who, at that time, cannot, under the laws of that State, prevent its collection, that revenue claim shall, at the request of the competent authority of that State, be accepted for purposes of collection by the competent authority of the other Contracting State. That revenue claim shall be collected by that other State in accordance with the provisions of its laws applicable to the enforcement and collection of its own taxes as if the revenue claim were a revenue claim of that other State.

4. When a revenue claim of a Contracting State is a claim in respect of which that State may, under its law, take measures of conservancy with a view to ensure its collection, that revenue claim shall, at the request of the competent authority of that State, be accepted for purposes of taking measures of conservancy by the competent authority of the other Contracting State. That other State shall take measures of conservancy in respect of that revenue claim in accordance with the provisions of its laws as if the revenue claim were a revenue claim of that other State even if, at the time when such measures are applied, the revenue claim is not enforceable in the first-mentioned State or is owed by a person who has a right to prevent its collection.

5. Notwithstanding the provisions of paragraphs 3 and 4, a revenue claim accepted by a Contracting State for purposes of paragraph 3 or 4 shall not, in that State, be subject to the time limits or accorded any priority applicable to a revenue claim under the laws of that

---

2 In some countries, national law, policy or administrative considerations may not allow or justify the type of assistance envisaged under this Article or may require that this type of assistance be restricted, e.g. to countries that have similar tax systems or tax administrations or as to the taxes covered. For that reason, the Article should only be included in the Convention where each State concludes that, based on the factors described in paragraph 1 of the Commentary on the Article, they can agree to provide assistance in the collection of taxes levied by the other State.

State by reason of its nature as such. In addition, a revenue claim accepted by a Contracting State for the purposes of paragraph 3 or 4 shall not, in that State, have any priority applicable to that revenue claim under the laws of the other Contracting State.

6. Proceedings with respect to the existence, validity or the amount of a revenue claim of a Contracting State shall not be brought before the courts or administrative bodies of the other Contracting State.

7. Where, at any time after a request has been made by a Contracting State under paragraph 3 or 4 and before the other Contracting State has collected and remitted the relevant revenue claim to the first-mentioned State, the relevant revenue claim ceases to be

(a) in the case of a request under paragraph 3, a revenue claim of the first-mentioned State that is enforceable under the laws of that State and is owed by a person who, at that time, cannot, under the laws of that State, prevent its collection, or
(b) in the case of a request under paragraph 4, a revenue claim of the first-mentioned State in respect of which that State may, under its laws, take measures of conservancy with a view to ensure its collection

the competent authority of the first-mentioned State shall promptly notify the competent authority of the other State of that fact and, at the option of the other State, the first-mentioned State shall either suspend or withdraw its request.

8. In no case shall the provisions of this Article be construed so as to impose on a Contracting State the obligation:

(a) to carry out administrative measures at variance with the laws and administrative practice of that or of the other Contracting State;
(b) to carry out measures which would be contrary to public policy (ordre public);
(c) to provide assistance if the other Contracting State has not pursued all reasonable measures of collection or conservancy, as the case may be, available under its laws or administrative practice;
(d) to provide assistance in those cases where the administrative burden for that State is clearly disproportionate to the benefit to be derived by the other Contracting State.

Article 28
Members of diplomatic missions and consular posts

Nothing in this Convention shall affect the fiscal privileges of members of diplomatic missions or consular posts under the general rules of international law or under the provisions of special agreements.

Article 29
Entitlement to benefits[3]

1. Except as otherwise provided in this Article, a resident of a Contracting State shall not be entitled to a benefit that would otherwise be accorded by this Convention (other than a

3 The drafting of this Article will depend on how the Contracting States decide to implement their common intention, reflected in the preamble of the Convention and incorporated in the minimum standard agreed to as part of the OECD-G20 Base Erosion and Profit Shifting project by particular countries, to eliminate double taxation without creating opportunities for non-taxation or reduced taxation through tax evasion or avoidance, including through treaty shopping arrangements.

benefit under para- graph 3 of Article 4, paragraph 2 of Article 9 or Article 25) unless such resident is a "qualified person", as defined in paragraph 2, at the time that the benefit would be accorded.

2. A resident of a Contracting State shall be a qualified person at a time when a benefit would otherwise be accorded by the Convention if, at that time, the resident is:

(a) an individual;

(b) that Contracting State, or a political subdivision or local authority thereof, or an agency or instrumentality of that State, political subdivision or local authority;

(c) a company or other entity, if, throughout the taxable period that includes that time, the principal class of its shares (and any dis- proportionate class of shares) is regularly traded on one or more recognised stock exchanges, and either:

  (i) its principal class of shares is primarily traded on one or more recognised stock exchanges located in the Contracting State of which the company or entity is a resident; or

  (ii) the company's or entity's primary place of management and control is in the Contracting State of which it is a resident;

(d) a company, if:

  (i) throughout the taxable period that includes that time, at least 50 per cent of the aggregate vote and value of the shares (and at least 50 per cent of the aggregate vote and value of any disproportionate class of shares) in the company is owned directly or indirectly by five or fewer companies or entities entitled to benefits under subparagraph c) of this paragraph, provided that, in the case of indirect ownership, each intermediate owner is a resident of the Contracting State from which a benefit under this Convention is being sought or is a qualifying intermediate owner; and

  (ii) with respect to benefits under this Convention other than under Article 10, less than 50 per cent of the company's gross income, and less than 50 per cent of the tested group's gross income, for the taxable period that includes that time, is paid or accrued, directly or indirectly, in the form of payments that are deductible in that taxable period for purposes of the taxes covered by this Convention in the company's Contracting State of residence (but not including arm's length payments in the ordinary course of business for services or tangible property, and in the case of a tested group, not including intra-group transactions) to persons that are not residents of either Contracting State entitled to the benefits of this Convention under subparagraph a), b), c) or e);

(e) a person, other than an individual, that

  (i) is a [agreed description of the relevant non-profit organisations found in each Contracting State],

  (ii) is a recognised pension fund[4] to which subdivision (i) of the definition of recognised pension fund in paragraph 1 of Article 3 applies, provided that more than 50 per cent of the beneficial interests in that person are owned by individuals resident of either Contracting State, or more than [... per cent] of the beneficial interests in that person are owned by individuals resident of either Contracting State or of any other State with respect to which the following conditions are met

4 As to incorporation of such a definition, see paragraph 14 of the Commentary on Article 29.

(*A*) individuals who are residents of that other State are entitled to the benefits of a comprehensive convention for the avoidance of double taxation between that other State and the State from which the benefits of this Convention are claimed, and

(*B*) with respect to income referred to in Articles 10 and 11 of this Convention, if the person were a resident of that other State entitled to all the benefits of that other convention, the person would be entitled, under such convention, to a rate of tax with respect to the particular class of income for which benefits are being claimed under this Convention that is at least as low as the rate applicable under this Convention; or

(*iii*) is a recognised pension fund to which subdivision (ii) of the definition of recognised pension fund in paragraph 1 of Article 3 applies, provided that it is established and operated exclusively or almost exclusively to invest funds for the benefit of entities or arrangements referred to in the preceding subdivision;

(*f*) a person other than an individual, if

(*i*) at that time and on at least half the days of a twelve-month period that includes that time, persons who are residents of that Contracting State and that are entitled to the benefits of this Convention under subparagraph a), b), c) or e) own, directly or indirectly, shares representing at least 50 per cent of the aggregate vote and value (and at least 50 per cent of the aggregate vote and value of any disproportionate class of shares) of the shares in the person, provided that, in the case of indirect ownership, each intermediate owner is a qualifying intermediate owner, and

(*ii*) less than 50 per cent of the person's gross income, and less than 50 per cent of the tested group's gross income, for the taxable period that includes that time, is paid or accrued, directly or indirectly, in the form of payments that are deductible for purposes of the taxes covered by this Convention in the person's Contracting State of residence (but not including arm's length payments in the ordinary course of business for services or tangible property, and in the case of a tested group, not including intra-group transactions), to persons that are not residents of either Contracting State entitled to the benefits of this Convention under subparagraph a), b), c) or e) of this paragraph; or

(*g*) [possible provision on collective investment vehicles];

3.

(*a*) A resident of a Contracting State shall be entitled to benefits under this Convention with respect to an item of income derived from the other Contracting State, regardless of whether the resident is a qualified person, if the resident is engaged in the active conduct of a business in the first-mentioned State (other than the business of making or managing investments for the resident's own account, unless these activities are banking, insurance or securities activities carried on by a bank or [list financial institutions similar to banks that the Contracting States agree to treat as such], insurance enterprise or registered securities dealer respectively), and the income derived from the other State emanates from, or is incidental to, that business. For purposes of this Article, the term "active conduct of a business" shall not include the following activities or any combination thereof:

(i) operating as a holding company;
(ii) providing overall supervision or administration of a group of companies;
(iii) providing group financing (including cash pooling); or
(iv) making or managing investments, unless these activities are carried on by a bank [list financial institutions similar to banks that the Contracting States agree to treat as such], insurance enterprise or registered securities dealer in the ordinary course of its business as such.

(b) If a resident of a Contracting State derives an item of income from a business activity conducted by that resident in the other Contracting State, or derives an item of income arising in the other State from a connected person, the conditions described in subparagraph a) shall be considered to be satisfied with respect to such item only if the business activity carried on by the resident in the first-mentioned State to which the item is related is substantial in relation to the same or complementary business activity carried on by the resident or such connected person in the other Contracting State. Whether a business activity is substantial for the purposes of this paragraph shall be determined based on all the facts and circumstances.

(c) For purposes of applying this paragraph, activities conducted by connected persons with respect to a resident of a Contracting State shall be deemed to be conducted by such resident.

4. [A rule providing so-called derivative benefits. The question of how the derivative benefits paragraph should be drafted in a convention that follows the detailed version is discussed in the Commentary.]

5. A company that is a resident of a Contracting State that functions as a headquarters company for a multinational corporate group consisting of such company and its direct and indirect subsidiaries shall be entitled to benefits under this Convention with respect to dividends and interest paid by members of its multinational corporate group, regardless of whether the resident is a qualified person. A company shall be considered a headquarters company for this purpose only if:

(a) such company's primary place of management and control is in the Contracting State of which it is a resident;

(b) the multinational corporate group consists of companies resident of, and engaged in the active conduct of a business in, at least four States, and the businesses carried on in each of the four States (or four groupings of States) generate at least 10 per cent of the gross income of the group;

(d) the businesses of the multinational corporate group that are carried on in any one State other than the Contracting State of residence of such company generate less than 50 per cent of the gross income of the group;

(e) no more than 25 per cent of such company's gross income is derived from the other Contracting State;
such company is subject to the same income taxation rules in its Contracting State of residence as persons described in para- graph 3 of this Article; and

(f) less than 50 per cent of such company's gross income, and less than 50 per cent of the tested group's gross income, is paid or accrued, directly or indirectly, in the form of payments that are deductible for purposes of the taxes covered by this Convention in the company's Contracting State of residence (but not including arm's length payments in the ordinary course of business for services or tangible property or payments in respect of financial obligations to a bank that is not a connected person with respect to such company, and in the case of a tested group, not including intra-group transactions) to persons that are not residents of either Contracting State entitled to the benefits of this Convention under subparagraph a), b), c) or e) of paragraph 2.

If the requirements of subparagraph b), c) or d) of this paragraph are not fulfilled for the relevant taxable period, they shall be deemed to be fulfilled if the required ratios are met when averaging the gross income of the preceding four taxable periods.

6. If a resident of a Contracting State is neither a qualified person pursuant to the provisions of paragraph 2 of this Article, nor entitled to benefits under paragraph 3, 4 or 5, the competent authority of the Contracting State in which benefits are denied under the previous provisions of this Article may, nevertheless, grant the benefits of this Convention, or benefits with respect to a specific item of income or capital, taking into account the object and purpose of this Convention, but only if such resident demonstrates to the satisfaction of such competent authority that neither its establishment, acquisition or maintenance, nor the conduct of its operations, had as one of its principal purposes the obtaining of benefits under this Convention. The competent authority of the Contracting State to which a request has been made, under this paragraph, by a resident of the other State, shall consult with the competent authority of that other State before either granting or denying the request.

7. For the purposes of this and the previous paragraphs of this Article:

(a) the term "recognised stock exchange" means:
  - *(i)* [list of stock exchanges agreed to at the time of signature]; and
  - *(ii)* any other stock exchange agreed upon by the competent authorities of the Contracting States;

(b) with respect to entities that are not companies, the term "shares" means interests that are comparable to shares;

(c) the term "principal class of shares" means the ordinary or common shares of the company or entity, provided that such class of shares represents the majority of the aggregate vote and value of the company or entity. If no single class of ordinary or common shares represents the majority of the aggregate vote and value of the company or entity, the "principal class of shares" are those classes that in the aggregate represent a majority of the aggregate vote and value;

(d) two persons shall be "connected persons" if one owns, directly or indirectly, at least 50 per cent of the beneficial interest in the other (or, in the case of a company, at least 50 per cent of the aggregate vote and value of the company's shares) or another person owns, directly or indirectly, at least 50 per cent of the beneficial interest (or, in the case of a company, at least 50 per cent of the aggregate vote and value of the company's shares) in each person. In any case, a person shall be connected to another if, based on all the relevant facts and circumstances, one has control of the other or both are under the control of the same person or persons.

(e) the term "equivalent beneficiary" means:
  - *(i)* a resident of any State, provided that:
    - *(A)* the resident is entitled to all the benefits of a comprehensive convention for the avoidance of double taxation between that State and the Contracting State

from which the benefits of this Convention are sought, under provisions substantially similar to subparagraph a), b), c) or e) of paragraph 2 or, when the benefit being sought is with respect to interest or dividends paid by a member of the resident's multinational corporate group, the resident is entitled to benefits under provisions substantially similar to paragraph 5 of this Article in such convention, provided that, if such convention does not contain a detailed limitation on benefits article, such convention shall be applied as if the provisions of sub-paragraphs a), b), c) and e) of paragraph 2 (including the definitions relevant to the application of the tests in such subparagraphs) were contained in such convention; and

(B) *(1)* with respect to income referred to in Article 10, 11, 12 or 12A if the resident had received such income directly, the resident would be entitled under such Convention, a provision of domestic law or any international agreement, to a rate of tax with respect to such income for which benefits are being sought under this Convention that is less than or equal to the rate applicable under this Convention. Regarding a company seeking, under paragraph 4, the benefits of Article 10 with respect to dividends, for purposes of this subclause:

(I) if the resident is an individual, and the company is engaged in the active conduct of a business in its Contracting State of residence that is substantial in relation, and similar or complementary, to the business that generated the earnings from which the dividend is paid, such individual shall be treated as if he or she were a company. Activities conducted by a person that is a connected person with respect to the company seeking benefits shall be deemed to be conducted by such company. Whether a business activity is substantial shall be determined based on all the facts and circumstances; and

(II) if the resident is a company (including an individual treated as a company), to determine whether the resident is entitled to a rate of tax that is less than or equal to the rate applicable under this Convention, the resident's indirect holding of the capital of the company paying the dividends shall be treated as a direct holding; or

(2) with respect to an item of income referred to in Article 7, 13 or 21 of this Convention, the resident is entitled to benefits under such Convention that are at least as favourable as the benefits that are being sought under this Convention; and

(C) notwithstanding that a resident may satisfy the requirements of clauses A) and B) of this subdivision, where the item of income has been derived through an entity that is treated as fiscally transparent under the laws of the Contracting State of residence of the company seeking benefits, if the item of income would not be treated as the income of the resident under a provision analogous to paragraph 2 of Article 1 had the resident, and not the company seeking benefits under paragraph 4 of this Article, itself owned the entity through which the income was derived by the company, such resident shall not be considered an equivalent beneficiary with respect to the item of income;

(ii) a resident of the same Contracting State as the company seeking benefits under paragraph 4 of this Article that is entitled to all the benefits of this Convention by reason of subparagraph a), b), c) or e) of paragraph 2 or, when the benefit being sought is with respect to interest or dividends paid by a member of the resident's multinational corporate group, the resident is entitled to benefits under paragraph 5, provided that, in the case of a resident described in paragraph 5, if the resident had received such interest or dividends directly, the resident would be entitled to a rate of tax with respect to such income that is less than or equal to the rate applicable under this Convention to the company seeking benefits under paragraph 4; or

(iii) a resident of the Contracting State from which the bene- fits of this Convention are sought that is entitled to all the benefits of this Convention by reason of subparagraph a), b), c) or e) of paragraph 2, provided that all such residents' ownership of the aggregate vote and value of the shares (and any disproportionate class of shares) of the company seeking benefits under paragraph 4 does not exceed 25 per cent of the total vote and value of the shares (and any disproportionate class of shares) of the company;

(f) the term "disproportionate class of shares" means any class of shares of a company or entity resident in one of the Contracting States that entitles the shareholder to disproportionately higher participation, through dividends, redemption payments or otherwise, in the earnings generated in the other Contracting State by particular assets or activities of the company;

(g) a company's or entity's "primary place of management and control" is in the Contracting State of which it is a resident only if:

(i) the executive officers and senior management employees of the company or entity exercise day-to-day responsibility for more of the strategic, financial and operational policy decision making for the company or entity and its direct and indirect subsidiaries, and the staff of such persons conduct more of the day-to-day activities necessary for preparing and making those decisions, in that Contracting State than in any other State; and

(ii) such executive officers and senior management employees exercise day-to-day responsibility for more of the strategic, financial and operational policy decision-making for the company or entity and its direct and indirect subsidiaries, and the staff of such persons conduct more of the day-to- day activities necessary for preparing and making those decisions, than the officers or employees of any other company or entity;

(h) the term "qualifying intermediate owner" means an intermediate owner that is either:

(i) a resident of a State that has in effect with the Contracting State from which a benefit under this Convention is being sought a comprehensive convention for the avoidance of double taxation; or

(ii) a resident of the same Contracting State as the company applying the test under subparagraph d) or f) of paragraph 2 or paragraph 4 to determine whether it is eligible for benefits under the Convention;

(i) the term "tested group" means the resident of a Contracting State that is applying the test under subparagraph d) or f) of paragraph 2 or under paragraph 4 or 5 to determine whether it is eligible for benefits under the Convention (the "tested resident"), and any company or permanent establishment that:

(i) participates as a member with the tested resident in a tax consolidation, fiscal unity or similar regime that requires members of the group to share profits or losses; or
(ii) shares losses with the tested resident pursuant to a group relief or other loss sharing regime in the relevant taxable period; [and]

(j) the term "gross income" means gross receipts as determined in the person's Contracting State of residence for the taxable period that includes the time when the benefit would be accorded, except that where a person is engaged in a business that includes the manufacture, production or sale of goods, "gross income" means such gross receipts reduced by the cost of goods sold, and where a person is engaged in a business of providing non-financial services, "gross income" means such gross receipts reduced by the direct costs of generating such receipts, provided that:
(i) except when relevant for determining benefits under Article 10 of this Convention, gross income shall not include the portion of any dividends that are effectively exempt from tax in the person's Contracting State of residence, whether through deductions or otherwise; and
(ii) except with respect to the portion of any dividend that is taxable, a tested group's gross income shall not take into account transactions between companies within the tested group; [and]

(k) [possible definition of "collective investment vehicle"].

8.

(a) Where
(i) an enterprise of a Contracting State derives income from the other Contracting State and the first-mentioned State treats such income as attributable to a permanent establishment of the enterprise situated in a third juris- diction, and
(ii) the profits attributable to that permanent establishment are exempt from tax in the first-mentioned State,

the benefits of this Convention shall not apply to any item of income on which the tax in the third jurisdiction is less than the lower of [rate to be determined bilaterally] of the amount of that item of income and 60 per cent of the tax that would be imposed in the first-mentioned State on that item of income if that permanent establishment were situated in the first-mentioned State. In such a case any income to which the provisions of this paragraph apply shall remain taxable according to the domestic law of the other State, notwithstanding any other provisions of the Convention.

(b) The preceding provisions of this paragraph shall not apply if the income derived from the other State emanates from, or is incidental to, the active conduct of a business carried on through the permanent establishment (other than the business of making, managing or simply holding investments for the enterprise's own account, unless these activities are banking, insurance or securities activities carried on by a bank, insurance enterprise or registered securities dealer, respectively).

(c) If benefits under this Convention are denied pursuant to the preceding provisions of this paragraph with respect to an item of income derived by a resident of a Contracting State, the competent authority of the other Contracting State may, nevertheless, grant these benefits with respect to that item of income if, in response to a request by such resident, such competent authority determines that granting such benefits is justified in light of the reasons such resident did not satisfy the requirements of this paragraph (such as the existence of losses). The competent authority of the Contracting State to which a request has been made under the preceding sentence shall consult with the competent authority of the other Contracting State before either granting or denying the request.

9. Notwithstanding the other provisions of this Convention, a benefit under this Convention shall not be granted in respect of an item of income or capital if it is reasonable to conclude, having regard to all relevant facts and circumstances, that obtaining that benefit was one of the principal purposes of any arrangement or transaction that resulted directly or indirectly in that benefit, unless it is established that granting that benefit in these circumstances would be in accordance with the object and purpose of the relevant provisions of this Convention.

Chapter VII
FINAL PROVISIONS

Article 30
Entry into force

1. This Convention shall be ratified and the instruments of ratification shall be exchanged at as soon as possible.

2. The Convention shall enter into force upon the exchange of instruments of ratification and its provisions shall have effect:

a) (in State A): ....

b) (in State B): ....

Article 31
Termination

This Convention shall remain in force until terminated by a Contracting State. Either Contracting State may terminate the Convention, through diplomatic channels, by giving notice of termination at least six months before the end of any calendar year after the year ... In such event, the Convention shall cease to have effect:

a) (in State A): ....

b) (in State B): ....

Terminal clause

NOTE: The provisions relating to the entry into force and termination and the terminal clause concerning the signing of the Convention shall be drafted in accordance with the constitutional procedure of both Contracting States.

Annex 3

OECD MODEL DOUBLE TAXATION CONVENTION ON ESTATES AND INHERITANCES AND ON GIFTS 1982 UPDATE

SUMMARY OF THE CONVENTION

TITLE OF THE CONVENTION

Convention between (State A) and (State B) for the avoidance of double taxation with respect to taxes on estates and inheritances and on gifts.

PREAMBLE OF THE CONVENTION[1]

Chapter I
SCOPE OF THE CONVENTION

Article 1
ESTATES, INHERITANCES AND GIFTS COVERED

This Convention shall apply:

a) to estates and inheritances where the deceased was domiciled, at the time of his death, in one or both of the Contracting States, and
b) to gifts where the donor was domiciled, at the time of the gift, in one or both of the Contracting States.

Article 2
TAXES COVERED

1. This Convention shall apply to taxes on estates and inheritances and on gifts imposed on behalf of a Contracting State or of its political subdivisions or local authorities, irrespective of the manner in which they are levied.

2. There shall be regarded as taxes on estates and inheritances taxes imposed by reason of death in the form of taxes on the corpus of the estate, of taxes on inheritances, of transfer duties, or of taxes on donationes mortis causa. There shall be regarded as taxes on gifts taxes imposed on transfers inter vivos only because such transfers are made for no, or less than full, consideration.

3. The existing taxes to which the Convention shall apply are:

a) (in State A): ....
b) (in State B): ....

4. The Convention shall apply also to any identical or substantially similar taxes which are imposed after the date of signature of the Convention in addition to, or in place of, the existing taxes. At the end of each year, the competent authorities of the Contracting States shall notify each other of changes which have been made in their respective taxation laws.

Chapter II
DEFINITIONS

Article 3
GENERAL DEFINITIONS

1. For the purposes of this Convention, unless the context otherwise requires:

a) the term "property which forms part of the estate of, or of a gift made by, a person domiciled in a Contracting State" includes any property the devolution or transfer of which, under the law of a Contracting State, is liable to a tax covered by the Convention;

---

1 Note: The Preamble of the Convention shall be drafted in accordance with the constitutional procedure of both Contracting States.

b) the term "competent authority" means:
   i) (in State A): ....
   ii) (in State B): ....

2. As regards the application of the Convention by a Contracting State, any term not defined therein shall, unless the context otherwise requires, have the meaning which it has under the law of that State concerning the taxes to which the Convention applies.

Article 4
FISCAL DOMICILE

1. For the purposes of this Convention, the term "person domiciled in a Contracting State" means any person whose estate or whose gift, under the law of that State, is liable to tax therein by reason of the domicile, residence or place of management of that person or any other criterion of a similar nature. However, this term does not include any person whose estate or whose gift is liable to tax in that State only in respect of property situated therein.

2. Where by reason of the provisions of paragraph 1 an individual is domiciled in both Contracting States, then his status shall be determined as follows:

a) he shall be deemed to be domiciled in the State in which he has a permanent home available to him; if he has a permanent home available to him in both States, he shall be deemed to be domiciled in the State with which his personal and economic relations are closer (centre of vital interests);
b) if the State in which he has his centre of vital interests cannot be determined, or if he has not a permanent home available to him in either State, he shall be deemed to be domiciled in the State in which he has an habitual abode;
c) if he has an habitual abode in both States or in neither of them, he shall be deemed to be domiciled in the State of which he is a national;
d) if he is a national of both States or of neither of them, the competent authorities of the Contracting States shall settle the question by mutual agreement.

3. Where by reason of the provisions of paragraph 1 a person other than an individual is domiciled in both Contracting States, then it shall be deemed to be domiciled in the State in which its place of effective management is situated.

Chapter III
TAXING RULES

Article 5
IMMOVABLE PROPERTY

1. Immovable property which forms part of the estate of, or of a gift made by, a person domiciled in a Contracting State and which is situated in the other Contracting State may be taxed in that other State.

2. The term "immovable property" shall have the meaning which it has under the law of the Contracting State in which the property in question is situated. The term shall in any case include property accessory to immovable property, livestock and equipment used in agriculture and forestry, rights to which the provisions of general law respecting landed property apply, usufruct of immovable property and rights to variable or fixed payments as consideration for the working of, or the right to work, mineral deposits, sources and other natural resources; ships, boats and aircraft shall not be regarded as immovable property.

3. The provisions of paragraph 1 shall also apply to immovable property of an enterprise and to immovable property used for the performance of professional services or other activities of an independent character.

Article 6
MOVABLE PROPERTY OF A PERMANENT ESTABLISHMENT OR A FIXED BASE

1. Movable property of an enterprise which forms part of the estate of, or of a gift made by, a person domiciled in a Contracting State, which is the business property of a permanent establishment situated in the other Contracting State, may be taxed in that other State.

2. For the purposes of this Convention, the term "permanent establishment" means a fixed place of business through which the business of an enterprise is wholly or partly carried on.

3. The term "permanent establishment" includes especially:

a) a place of management;
b) a branch;
c) an office;
d) a factory;
e) a workshop; and
f) a mine, an oil or gas well, a quarry or any other place of extraction of natural resources.

4. A building site or construction or installation project constitutes a permanent establishment only if it lasts more than twelve months.

5. Notwithstanding the preceding provisions of this Article, the term "permanent establishment" shall be deemed not to include:

a) the use of facilities solely for the purpose of storage, display or delivery of goods or merchandise belonging to the enterprise;
b) the maintenance of a stock of goods or merchandise belonging to the enterprise solely for the purpose of storage, display or delivery;
c) the maintenance of a stock of goods or merchandise belonging to the enterprise solely for the purpose of processing by another enterprise;
d) the maintenance of a fixed place of business solely for the purpose of purchasing goods or merchandise, or of collecting information, for the enterprise;
e) the maintenance of a fixed place of business solely for the purpose of carrying on for the enterprise any other activity of a preparatory or auxiliary character; or
f) the maintenance of a fixed place of business solely for any combination of activities mentioned in subparagraphs a) to e), provided that the overall activity of the fixed place of business resulting from this combination is of a preparatory or auxiliary character.

6. Movable property which forms part of the estate of, or of a gift made by, a person domiciled in a Contracting State, used for the performance of professional services or other activities of an independent character and pertaining to a fixed base situated in the other Contracting State, may be taxed in that other State.

Article 7
OTHER PROPERTY

Property, wherever situated, which forms part of the estate of, or of a gift made by, a person domiciled in a Contracting State, and not dealt with in Articles 5 and 6, shall be taxable only in that State.

Article 8
DEDUCTION OF DEBTS

1. Debts especially secured on any property referred to in Article 5 shall be deducted from the value of that property. Debts, not being especially secured on any property referred to in Article 5, which are represented by the acquisition, conversion, repair or upkeep of any such property, shall be deducted from the value of that property.

2. Subject to the provisions of paragraph 1, debts pertaining to a permanent establishment referred to in paragraph 1 of Article 6, or to a fixed base referred to in paragraph 6 of Article 6, shall be deducted from the value of the permanent establishment or the fixed base as the case may be.

3. Other debts shall be deducted from the value of property to which the provisions of Article 7 apply.

4. If a debt exceeds the value of the property from which it is deductible in a Contracting State, according to the provisions of paragraphs 1 or 2, the excess shall be deducted from the value of any other property taxable in that State.

5. Any excess still remaining in one Contracting State after the deductions referred to in paragraphs 3 or 4 shall be deducted from the value of the property liable to tax in the other Contracting State.

6. Where the provisions of paragraphs 1 to 5 would oblige one Contracting State to deduct debts to an extent greater than that provided for under its law, those provisions shall apply only to the extent that the other Contracting State is not obliged to deduct the same debts under its own law.

Chapter IV
METHODS FOR ELIMINATING DOUBLE TAXATION

Article 9A
EXEMPTION METHOD

1. The Contracting State in which the deceased was domiciled at his death, or the donor was domiciled at the time of the gift, shall exempt from tax any property which, in relation to the same event and in accordance with the provisions of this Convention, may be taxed in the other Contracting State.

2. The former Contracting State shall also exempt from tax any property which, in relation to a previous gift and in accordance with the provisions of the Convention, may have been taxed in the other Contracting State. That former State, however, shall not exempt from tax any property which was taxable in that State in accordance with the provisions of Articles 5 or 6 of the Convention.

3. In each case the former Contracting State may take the exempted property into account in calculating the amount of tax on any remaining property.

Article 9B
CREDIT METHOD

1. The Contracting State in which the deceased was domiciled at his death, or the donor was domiciled at the time of the gift, shall allow as a deduction from the tax calculated according to its law an amount equal to the tax paid in the other Contracting State on any property which, in relation to the same event and in accordance with the provisions of this Convention, may be taxed in that other State.

2. The former Contracting State shall also allow as a deduction from such tax an amount equal to the tax which has been paid in the other Contracting State on a previous gift in accordance with the provisions of the Convention to the extent that such a deduction has not been allowed under the provisions of paragraph 1 at the time of that gift. That former State, however, shall not allow a deduction in respect of tax paid on property which was taxable in that State in accordance with the provisions of Articles 5 or 6 of the Convention.

3. The deductions referred to in paragraphs 1 and 2 shall not, however, exceed that part of the tax of the former Contracting State, as computed before any deduction is made, which is attributable to the property in respect of which the deduction is to be allowed.

Chapter V
SPECIAL PROVISIONS

Article 10
NON-DISCRIMINATION

1. Nationals of a Contracting State, wherever they are domiciled, shall not be subjected in the other Contracting State to any taxation, or any requirement connected therewith, which is other or more burdensome than the taxation and connected requirements to which nationals of that other State in the same circumstances are or may be subjected.

2. The term "nationals" means:

a) all individuals possessing the nationality of a Contracting State;
b) all legal persons, partnerships and associations deriving their status as such from the law in force in a Contracting State.

3. Stateless persons who are domiciled in a Contracting State shall not be subjected in either Contracting State to any taxation, or any requirement connected therewith, which is other or more burdensome than the taxation and connected requirements to which nationals of the State concerned in the same circumstances are or may be subjected.

4. The provisions of this Article shall, notwithstanding the provisions of Article 2, apply to taxes of every kind and description.

Article 11
MUTUAL AGREEMENT PROCEDUI

1. Where a person considers that the actions of one or both of the Contracting States result or will result for him in taxation not in accordance with t'\e provisions of this Convention, he may, irrespective of the remedies provided by the domestic laws of those States, present his case to the competent authority of either Contracting State. The case must be presented within three years from the first notification of the action resulting in taxation not in accordance with the provisions of the Convention.

2. The competent authority, if the objection appears to it to be justified and if it is not itself able to arrive at a satisfactory solution, shall endeavour to resolve the case by mutual agreement with the competent authority of the other Contracting State, with a view to the avoidance of taxation which is not in accordance with the provisions of the Convention. Any agreement reached shall be implemented notwithstanding any time limits in the domestic laws of the Contracting States.

3. The competent authorities of the Contracting States shall endeavour to resolve by mutual agreement any difficulties or doubts arising as to the interpretation or application of the Convention. They may also consult together for the elimination of double taxation in cases not provided for in the Convention.

4. The competent authorities of the Contracting States may communicate with each other directly for the purpose of reaching an agreement in the sense of the preceding paragraphs. When it seems advisable in order to reach agreement to have an oral exchange of opinions, such exchange may take place through a Commission consisting of representatives of the competent authorities of the Contracting States.

Article 12
EXCHANGE OF INFORMATION

1. The competent authorities of the Contracting States shall exchange such information as is necessary for carrying out the provisions of this Convention or of the domestic laws of the Contracting States concerning taxes covered by the Convention insofar as the taxation thereunder is not contrary to the Convention. The exchange of information is not restricted by Article 1. Any information received by a Contracting State shall be treated as secret in the same manner as information obtained under the domestic laws of that State and shall be disclosed only to persons or authorities (including courts and administrative bodies) involved in the assessment or collection of, the enforcement or prosecution in respect of, or the determination of appeals in relation to, the taxes covered by the Convention. Such persons or authorities shall use the information only for such purposes. They may disclose the information in public court proceedings or in judicial decisions.

2. In no case shall the provisions of paragraph 1 be construed so as to impose on a Contracting State the obligation:

a) to carry out administrative measures at variance with the laws or administrative practice of that or of the other State;
b) to supply information which is not obtainable under the laws, or in the normal course of the administration, of that or of the other State;
c) to supply information which would disclose any trade, business, industrial, commercial or professional secret or trade process, or information, the disclosure of which would be contrary to public policy (ordre public).

Article 13
DIPLOMATIC AGENTS AND CONSULAR OFFICERS

Nothing in this Convention shall affect the fiscal privileges of diplomatic agents or consular officers under the general rules of international law or under the provisions of special agreements.

Article 14
TERRITORIAL EXTENSION

1. This Convention may be extended, either in its entirety or with any necessary modifications, [to any part of the territory of (State A) or of (State B) which is specifically excluded from the application of the Convention or][2] to any State or territory for whose international relations (State A) or (State B) is responsible, which imposes taxes substantially similar in character to those to which the Convention applies. Any such extension shall take effect from such date and subject to such modifications and conditions, including conditions as to termination, as may be specified and agreed between the Contracting States in notes to be exchanged through diplomatic channels or in any other manner in accordance with their constitutional procedures.

2. Unless otherwise agreed by both Contracting States, the termination of the Convention by one of them under Article 16 shall also terminate, in the manner provided for in that Article, the application of the Convention [to any part of the territory of (State A) or of (State B) or] to any State or territory to which it has been extended under this Article.

Chapter VI
FINAL PROVISIONS

Article 15
ENTRY INTO FORCE

1. This Convention shall be ratified and the instruments of ratification shall be exchanged at as soon as possible.

2. The Convention shall enter into force upon the exchange of instruments of ratification and its provisions shall have effect:

a) (in State A)
b) (in State B)

Article 16
TERMINATION

This Convention shall remain in force until terminated by a Contracting State. Either Contracting State may terminate the Convention, through diplomatic channels, by giving notice of termination at least six months before the end of any calendar year after the year In such event, the Convention shall cease to have effect:

a) (in State A)
b) (In State B)

TERMINAL CLAUSE[3]

2 Note : The words between square brackets are of relevance when, by special provision, a part of the territory of a Contracting State is excluded from the application of the Convention.

3 Note: The terminal clause shall be drafted in accordance with the constitutional procedure of both Contracting States.

Annex 4

OECD/G20
(MLI)
MULTILATERAL CONVENTION TO IMPLEMENT TAX TREATY RELATED MEASURES TO PREVENT BASE EROSION AND PROFIT SHIFTING
(2016)

The Parties to this Convention,

Recognising that governments lose substantial corporate tax revenue because of aggressive international tax planning that has the effect of artificially shifting profits to locations where they are subject to non-taxation or reduced taxation;

Mindful that base erosion and profit shifting (hereinafter referred to as "BEPS") is a pressing issue not only for industrialised countries but also for emerging economies and developing countries;

Recognising the importance of ensuring that profits are taxed where substantive economic activities generating the profits are carried out and where value is created;

Welcoming the package of measures developed under the OECD/G20 BEPS project (hereinafter referred to as the "OECD/G20 BEPS package");

Noting that the OECD/G20 BEPS package included tax treaty-related measures to address certain hybrid mismatch arrangements, prevent treaty abuse, address artificial avoidance of permanent establishment status, and improve dispute resolution;

Conscious of the need to ensure swift, co-ordinated and consistent implementation of the treaty-related BEPS measures in a multilateral context;

Noting the need to ensure that existing agreements for the avoidance of double taxation on income are interpreted to eliminate double taxation with respect to the taxes covered by those agreements without creating opportunities for non-taxation or reduced taxation through tax evasion or avoidance (including through treaty-shopping arrangements aimed at obtaining reliefs provided in those agreements for the indirect benefit of residents of third jurisdictions);

Recognising the need for an effective mechanism to implement agreed changes in a synchronised and efficient manner across the network of existing agreements for the avoidance of double taxation on income without the need to bilaterally renegotiate each such agreement;

Have agreed as follows

PART I.
SCOPE AND INTERPRETATION OF TERMS

Article 1
Scope of the Convention

This Convention modifies all Covered Tax Agreements as defined in subparagraph a) of paragraph 1 of Article 2 (Interpretation of Terms).

Article 2
Interpretation of Terms

1. For the purpose of this Convention, the following definitions apply:

a) The term "Covered Tax Agreement" means an agreement for the avoidance of double taxation with respect to taxes on income (whether or not other taxes are also covered):
   i) that is in force between two or more:
      A) Parties; and/or
      B) jurisdictions or territories which are parties to an agreement described above and for whose international relations a Party is responsible; and
   ii) with respect to which each such Party has made a notification to the Depositary listing the agreement as well as any amending or accompanying instruments thereto (identified by title, names of the parties, date of signature, and, if applicable at the time of the notification, date of entry into force) as an agreement which it wishes to be covered by this Convention.
b) The term "Party" means:
   i) A State for which this Convention is in force pursuant to Article 34 (Entry into Force); or
   ii) A jurisdiction which has signed this Convention pursuant to subparagraph b) or c) of paragraph 1 of Article 27 (Signature and Ratification, Acceptance or Approval) and for which this Convention is in force pursuant to Article 34 (Entry into Force).
c) The term "Contracting Jurisdiction" means a party to a Covered Tax Agreement.
d) The term "Signatory" means a State or jurisdiction which has signed this Convention but for which the Convention is not yet in force.

2. As regards the application of this Convention at any time by a Party, any term not defined herein shall, unless the context otherwise requires, have the meaning that it has at that time under the relevant Covered Tax Agreement.

PART II.
HYBRID MISMATCHES

Article 3
Transparent Entities

1. For the purposes of a Covered Tax Agreement, income derived by or through an entity or arrangement that is treated as wholly or partly fiscally transparent under the tax law of either Contracting Jurisdiction shall be considered to be income of a resident of a Contracting Jurisdiction but only to the extent that the income is treated, for purposes of taxation by that Contracting Jurisdiction, as the income of a resident of that Contracting Jurisdiction.

2. Provisions of a Covered Tax Agreement that require a Contracting Jurisdiction to exempt from income tax or provide a deduction or credit equal to the income tax paid with respect to income derived by a resident of that Contracting Jurisdiction which may be taxed in the other Contracting Jurisdiction according to the provisions of the Covered Tax Agreement shall not apply to the extent that such provisions allow taxation by that other Contracting Jurisdiction solely because the income is also income derived by a resident of that other Contracting Jurisdiction.

3. With respect to Covered Tax Agreements for which one or more Parties has made the reservation described in subparagraph a) of paragraph 3 of Article 11 (Application of Tax Agreements to Restrict a Party's Right to Tax its Own Residents), the following sentence will be added at the end of paragraph 1: "In no case shall the provisions of this paragraph be construed to affect a Contracting Jurisdiction's right to tax the residents of that Contracting Jurisdiction."

4. Paragraph 1 (as it may be modified by paragraph 3) shall apply in place of or in the absence of provisions of a Covered Tax Agreement to the extent that they address whether income derived by or through entities or arrangements that are treated as fiscally transparent under the tax law of either Contracting Jurisdiction (whether through a general rule or by identifying in detail the treatment of specific fact patterns and types of entities or arrangements) shall be treated as income of a resident of a Contracting Jurisdiction.

5. A Party may reserve the right:

a) for the entirety of this Article not to apply to its Covered Tax Agreements;
b) for paragraph 1 not to apply to its Covered Tax Agreements that already contain a provision described in paragraph 4;
c) for paragraph 1 not to apply to its Covered Tax Agreements that already contain a provision described in paragraph 4 which denies treaty benefits in the case of income derived by or through an entity or arrangement established in a third jurisdiction;
d) for paragraph 1 not to apply to its Covered Tax Agreements that already contain a provision described in paragraph 4 which identifies in detail the treatment of specific fact patterns and types of entities or arrangements;
e) for paragraph 1 not to apply to its Covered Tax Agreements that already contain a provision described in paragraph 4 which identifies in detail the treatment of specific fact patterns and types of entities or arrangements and denies treaty benefits in the case of income derived by or through an entity or arrangement established in a third jurisdiction;
f) for paragraph 2 not to apply to its Covered Tax Agreements;
g) for paragraph 1 to apply only to its Covered Tax Agreements that already contain a provision described in paragraph 4 which identifies in detail the treatment of specific fact patterns and types of entities or arrangements.

6. Each Party that has not made a reservation described in subparagraph a) or b) of paragraph 5 shall notify the Depositary of whether each of its Covered Tax Agreements contains a provision described in paragraph 4 that is not subject to a reservation under subparagraphs c) through e) of paragraph 5, and if so, the article and paragraph number of each such provision. In the case of a Party that has made the reservation described in subparagraph g) of paragraph 5, the notification pursuant to the preceding sentence shall be limited to Covered Tax Agreements that are subject to that reservation. Where all Contracting Jurisdictions have made such a notification with respect to a provision of a Covered Tax Agreement, that provision shall be replaced by the provisions of paragraph 1 (as it may be modified by paragraph 3) to the extent provided in paragraph 4. In other cases, paragraph 1 (as it may be modified by paragraph 3) shall supersede the provisions of the Covered Tax Agreement only to the extent that those provisions are incompatible with paragraph 1 (as it may be modified by paragraph 3).

Article 4
Dual Resident Entities

1. Where by reason of the provisions of a Covered Tax Agreement a person other than an individual is a resident of more than one Contracting Jurisdiction, the competent authorities of the Contracting Jurisdictions shall endeavour to determine by mutual agreement the Contracting Jurisdiction of which such person shall be deemed to be a resident for the purposes of the Covered Tax Agreement, having regard to its place of effective management, the place where it is incorporated or otherwise constituted and any other relevant factors. In the absence of such agreement, such person shall not be entitled to any relief or exemption from tax provided by the Covered Tax Agreement except to the extent and in such manner as may be agreed upon by the competent authorities of the Contracting Jurisdictions.

2. Paragraph 1 shall apply in place of or in the absence of provisions of a Covered Tax Agreement that provide rules for determining whether a person other than an individual shall be treated as a resident of one of the Contracting Jurisdictions in cases in which that person would otherwise be treated as a resident of more than one Contracting Jurisdiction. Paragraph 1 shall not apply, however, to provisions of a Covered Tax Agreement specifically addressing the residence of companies participating in dual-listed company arrangements.

3. A Party may reserve the right:

a) for the entirety of this Article not to apply to its Covered Tax Agreements;
b) for the entirety of this Article not to apply to its Covered Tax Agreements that already address cases where a person other than an individual is a resident of more than one Contracting Jurisdiction by requiring the competent authorities of the Contracting Jurisdictions to endeavour to reach mutual agreement on a single Contracting Jurisdiction of residence;
c) for the entirety of this Article not to apply to its Covered Tax Agreements that already address cases where a person other than an individual is a resident of more than one Contracting Jurisdiction by denying treaty benefits without requiring the competent authorities of the Contracting Jurisdictions to endeavour to reach mutual agreement on a single Contracting Jurisdiction of residence;
d) for the entirety of this Article not to apply to its Covered Tax Agreements that already address cases where a person other than an individual is a resident of more than one Contracting Jurisdiction by requiring the competent authorities of the Contracting Jurisdictions to endeavour to reach mutual agreement on a single Contracting Jurisdiction of residence, and that set out the treatment of that person under the Covered Tax Agreement where such an agreement cannot be reached;
e) to replace the last sentence of paragraph 1 with the following text for the purposes of its Covered Tax Agreements: "In the absence of such agreement, such person shall not be entitled to any relief or exemption from tax provided by the Covered Tax Agreement.";
f) for the entirety of this Article not to apply to its Covered Tax Agreements with Parties that have made the reservation described in subparagraph e).

4. Each Party that has not made a reservation described in subparagraph a) of paragraph 3 shall notify the Depositary of whether each of its Covered Tax Agreements contains a provision described in paragraph 2 that is not subject to a reservation under subparagraphs b) through d) of paragraph 3, and if so, the article and paragraph number of each such provision. Where all Contracting Jurisdictions have made such a notification with respect to a provision of a Covered Tax Agreement, that provision shall be replaced by the provisions of paragraph 1. In other cases, paragraph 1 shall supersede the provisions of the Covered Tax Agreement only to the extent that those provisions are incompatible with paragraph 1.

Article 5
Application of Methods for Elimination of Double Taxation

1. A Party may choose to apply either paragraphs 2 and 3 (Option A), paragraphs 4 and 5 (Option B), or paragraphs 6 and 7 (Option C), or may choose to apply none of the Options. Where each Contracting Jurisdiction to a Covered Tax Agreement chooses a different Option (or where one Contracting Jurisdiction chooses to apply an Option and the other chooses to apply none of the Options), the Option chosen by each Contracting Jurisdiction shall apply with respect to its own residents.

Option A

2. Provisions of a Covered Tax Agreement that would otherwise exempt income derived or capital owned by a resident of a Contracting Jurisdiction from tax in that Contracting Jurisdiction for the purpose of eliminating double taxation shall not apply where the other Contracting Jurisdiction applies the provisions of the Covered Tax Agreement to exempt such income or capital from tax or to limit the rate at which such income or capital may be taxed. In the latter case, the first-mentioned Contracting Jurisdiction shall allow as a deduction from the tax on the income or capital of that resident an amount equal to the tax paid in that other Contracting Jurisdiction. Such deduction shall not, however, exceed that part of the tax, as computed before the deduction is given, which is attributable to such items of income or capital which may be taxed in that other Contracting Jurisdiction.

3. Paragraph 2 shall apply to a Covered Tax Agreement that would otherwise require a Contracting Jurisdiction to exempt income or capital described in that paragraph.

Option B

4. Provisions of a Covered Tax Agreement that would otherwise exempt income derived by a resident of a Contracting Jurisdiction from tax in that Contracting Jurisdiction for the purpose of eliminating double taxation because such income is treated as a dividend by that Contracting Jurisdiction shall not apply where such income gives rise to a deduction for the purpose of determining the taxable profits of a resident of the other Contracting Jurisdiction under the laws of that other Contracting Jurisdiction. In such case, the first-mentioned Contracting Jurisdiction shall allow as a deduction from the tax on the income of that resident an amount equal to the income tax paid in that other Contracting Jurisdiction. Such deduction shall not, however, exceed that part of the income tax, as computed before the deduction is given, which is attributable to such income which may be taxed in that other Contracting Jurisdiction.

5. Paragraph 4 shall apply to a Covered Tax Agreement that would otherwise require a Contracting Jurisdiction to exempt income described in that paragraph.

Option C

6.

a) Where a resident of a Contracting Jurisdiction derives income or owns capital which may be taxed in the other Contracting Jurisdiction in accordance with the provisions of a Covered Tax Agreement (except to the extent that these provisions allow taxation by that other Contracting Jurisdiction solely because the income is also income derived by a resident of that other Contracting Jurisdiction), the first-mentioned Contracting Jurisdiction shall allow:
   i) as a deduction from the tax on the income of that resident, an amount equal to the income tax paid in that other Contracting Jurisdiction;
   ii) as a deduction from the tax on the capital of that resident, an amount equal to the capital tax paid in that other Contracting Jurisdiction.

   Such deduction shall not, however, exceed that part of the income tax or capital tax, as computed before the deduction is given, which is attributable to the income or the capital which may be taxed in that other Contracting Jurisdiction.
b) Where in accordance with any provision of the Covered Tax Agreement income derived or capital owned by a resident of a Contracting Jurisdiction is exempt from tax in that Contracting Jurisdiction, such Contracting Jurisdiction may nevertheless, in calculating the amount of tax on the remaining income or capital of such resident, take into account the exempted income or capital.

7. Paragraph 6 shall apply in place of provisions of a Covered Tax Agreement that, for purposes of eliminating double taxation, require a Contracting Jurisdiction to exempt from tax in that Contracting Jurisdiction income derived or capital owned by a resident of that Contracting Jurisdiction which, in accordance with the provisions of the Covered Tax Agreement, may be taxed in the other Contracting Jurisdiction.

8. A Party that does not choose to apply an Option under paragraph 1 may reserve the right for the entirety of this Article not to apply with respect to one or more identified Covered Tax Agreements (or with respect to all of its Covered Tax Agreements).

9. A Party that does not choose to apply Option C may reserve the right, with respect to one or more identified Covered Tax Agreements (or with respect to all of its Covered Tax Agreements), not to permit the other Contracting Jurisdiction(s) to apply Option C.

10. Each Party that chooses to apply an Option under paragraph 1 shall notify the Depositary of its choice of Option. Such notification shall also include:

a) in the case of a Party that chooses to apply Option A, the list of its Covered Tax Agreements which contain a provision described in paragraph 3, as well as the article and paragraph number of each such provision;
b) in the case of a Party that chooses to apply Option B, the list of its Covered Tax Agreements which contain a provision described in paragraph 5, as well as the article and paragraph number of each such provision;
c) in the case of a Party that chooses to apply Option C, the list of its Covered Tax Agreements which contain a provision described in paragraph 7, as well as the article and paragraph number of each such provision.

An Option shall apply with respect to a provision of a Covered Tax Agreement only where the Party that has chosen to apply that Option has made such a notification with respect to that provision.

PART III.
TREATY ABUSE

Article 6
Purpose of a Covered Tax Agreement

1. A Covered Tax Agreement shall be modified to include the following preamble text:

"Intending to eliminate double taxation with respect to the taxes covered by this agreement without creating opportunities for non-taxation or reduced taxation through tax evasion or avoidance (including through treaty-shopping arrangements aimed at obtaining reliefs provided in this agreement for the indirect benefit of residents of third jurisdictions),".

2. The text described in paragraph 1 shall be included in a Covered Tax Agreement in place of or in the absence of preamble language of the Covered Tax Agreement referring to an intent to eliminate double taxation, whether or not that language also refers to the intent not to create opportunities for non-taxation or reduced taxation.

3. A Party may also choose to include the following preamble text with respect to its Covered Tax Agreements that do not contain preamble language referring to a desire to develop an economic relationship or to enhance co-operation in tax matters:

"Desiring to further develop their economic relationship and to enhance their co-operation in tax matters,".

4. A Party may reserve the right for paragraph 1 not to apply to its Covered Tax Agreements that already contain preamble language describing the intent of the Contracting Jurisdictions to eliminate double taxation without creating opportunities for non-taxation or reduced taxation, whether that language is limited to cases of tax evasion or avoidance (including through treaty-shopping arrangements aimed at obtaining reliefs provided in the Covered Tax Agreement for the indirect benefit of residents of third jurisdictions) or applies more broadly.

5. Each Party shall notify the Depositary of whether each of its Covered Tax Agreements, other than those that are within the scope of a reservation under paragraph 4, contains preamble language described in paragraph 2, and if so, the text of the relevant preambular paragraph. Where all Contracting Jurisdictions have made such a notification with respect to that preamble language, such preamble language shall be replaced by the text described in paragraph 1. In other cases, the text described in paragraph 1 shall be included in addition to the existing preamble language.

6. Each Party that chooses to apply paragraph 3 shall notify the Depositary of its choice. Such notification shall also include the list of its Covered Tax Agreements that do not already contain preamble language referring to a desire to develop an economic relationship or to enhance co-operation in tax matters. The text described in paragraph 3 shall be included in a Covered Tax Agreement only where all Contracting Jurisdictions have chosen to apply that paragraph and have made such a notification with respect to the Covered Tax Agreement.

Article 7
Prevention of Treaty Abuse

1. Notwithstanding any provisions of a Covered Tax Agreement, a benefit under the Covered Tax Agreement shall not be granted in respect of an item of income or capital if it is

reasonable to conclude, having regard to all relevant facts and circumstances, that obtaining that benefit was one of the principal purposes of any arrangement or transaction that resulted directly or indirectly in that benefit, unless it is established that granting that benefit in these circumstances would be in accordance with the object and purpose of the relevant provisions of the Covered Tax Agreement.

2. Paragraph 1 shall apply in place of or in the absence of provisions of a Covered Tax Agreement that deny all or part of the benefits that would otherwise be provided under the Covered Tax Agreement where the principal purpose or one of the principal purposes of any arrangement or transaction, or of any person concerned with an arrangement or transaction, was to obtain those benefits.

3. A Party that has not made the reservation described in subparagraph a) of paragraph 15 may also choose to apply paragraph 4 with respect to its Covered Tax Agreements.

4. Where a benefit under a Covered Tax Agreement is denied to a person under provisions of the Covered Tax Agreement (as it may be modified by this Convention) that deny all or part of the benefits that would otherwise be provided under the Covered Tax Agreement where the principal purpose or one of the principal purposes of any arrangement or transaction, or of any person concerned with an arrangement or transaction, was to obtain those benefits, the competent authority of the Contracting Jurisdiction that would otherwise have granted this benefit shall nevertheless treat that person as being entitled to this benefit, or to different benefits with respect to a specific item of income or capital, if such competent authority, upon request from that person and after consideration of the relevant facts and circumstances, determines that such benefits would have been granted to that person in the absence of the transaction or arrangement. The competent authority of the Contracting Jurisdiction to which a request has been made under this paragraph by a resident of the other Contracting Jurisdiction shall consult with the competent authority of that other Contracting Jurisdiction before rejecting the request.

5. Paragraph 4 shall apply to provisions of a Covered Tax Agreement (as it may be modified by this Convention) that deny all or part of the benefits that would otherwise be provided under the Covered Tax Agreement where the principal purpose or one of the principal purposes of any arrangement or transaction, or of any person concerned with an arrangement or transaction, was to obtain those benefits.

6. A Party may also choose to apply the provisions contained in paragraphs 8 through 13 (hereinafter referred to as the "Simplified Limitation on Benefits Provision") to its Covered Tax Agreements by making the notification described in subparagraph c) of paragraph 17. The Simplified Limitation on Benefits Provision shall apply with respect to a Covered Tax Agreement only where all Contracting Jurisdictions have chosen to apply it.

7. In cases where some but not all of the Contracting Jurisdictions to a Covered Tax Agreement choose to apply the Simplified Limitation on Benefits Provision pursuant to paragraph 6, then, notwithstanding the provisions of that paragraph, the Simplified Limitation on Benefits Provision shall apply with respect to the granting of benefits under the Covered Tax Agreement:

a) by all Contracting Jurisdictions, if all of the Contracting Jurisdictions that do not choose pursuant to paragraph 6 to apply the Simplified Limitation on Benefits Provision agree to such application by choosing to apply this subparagraph and notifying the Depositary accordingly; or

b) only by the Contracting Jurisdictions that choose to apply the Simplified Limitation on Benefits Provision, if all of the Contracting Jurisdictions that do not choose pursuant to paragraph 6 to apply the Simplified Limitation on Benefits Provision agree to such application by choosing to apply this subparagraph and notifying the Depositary accordingly.

Simplified Limitation on Benefits Provision

8. Except as otherwise provided in the Simplified Limitation on Benefits Provision, a resident of a Contracting Jurisdiction to a Covered Tax Agreement shall not be entitled to a benefit that would otherwise be accorded by the Covered Tax Agreement, other than a benefit under provisions of the Covered Tax Agreement:

a) which determine the residence of a person other than an individual which is a resident of more than one Contracting Jurisdiction by reason of provisions of the Covered Tax Agreement that define a resident of a Contracting Jurisdiction;
b) which provide that a Contracting Jurisdiction will grant to an enterprise of that Contracting Jurisdiction a corresponding adjustment following an initial adjustment made by the other Contacting Jurisdiction, in accordance with the Covered Tax Agreement, to the amount of tax charged in the first-mentioned Contracting Jurisdiction on the profits of an associated enterprise; or
c) which allow residents of a Contracting Jurisdiction to request that the competent authority of that Contracting Jurisdiction consider cases of taxation not in accordance with the Covered Tax Agreement,

unless such resident is a “qualified person”, as defined in paragraph 9 at the time that the benefit would be accorded.

9. A resident of a Contracting Jurisdiction to a Covered Tax Agreement shall be a qualified person at a time when a benefit would otherwise be accorded by the Covered Tax Agreement if, at that time, the resident is:

a) an individual;
b) that Contracting Jurisdiction, or a political subdivision or local authority thereof, or an agency or instrumentality of any such Contracting Jurisdiction, political subdivision or local authority;
c) a company or other entity, if the principal class of its shares is regularly traded on one or more recognised stock exchanges;
d) a person, other than an individual, that:
    i) is a non-profit organisation of a type that is agreed to by the Contracting Jurisdictions through an exchange of diplomatic notes; or
    ii) is an entity or arrangement established in that Contracting Jurisdiction that is treated as a separate person under the taxation laws of that Contracting Jurisdiction and:
        A) that is established and operated exclusively or almost exclusively to administer or provide retirement benefits and ancillary or incidental benefits to individuals and that is regulated as such by that Contracting Jurisdiction or one of its political subdivisions or local authorities; or
        B) that is established and operated exclusively or almost exclusively to invest funds for the benefit of entities or arrangements referred to in subdivision A);

e) a person other than an individual, if, on at least half the days of a twelve-month period that includes the time when the benefit would otherwise be accorded, persons who are residents of that Contracting Jurisdiction and that are entitled to benefits of the Covered Tax Agreement under subparagraphs a) to d) own, directly or indirectly, at least 50 per cent of the shares of the person.

10.

a) A resident of a Contracting Jurisdiction to a Covered Tax Agreement will be entitled to benefits of the Covered Tax Agreement with respect to an item of income derived from the other Contracting Jurisdiction, regardless of whether the resident is a qualified person, if the resident is engaged in the active conduct of a business in the first-mentioned Contracting Jurisdiction, and the income derived from the other Contracting Jurisdiction emanates from, or is incidental to, that business. For purposes of the Simplified Limitation on Benefits Provision, the term "active conduct of a business" shall not include the following activities or any combination thereof:
   i) operating as a holding company;
   ii) providing overall supervision or administration of a group of companies;
   iii) providing group financing (including cash pooling); or
   iv) making or managing investments, unless these activities are carried on by a bank, insurance company or registered securities dealer in the ordinary course of its business as such.

b) If a resident of a Contracting Jurisdiction to a Covered Tax Agreement derives an item of income from a business activity conducted by that resident in the other Contracting Jurisdiction, or derives an item of income arising in the other Contracting Jurisdiction from a connected person, the conditions described in subparagraph a) shall be considered to be satisfied with respect to such item only if the business activity carried on by the resident in the first-mentioned Contracting Jurisdiction to which the item is related is substantial in relation to the same activity or a complementary business activity carried on by the resident or such connected person in the other Contracting Jurisdiction. Whether a business activity is substantial for the purposes of this subparagraph shall be determined based on all the facts and circumstances.

c) For purposes of applying this paragraph, activities conducted by connected persons with respect to a resident of a Contracting Jurisdiction to a Covered Tax Agreement shall be deemed to be conducted by such resident.

11. A resident of a Contracting Jurisdiction to a Covered Tax Agreement that is not a qualified person shall also be entitled to a benefit that would otherwise be accorded by the Covered Tax Agreement with respect to an item of income if, on at least half of the days of any twelve-month period that includes the time when the benefit would otherwise be accorded, persons that are equivalent beneficiaries own, directly or indirectly, at least 75 per cent of the beneficial interests of the resident.

12. If a resident of a Contracting Jurisdiction to a Covered Tax Agreement is neither a qualified person pursuant to the provisions of paragraph 9, nor entitled to benefits under paragraph 10 or 11, the competent authority of the other Contracting Jurisdiction may, nevertheless, grant the benefits of the Covered Tax Agreement, or benefits with respect to a specific item of income, taking into account the object and purpose of the Covered Tax

Agreement, but only if such resident demonstrates to the satisfaction of such competent authority that neither its establishment, acquisition or maintenance, nor the conduct of ist operations, had as one of its principal purposes the obtaining of benefits under the Covered Tax Agreement. Before either granting or denying a request made under this paragraph by a resident of a Contracting Jurisdiction, the competent authority of the other Contracting Jurisdiction to which the request has been made shall consult with the competent authority of the first-mentioned Contracting Jurisdiction.

13. For the purposes of the Simplified Limitation on Benefits Provision:

a) the term "recognised stock exchange" means:
   i) any stock exchange established and regulated as such under the laws of either Contracting Jurisdiction; and
   ii) any other stock exchange agreed upon by the competent authorities of the Contracting Jurisdictions;
b) the term "principal class of shares" means the class or classes of shares of a company which represents the majority of the aggregate vote and value of the company or the class or classes of beneficial interests of an entity which represents in the aggregate a majority of the aggregate vote and value of the entity;
c) the term "equivalent beneficiary" means any person who would be entitled to benefits with respect to an item of income accorded by a Contracting Jurisdiction to a Covered Tax Agreement under the domestic law of that Contracting Jurisdiction, the Covered Tax Agreement or any other international instrument which are equivalent to, or more favourable than, benefits to be accorded to that item of income under the Covered Tax Agreement; for the purposes of determining whether a person is an equivalent beneficiary with respect to dividends, the person shall be deemed to hold the same capital of the company paying the dividends as such capital the company claiming the benefit with respect to the dividends holds;
d) with respect to entities that are not companies, the term "shares" means interests that are comparable to shares;
e) two persons shall be "connected persons" if one owns, directly or indirectly, at least 50 per cent of the beneficial interest in the other (or, in the case of a company, at least 50 per cent of the aggregate vote and value of the company's shares) or another person owns, directly or indirectly, at least 50 per cent of the beneficial interest (or, in the case of a company, at least 50 per cent of the aggregate vote and value of the company's shares) in each person; in any case, a person shall be connected to another if, based on all the relevant facts and circumstances, one has control of the other or both are under the control of the same person or persons.

14. The Simplified Limitation on Benefits Provision shall apply in place of or in the absence of provisions of a Covered Tax Agreement that would limit the benefits of the Covered Tax Agreement (or that would limit benefits other than a benefit under the provisions of the Covered Tax Agreement relating to residence, associated enterprises or non-discrimination or a benefit that is not restricted solely to residents of a Contracting Jurisdiction) only to a resident that qualifies for such benefits by meeting one or more categorical tests.

15. A Party may reserve the right:

a) for paragraph 1 not to apply to its Covered Tax Agreements on the basis that it intends to adopt a combination of a detailed limitation on benefits provision and either rules to address conduit financing structures or a principal purpose test, thereby meeting the minimum standard for preventing treaty abuse under the OECD/G20 BEPS package; in such cases, the Contracting Jurisdictions shall endeavour to reach a mutually satisfactory solution which meets the minimum standard;

b) for paragraph 1 (and paragraph 4, in the case of a Party that has chosen to apply that paragraph) not to apply to its Covered Tax Agreements that already contain provisions that deny all of the benefits that would otherwise be provided under the Covered Tax Agreement where the principal purpose or one of the principal purposes of any arrangement or transaction, or of any person concerned with an arrangement or transaction, was to obtain those benefits;

c) for the Simplified Limitation on Benefits Provision not to apply to its Covered Tax Agreements that already contain the provisions described in paragraph 14.

16. Except where the Simplified Limitation on Benefits Provision applies with respect to the granting of benefits under a Covered Tax Agreement by one or more Parties pursuant to paragraph 7, a Party that chooses pursuant to paragraph 6 to apply the Simplified Limitation on Benefits Provision may reserve the right for the entirety of this Article not to apply with respect to its Covered Tax Agreements for which one or more of the other Contracting Jurisdictions has not chosen to apply the Simplified Limitation on Benefits Provision. In such cases, the Contracting Jurisdictions shall endeavour to reach a mutually satisfactory solution which meets the minimum standard for preventing treaty abuse under the OECD/G20 BEPS package.

17.

a) Each Party that has not made the reservation described in subparagraph a) of paragraph 15 shall notify the Depositary of whether each of its Covered Tax Agreements that is not subject to a reservation described in subparagraph b) of paragraph 15 contains a provision described in paragraph 2, and if so, the article and paragraph number of each such provision. Where all Contracting Jurisdictions have made such a notification with respect to a provision of a Covered Tax Agreement, that provision shall be replaced by the provisions of paragraph 1 (and where applicable, paragraph 4). In other cases, paragraph 1 (and where applicable, paragraph 4) shall supersede the provisions of the Covered Tax Agreement only to the extent that those provisions are incompatible with paragraph 1 (and where applicable, paragraph 4). A Party making a notification under this subparagraph may also include a statement that while such Party accepts the application of paragraph 1 alone as an interim measure, it intends where possible to adopt a limitation on benefits provision, in addition to or in replacement of paragraph 1, through bilateral negotiation.

b) Each Party that chooses to apply paragraph 4 shall notify the Depositary of its choice. Paragraph 4 shall apply to a Covered Tax Agreement only where all Contracting Jurisdictions have made such a notification.

c) Each Party that chooses to apply the Simplified Limitation on Benefits Provision pursuant to paragraph 6 shall notify the Depositary of its choice. Unless such Party has made the reservation described in subparagraph c) of paragraph 15, such notification shall also include the list of its Covered Tax Agreements which contain a provision described in paragraph 14, as well as the article and paragraph number of each such provision.

d) Each Party that does not choose to apply the Simplified Limitation on Benefits Provision pursuant to paragraph 6, but chooses to apply either subparagraph a) or b) of paragraph 7 shall notify the Depositary of its choice of subparagraph. Unless such Party has made the reservation described in subparagraph c) of paragraph 15, such notification shall also include the list of its Covered Tax Agreements which contain a provision described in paragraph 14, as well as the article and paragraph number of each such provision.
e) Where all Contracting Jurisdictions have made a notification under subparagraph c) or d) with respect to a provision of a Covered Tax Agreement, that provision shall be replaced by the Simplified Limitation on Benefits Provision. In other cases, the Simplified Limitation on Benefits Provision shall supersede the provisions of the Covered Tax Agreement only to the extent that those provisions are incompatible with the Simplified Limitation on Benefits Provision.

Article 8
Dividend Transfer Transactions

1. Provisions of a Covered Tax Agreement that exempt dividends paid by a company which is a resident of a Contracting Jurisdiction from tax or that limit the rate at which such dividends may be taxed, provided that the beneficial owner or the recipient is a company which is a resident of the other Contracting Jurisdiction and which owns, holds or controls more than a certain amount of the capital, shares, stock, voting power, voting rights or similar ownership interests of the company paying the dividends, shall apply only if the ownership conditions described in those provisions are met throughout a 365 day period that includes the day of the payment of the dividends (for the purpose of computing that period, no account shall be taken of changes of ownership that would directly result from a corporate reorganisation, such as a merger or divisive reorganisation, of the company that holds the shares or that pays the dividends).

2. The minimum holding period provided in paragraph 1 shall apply in place of or in the absence of a minimum holding period in provisions of a Covered Tax Agreement described in paragraph 1.

3. A Party may reserve the right:

a) for the entirety of this Article not to apply to its Covered Tax Agreements;
b) for the entirety of this Article not to apply to its Covered Tax Agreements to the extent that the provisions described in paragraph 1 already include:
   i) a minimum holding period;
   ii) a minimum holding period shorter than a 365 day period; or
   iii) a minimum holding period longer than a 365 day period.

4. Each Party that has not made a reservation described in subparagraph a) of paragraph 3 shall notify the Depositary of whether each of its Covered Tax Agreements contains a provision described in paragraph 1 that is not subject to a reservation described in subparagraph b) of paragraph 3, and if so, the article and paragraph number of each such provision. Paragraph 1 shall apply with respect to a provision of a Covered Tax Agreement only where all Contracting Jurisdictions have made such a notification with respect to that provision.

Article 9
Capital Gains from Alienation of Shares or Interests of Entities Deriving their Value Principally from Immovable Property

1. Provisions of a Covered Tax Agreement providing that gains derived by a resident of a Contracting Jurisdiction from the alienation of shares or other rights of participation in an entity may be taxed in the other Contracting Jurisdiction provided that these shares or rights derived more than a certain part of their value from immovable property (real property) situated in that other Contracting Jurisdiction (or provided that more than a certain part of the property of the entity consists of such immovable property (real property)):

a) shall apply if the relevant value threshold is met at any time during the 365 days preceding the alienation; and
b) shall apply to shares or comparable interests, such as interests in a partnership or trust (to the extent that such shares or interests are not already covered) in addition to any shares or rights already covered by the provisions.

2. The period provided in subparagraph a) of paragraph 1 shall apply in place of or in the absence of a time period for determining whether the relevant value threshold in provisions of a Covered Tax Agreement described in paragraph 1 was met.

3. A Party may also choose to apply paragraph 4 with respect to its Covered Tax Agreements.

4. For purposes of a Covered Tax Agreement, gains derived by a resident of a Contracting Jurisdiction from the alienation of shares or comparable interests, such as interests in a partnership or trust, may be taxed in the other Contracting Jurisdiction if, at any time during the 365 days preceding the alienation, these shares or comparable interests derived more than 50 per cent of their value directly or indirectly from immovable property (real property) situated in that other Contracting Jurisdiction.

5. Paragraph 4 shall apply in place of or in the absence of provisions of a Covered Tax Agreement providing that gains derived by a resident of a Contracting Jurisdiction from the alienation of shares or other rights of participation in an entity may be taxed in the other Contracting Jurisdiction provided that these shares or rights derived more than a certain part of their value from immovable property (real property) situated in that other Contracting Jurisdiction, or provided that more than a certain part of the property of the entity consists of such immovable property (real property).

6. A Party may reserve the right:

a) for paragraph 1 not to apply to its Covered Tax Agreements;
b) for subparagraph a) of paragraph 1 not to apply to its Covered Tax Agreements;
c) for subparagraph b) of paragraph 1 not to apply to its Covered Tax Agreements;
d) for subparagraph a) of paragraph 1 not to apply to its Covered Tax Agreements that already contain a provision of the type described in paragraph 1 that includes a period for determining whether the relevant value threshold was met;
e) for subparagraph b) of paragraph 1 not to apply to its Covered Tax Agreements that already contain a provision of the type described in paragraph 1 that applies to the alienation of interests other than shares;
f) for paragraph 4 not to apply to its Covered Tax Agreements that already contain the provisions described in paragraph 5.

7. Each Party that has not made the reservation described in subparagraph a) of paragraph 6 shall notify the Depositary of whether each of its Covered Tax Agreements contains a provision described in paragraph 1, and if so, the article and paragraph number of each such provision. Paragraph 1 shall apply with respect to a provision of a Covered Tax Agreement only where all Contracting Jurisdictions have made a notification with respect to that provision.

8. Each Party that chooses to apply paragraph 4 shall notify the Depositary of its choice. Paragraph 4 shall apply to a Covered Tax Agreement only where all Contracting Jurisdictions have made such a notification. In such case, paragraph 1 shall not apply with respect to that Covered Tax Agreement. In the case of a Party that has not made the reservation described in subparagraph f) of paragraph 6 and has made the reservation described in subparagraph a) of paragraph 6, such notification shall also include the list of its Covered Tax Agreements which contain a provision described in paragraph 5, as well as the article and paragraph number of each such provision. Where all Contracting Jurisdictions have made a notification with respect to a provision of a Covered Tax Agreement under this paragraph or paragraph 7, that provision shall be replaced by the provisions of paragraph 4. In other cases, paragraph 4 shall supersede the provisions of the Covered Tax Agreement only to the extent that those provisions are incompatible with paragraph 4.

Article 10
Anti-abuse Rule for Permanent Establishments Situated in Third Jurisdictions

1. Where:

a) an enterprise of a Contracting Jurisdiction to a Covered Tax Agreement derives income from the other Contracting Jurisdiction and the first-mentioned Contracting Jurisdiction treats such income as attributable to a permanent establishment of the enterprise situated in a third jurisdiction; and
b) the profits attributable to that permanent establishment are exempt from tax in the first-mentioned Contracting Jurisdiction,

the benefits of the Covered Tax Agreement shall not apply to any item of income on which the tax in the third jurisdiction is less than 60 per cent of the tax that would be imposed in the first-mentioned Contracting Jurisdiction on that item of income if that permanent establishment were situated in the first- mentioned Contracting Jurisdiction. In such a case, any income to which the provisions of this paragraph apply shall remain taxable according to the domestic law of the other Contracting Jurisdiction, notwithstanding any other provisions of the Covered Tax Agreement.

2. Paragraph 1 shall not apply if the income derived from the other Contracting Jurisdiction described in paragraph 1 is derived in connection with or is incidental to the active conduct of a business carried on through the permanent establishment (other than the business of making, managing or simply holding investments for the enterprise's own account, unless these activities are banking, insurance or securities activities carried on by a bank, insurance enterprise or registered securities dealer, respectively).

3. If benefits under a Covered Tax Agreement are denied pursuant to paragraph 1 with respect to an item of income derived by a resident of a Contracting Jurisdiction, the competent authority of the other Contracting Jurisdiction may, nevertheless, grant these benefits

with respect to that item of income if, in response to a request by such resident, such competent authority determines that granting such benefits is justified in light of the reasons such resident did not satisfy the requirements of paragraphs 1 and 2. The competent authority of the Contracting Jurisdiction to which a request has been made under the preceding sentence by a resident of the other Contracting Jurisdiction shall consult with the competent authority of that other Contracting Jurisdiction before either granting or denying the request.

4. Paragraphs 1 through 3 shall apply in place of or in the absence of provisions of a Covered Tax Agreement that deny or limit benefits that would otherwise be granted to an enterprise of a Contracting Jurisdiction which derives income from the other Contracting Jurisdiction that is attributable to a permanent establishment of the enterprise situated in a third jurisdiction.

5. A Party may reserve the right:

a) for the entirety of this Article not to apply to its Covered Tax Agreements;
b) for the entirety of this Article not to apply to its Covered Tax Agreements that already contain the provisions described in paragraph 4;
c) for this Article to apply only to its Covered Tax Agreements that already contain the provisions described in paragraph 4.

6. Each Party that has not made the reservation described in subparagraph a) or b) of paragraph 5 shall notify the Depositary of whether each of its Covered Tax Agreements contains a provision described in paragraph 4, and if so, the article and paragraph number of each such provision. Where all Contracting Jurisdictions have made such a notification with respect to a provision of a Covered Tax Agreement, that provision shall be replaced by the provisions of paragraphs 1 through 3. In other cases, paragraphs 1 through 3 shall supersede the provisions of the Covered Tax Agreement only to the extent that those provisions are incompatible with those paragraphs.

Article 11
Application of Tax Agreements to Restrict a Party's Right to Tax its Own Residents

1. A Covered Tax Agreement shall not affect the taxation by a Contracting Jurisdiction of its residents, except with respect to the benefits granted under provisions of the Covered Tax Agreement:

a) which require that Contracting Jurisdiction to grant to an enterprise of that Contracting Jurisdiction a correlative or corresponding adjustment following an initial adjustment made by the other Contracting Jurisdiction, in accordance with the Covered Tax Agreement, to the amount of tax charged in the first-mentioned Contracting Jurisdiction on the profits of a permanent establishment of the enterprise or the profits of an associated enterprise;
b) which may affect how that Contracting Jurisdiction taxes an individual who is a resident of that Contracting Jurisdiction if that individual derives income in respect of services rendered to the other Contracting Jurisdiction or a political subdivision or local authority or other comparable body thereof;
c) which may affect how that Contracting Jurisdiction taxes an individual who is a resident of that Contracting Jurisdiction if that individual is also a student, business apprentice or trainee, or a teacher, professor, lecturer, instructor, researcher or research scholar who meets the conditions of the Covered Tax Agreement;

d) which require that Contracting Jurisdiction to provide a tax credit or tax exemption to residents of that Contracting Jurisdiction with respect to the income that the other Contracting Jurisdiction may tax in accordance with the Covered Tax Agreement (including profits that are attributable to a permanent establishment situated in that other Contracting Jurisdiction in accordance with the Covered Tax Agreement);
e) which protect residents of that Contracting Jurisdiction against certain discriminatory taxation practices by that Contracting Jurisdiction;
f) which allow residents of that Contracting Jurisdiction to request that the competent authority of that or either Contracting Jurisdiction consider cases of taxation not in accordance with the Covered Tax Agreement;
g) which may affect how that Contracting Jurisdiction taxes an individual who is a resident of that Contracting Jurisdiction when that individual is a member of a diplomatic mission, government mission or consular post of the other Contracting Jurisdiction;
h) which provide that pensions or other payments made under the social security legislation of the other Contracting Jurisdiction shall be taxable only in that other Contracting Jurisdiction;
i) which provide that pensions and similar payments, annuities, alimony payments or other maintenance payments arising in the other Contracting Jurisdiction shall be taxable only in that other Contracting Jurisdiction; or
j) which otherwise expressly limit a Contracting Jurisdiction's right to tax its own residents or provide expressly that the Contracting Jurisdiction in which an item of income arises has the exclusive right to tax that item of income.

2. Paragraph 1 shall apply in place of or in the absence of provisions of a Covered Tax Agreement stating that the Covered Tax Agreement would not affect the taxation by a Contracting Jurisdiction of its residents.

3. A Party may reserve the right:

a) for the entirety of this Article not to apply to its Covered Tax Agreements;
b) for the entirety of this Article not to apply to its Covered Tax Agreements that already contain the provisions described in paragraph 2.

4. Each Party that has not made the reservation described in subparagraph a) or b) of paragraph 3 shall notify the Depositary of whether each of its Covered Tax Agreements contains a provision described in paragraph 2, and if so, the article and paragraph number of each such provision. Where all Contracting Jurisdictions have made such a notification with respect to a provision of a Covered Tax Agreement, that provision shall be replaced by the provisions of paragraph 1. In other cases, paragraph 1 shall supersede the provisions of the Covered Tax Agreement only to the extent that those provisions are incompatible with paragraph 1.

PART IV.
AVOIDANCE OF PERMANENT ESTABLISHMENT STATUS

Article 12
Artificial Avoidance of Permanent Establishment Status through Commissionnaire Arrangements and Similar Strategies

1. Notwithstanding the provisions of a Covered Tax Agreement that define the term "permanent establishment", but subject to paragraph 2, where a person is acting in a Contracting

Jurisdiction to a Covered Tax Agreement on behalf of an enterprise and, in doing so, habitually concludes contracts, or habitually plays the principal role leading to the conclusion of contracts that are routinely concluded without material modification by the enterprise, and these contracts are:

a) in the name of the enterprise; or
b) for the transfer of the ownership of, or for the granting of the right to use, property owned by that enterprise or that the enterprise has the right to use; or
c) for the provision of services by that enterprise,

that enterprise shall be deemed to have a permanent establishment in that Contracting Jurisdiction in respect of any activities which that person undertakes for the enterprise unless these activities, if they were exercised by the enterprise through a fixed place of business of that enterprise situated in that Contracting Jurisdiction, would not cause that fixed place of business to be deemed to constitute a permanent establishment under the definition of permanent establishment included in the Covered Tax Agreement (as it may be modified by this Convention).

2. Paragraph 1 shall not apply where the person acting in a Contracting Jurisdiction to a Covered Tax Agreement on behalf of an enterprise of the other Contracting Jurisdiction carries on business in the first-mentioned Contracting Jurisdiction as an independent agent and acts for the enterprise in the ordinary course of that business. Where, however, a person acts exclusively or almost exclusively on behalf of one or more enterprises to which it is closely related, that person shall not be considered to be an independent agent within the meaning of this paragraph with respect to any such enterprise.

3.

a) Paragraph 1 shall apply in place of provisions of a Covered Tax Agreement that describe the conditions under which an enterprise shall be deemed to have a permanent establishment in a Contracting Jurisdiction (or a person shall be deemed to be a permanent establishment in a Contracting Jurisdiction) in respect of an activity which a person other than an agent of an independent status undertakes for the enterprise, but only to the extent that such provisions address the situation in which such person has, and habitually exercises, in that Contracting Jurisdiction an authority to conclude contracts in the name of the enterprise.
b) Paragraph 2 shall apply in place of provisions of a Covered Tax Agreement that provide that an enterprise shall not be deemed to have a permanent establishment in a Contracting Jurisdiction in respect of an activity which an agent of an independent status undertakes for the enterprise.

4. A Party may reserve the right for the entirety of this Article not to apply to its Covered Tax Agreements.

5. Each Party that has not made a reservation described in paragraph 4 shall notify the Depositary of whether each of its Covered Tax Agreements contains a provision described in subparagraph a) of paragraph 3, as well as the article and paragraph number of each such provision. Paragraph 1 shall apply with respect to a provision of a Covered Tax Agreement only where all Contracting Jurisdictions have made a notification with respect to that provision.

6. Each Party that has not made a reservation described in paragraph 4 shall notify the Depositary of whether each of its Covered Tax Agreements contains a provision described in subparagraph b) of paragraph 3, as well as the article and paragraph number of each such provision. Paragraph 2 shall apply with respect to a provision of a Covered Tax Agreement only where all Contracting Jurisdictions have made such a notification with respect to that provision.

Article 13
Artificial Avoidance of Permanent Establishment Status through the Specific Activity Exemptions

1. A Party may choose to apply paragraph 2 (Option A) or paragraph 3 (Option B) or to apply neither Option.

Option A

2. Notwithstanding the provisions of a Covered Tax Agreement that define the term "permanent establishment", the term "permanent establishment" shall be deemed not to include:

a) the activities specifically listed in the Covered Tax Agreement (prior to modification by this Convention) as activities deemed not to constitute a permanent establishment, whether or not that exception from permanent establishment status is contingent on the activity being of a preparatory or auxiliary character;
b) the maintenance of a fixed place of business solely for the purpose of carrying on, for the enterprise, any activity not described in subparagraph a);
c) the maintenance of a fixed place of business solely for any combination of activities mentioned in subparagraphs a) and b),

provided that such activity or, in the case of subparagraph c), the overall activity of the fixed place of business, is of a preparatory or auxiliary character.

Option B

3. Notwithstanding the provisions of a Covered Tax Agreement that define the term "permanent establishment", the term "permanent establishment" shall be deemed not to include:

a) the activities specifically listed in the Covered Tax Agreement (prior to modification by this Convention) as activities deemed not to constitute a permanent establishment, whether or not that exception from permanent establishment status is contingent on the activity being of a preparatory or auxiliary character, except to the extent that the relevant provision of the Covered Tax Agreement provides explicitly that a specific activity shall be deemed not to constitute a permanent establishment provided that the activity is of a preparatory or auxiliary character;
b) the maintenance of a fixed place of business solely for the purpose of carrying on, for the enterprise, any activity not described in subparagraph a), provided that this activity is of a preparatory or auxiliary character;
c) the maintenance of a fixed place of business solely for any combination of activities mentioned in subparagraphs a) and b), provided that the overall activity of the fixed place of business resulting from this combination is of a preparatory or auxiliary character.

4. A provision of a Covered Tax Agreement (as it may be modified by paragraph 2 or 3) that lists specific activities deemed not to constitute a permanent establishment shall not apply to a fixed place of business that is used or maintained by an enterprise if the same enterprise or a closely related enterprise carries on business activities at the same place or at another place in the same Contracting Jurisdiction and:

a) that place or other place constitutes a permanent establishment for the enterprise or the closely related enterprise under the provisions of a Covered Tax Agreement defining a permanent establishment; or
b) the overall activity resulting from the combination of the activities carried on by the two enterprises at the same place, or by the same enterprise or closely related enterprises at the two places, is not of a preparatory or auxiliary character,

provided that the business activities carried on by the two enterprises at the same place, or by the same enterprise or closely related enterprises at the two places, constitute complementary functions that are part of a cohesive business operation.

5.

a) Paragraph 2 or 3 shall apply in place of the relevant parts of provisions of a Covered Tax Agreement that list specific activities that are deemed not to constitute a permanent establishment even if the activity is carried on through a fixed place of business (or provisions of a Covered Tax Agreement that operate in a comparable manner).
b) Paragraph 4 shall apply to provisions of a Covered Tax Agreement (as they may be modified by paragraph 2 or 3) that list specific activities that are deemed not to constitute a permanent establishment even if the activity is carried on through a fixed place of business (or provisions of a Covered Tax Agreement that operate in a comparable manner).

6. A Party may reserve the right:

a) for the entirety of this Article not to apply to its Covered Tax Agreements;
b) for paragraph 2 not to apply to its Covered Tax Agreements that explicitly state that a list of specific activities shall be deemed not to constitute a permanent establishment only if each of the activities is of a preparatory or auxiliary character;
c) for paragraph 4 not to apply to its Covered Tax Agreements.

7. Each Party that chooses to apply an Option under paragraph 1 shall notify the Depositary of its choice of Option. Such notification shall also include the list of its Covered Tax Agreements which contain a provision described in subparagraph a) of paragraph 5, as well as the article and paragraph number of each such provision. An Option shall apply with respect to a provision of a Covered Tax Agreement only where all Contracting Jurisdictions have chosen to apply the same Option and have made such a notification with respect to that provision.

8. Each Party that has not made a reservation described in subparagraph a) or c) of paragraph 6 and does not choose to apply an Option under paragraph 1 shall notify the Depositary of whether each of its Covered Tax Agreements contains a provision described in subparagraph b) of paragraph 5, as well as the article and paragraph number of each such provision. Paragraph 4 shall apply with respect to a provision of a Covered Tax Agreement only where all Contracting Jurisdictions have made a notification with respect to that provision under this paragraph or paragraph 7.

Article 14
Splitting-up of Contracts

1. For the sole purpose of determining whether the period (or periods) referred to in a provision of a Covered Tax Agreement that stipulates a period (or periods) of time after which specific projects or activities shall constitute a permanent establishment has been exceeded:

a) where an enterprise of a Contracting Jurisdiction carries on activities in the other Contracting Jurisdiction at a place that constitutes a building site, construction project, installation project or other specific project identified in the relevant provision of the Covered Tax Agreement, or carries on supervisory or consultancy activities in connection with such a place, in the case of a provision of a Covered Tax Agreement that refers to such activities, and these activities are carried on during one or more periods of time that, in the aggregate, exceed 30 days without exceeding the period or periods referred to in the relevant provision of the Covered Tax Agreement; and
b) where connected activities are carried on in that other Contracting Jurisdiction at (or, where the relevant provision of the Covered Tax Agreement applies to supervisory or consultancy activities, in connection with) the same building site, construction or installation project, or other place identified in the relevant provision of the Covered Tax Agreement during different periods of time, each exceeding 30 days, by one or more enterprises closely related to the first-mentioned enterprise,

these different periods of time shall be added to the aggregate period of time during which the first-mentioned enterprise has carried on activities at that building site, construction or installation project, or other place identified in the relevant provision of the Covered Tax Agreement.

2. Paragraph 1 shall apply in place of or in the absence of provisions of a Covered Tax Agreement to the extent that such provisions address the division of contracts into multiple parts to avoid the application of a time period or periods in relation to the existence of a permanent establishment for specific projects or activities described in paragraph 1.

3. A Party may reserve the right:

a) for the entirety of this Article not to apply to its Covered Tax Agreements;
b) for the entirety of this Article not to apply with respect to provisions of its Covered Tax Agreements relating to the exploration for or exploitation of natural resources.

4. Each Party that has not made a reservation described in subparagraph a) of paragraph 3 shall notify the Depositary of whether each of its Covered Tax Agreements contains a provision described in paragraph 2 that is not subject to a reservation under subparagraph b) of paragraph 3, and if so, the article and paragraph number of each such provision. Where all Contracting Jurisdictions have made such a notification with respect to a provision of a Covered Tax Agreement, that provision shall be replaced by the provisions of paragraph 1 to the extent provided in paragraph 2. In other cases, paragraph 1 shall supersede the provisions of the Covered Tax Agreement only to the extent that those provisions are incompatible with paragraph 1.

Article 15
Definition of a Person Closely Related to an Enterprise

1. For the purposes of the provisions of a Covered Tax Agreement that are modified by paragraph 2 of Article 12 (Artificial Avoidance of Permanent Establishment Status through

Commissionnaire Arrangements and Similar Strategies), paragraph 4 of Article 13 (Artificial Avoidance of Permanent Establishment Status through the Specific Activity Exemptions), or paragraph 1 of Article 14 (Splitting-up of Contracts), a person is closely related to an enterprise if, based on all the relevant facts and circumstances, one has control of the other or both are under the control of the same persons or enterprises. In any case, a person shall be considered to be closely related to an enterprise if one possesses directly or indirectly more than 50 per cent of the beneficial interest in the other (or, in the case of a company, more than 50 per cent of the aggregate vote and value of the company's shares or of the beneficial equity interest in the company) or if another person possesses directly or indirectly more than 50 per cent of the beneficial interest (or, in the case of a company, more than 50 per cent of the aggregate vote and value of the company's shares or of the beneficial equity interest in the company) in the person and the enterprise.

2. A Party that has made the reservations described in paragraph 4 of Article 12 (Artificial Avoidance of Permanent Establishment Status through Commissionnaire Arrangements and Similar Strategies), subparagraph a) or c) of paragraph 6 of Article 13 (Artificial Avoidance of Permanent Establishment Status through the Specific Activity Exemptions), and subparagraph a) of paragraph 3 of Article 14 (Splitting-up of Contracts) may reserve the right for the entirety of this Article not to apply to the Covered Tax Agreements to which those reservations apply.

PART V.
IMPROVING DISPUTE RESOLUTION

Article 16
Mutual Agreement Procedure

1. Where a person considers that the actions of one or both of the Contracting Jurisdictions result or will result for that person in taxation not in accordance with the provisions of the Covered Tax Agreement, that person may, irrespective of the remedies provided by the domestic law of those Contracting Jurisdictions, present the case to the competent authority of either Contracting Jurisdiction. The case must be presented within three years from the first notification of the action resulting in taxation not in accordance with the provisions of the Covered Tax Agreement.

2. The competent authority shall endeavour, if the objection appears to it to be justified and if it is not itself able to arrive at a satisfactory solution, to resolve the case by mutual agreement with the competent authority of the other Contracting Jurisdiction, with a view to the avoidance of taxation which is not in accordance with the Covered Tax Agreement. Any agreement reached shall be implemented notwithstanding any time limits in the domestic law of the Contracting Jurisdictions.

3. The competent authorities of the Contracting Jurisdictions shall endeavour to resolve by mutual agreement any difficulties or doubts arising as to the interpretation or application of the Covered Tax Agreement. They may also consult together for the elimination of double taxation in cases not provided for in the Covered Tax Agreement.

4.

a) i) The first sentence of paragraph 1 shall apply in place of or in the absence of provisions of a Covered Tax Agreement (or parts thereof) that provide that where a person considers that the actions of one or both of the Contracting Jurisdiction result or will result for that person in taxation not in accordance with the provisions of the Covered Tax Agreement, that person may, irrespective of the remedies provided by the domestic law of those Contracting Jurisdictions, present the case to the competent authority of the Contracting Jurisdiction of which that person is a resident including provisions under which, if the case presented by that person comes under the provisions of a Covered Tax Agreement relating to non-discrimination based on nationality, the case may be presented to the competent authority of the Contracting Jurisdiction of which that person is a national.

ii) The second sentence of paragraph 1 shall apply in place of provisions of a Covered Tax Agreement that provide that a case referred to in the first sentence of paragraph 1 must be presented within a specific time period that is shorter than three years from the first notification of the action resulting in taxation not in accordance with the provisions of the Covered Tax Agreement, or in the absence of a provision of a Covered Tax Agreement describing the time period within which such a case must be presented.

b) i) The first sentence of paragraph 2 shall apply in the absence of provisions of a Covered Tax Agreement that provide that the competent authority that is presented with the case by the person referred to in paragraph 1 shall endeavour, if the objection appears to it to be justified and if it is not itself able to arrive at a satisfactory solution, to resolve the case by mutual agreement with the competent authority of the other Contracting Jurisdiction, with a view to the avoidance of taxation which is not in accordance with the Covered Tax Agreement.

ii) The second sentence of paragraph 2 shall apply in the absence of provisions of a Covered Tax Agreement providing that any agreement reached shall be implemented notwithstanding any time limits in the domestic law of the Contracting Jurisdictions.

c) i) The first sentence of paragraph 3 shall apply in the absence of provisions of a Covered Tax Agreement that provide that the competent authorities of the Contracting Jurisdictions shall endeavour to resolve by mutual agreement any difficulties or doubts arising as to the interpretation or application of the Covered Tax Agreement.

ii) The second sentence of paragraph 3 shall apply in the absence of provisions of a Covered Tax Agreement that provide that the competent authorities of the Contracting Jurisdictions may also consult together for the elimination of double taxation in cases not provided for in the Covered Tax Agreement.

5. A Party may reserve the right:

a) for the first sentence of paragraph 1 not to apply to its Covered Tax Agreements on the basis that it intends to meet the minimum standard for improving dispute resolution under the OECD/G20 BEPS Package by ensuring that under each of its Covered Tax Agreements (other than a Covered Tax Agreement that permits a person to present a case to the competent authority of either Contracting Jurisdiction), where a person considers that the actions of one or both of the Contracting Jurisdictions result or will result for that person in taxation not in accordance with the provisions of the Covered Tax Agreement, irrespective of the remedies provided by the domestic law of those Contracting Jurisdictions, that person may present the case to the competent authority of the Contracting Jurisdiction of which the person is a resident or, if the case presented by that person comes under a provision of a Covered Tax Agreement relating to non-discrimination based on nationality, to that of the Contracting Jurisdiction of which that person is a national; and the competent authority of that Contracting Jurisdiction will implement a bilateral notification or consultation process with the competent authority of the other Contracting Jurisdiction for cases in which the competent authority to which the mutual agreement procedure case was presented does not consider the taxpayer's objection to be justified;

b) for the second sentence of paragraph 1 not to apply to its Covered Tax Agreements that do not provide that the case referred to in the first sentence of paragraph 1 must be presented within a specific time period on the basis that it intends to meet the minimum standard for improving dispute resolution under the OECD/G20 BEPS package by ensuring that for the purposes of all such Covered Tax Agreements the taxpayer referred to in paragraph 1 is allowed to present the case within a period of at least three years from the first notification of the action resulting in taxation not in accordance with the provisions of the Covered Tax Agreement;

c) for the second sentence of paragraph 2 not to apply to its Covered Tax Agreements on the basis that for the purposes of all of its Covered Tax Agreements:
   i) any agreement reached via the mutual agreement procedure shall be implemented notwithstanding any time limits in the domestic laws of the Contracting Jurisdictions; or
   ii) it intends to meet the minimum standard for improving dispute resolution under the OECD/G20 BEPS package by accepting, in its bilateral treaty negotiations, a treaty provision providing that:
      A) the Contracting Jurisdictions shall make no adjustment to the profits that are attributable to a permanent establishment of an enterprise of one of the Contracting Jurisdictions after a period that is mutually agreed between both Contracting Jurisdictions from the end of the taxable year in which the profits would have been attributable to the permanent establishment (this provision shall not apply in the case of fraud, gross negligence or wilful default); and
      B) the Contracting Jurisdictions shall not include in the profits of an enterprise, and tax accordingly, profits that would have accrued to the enterprise but that by reason of the conditions referred to in a provision in the Covered Tax Agreement relating to associated enterprises have not so accrued, after a period that is mutually agreed between both Contracting Jurisdictions from the end of the taxable year in which the profits would have accrued to the enterprise (this provision shall not apply in the case of fraud, gross negligence or wilful default).

6.

a) Each Party that has not made a reservation described in subparagraph a) of paragraph 5 shall notify the Depositary of whether each of its Covered Tax Agreements contains a provision described in clause i) of subparagraph a) of paragraph 4, and if so, the article and paragraph number of each such provision. Where all Contracting Jurisdictions have made a notification with respect to a provision of a Covered Tax Agreement, that provision shall be replaced by the first sentence of paragraph 1. In other cases, the first sentence of paragraph 1 shall supersede the provisions of the Covered Tax Agreement only to the extent that those provisions are incompatible with that sentence.

b) Each Party that has not made the reservation described in subparagraph b) of paragraph 5 shall notify the Depositary of:
   i) the list of its Covered Tax Agreements which contain a provision that provides that a case referred to in the first sentence of paragraph 1 must be presented within a specific time period that is shorter than three years from the first notification of the action resulting in taxation not in accordance with the provisions of the Covered Tax Agreement, as well as the article and paragraph number of each such provision; a provision of a Covered Tax Agreement shall be replaced by the second sentence of paragraph 1 where all Contracting Jurisdictions have made such a notification with respect to that provision; in other cases, subject to clause ii), the second sentence of paragraph 1 shall supersede the provisions of the Covered Tax Agreement only to the extent that those provisions are incompatible with the second sentence of paragraph 1;
   ii) the list of its Covered Tax Agreements which contain a provision that provides that a case referred to in the first sentence of paragraph 1 must be presented within a specific time period that is at least three years from the first notification of the action resulting in taxation not in accordance with the provisions of the Covered Tax Agreement, as well as the article and paragraph number of each such provision; the second sentence of paragraph 1 shall not apply to a Covered Tax Agreement where any Contracting Jurisdiction has made such a notification with respect to that Covered Tax Agreement.
c) Each Party shall notify the Depositary of:
   i) the list of its Covered Tax Agreements which do not contain a provision described in clause i) of subparagraph b) of paragraph 4; the first sentence of paragraph 2 shall apply to a Covered Tax Agreement only where all Contracting Jurisdictions have made such a notification with respect to that Covered Tax Agreement;
   ii) in the case of a Party that has not made the reservation described in subparagraph c) of paragraph 5, the list of its Covered Tax Agreements which do not contain a provision described in clause ii) of subparagraph b) of paragraph 4; the second sentence of paragraph 2 shall apply to a Covered Tax Agreement only where all Contracting Jurisdictions have made such a notification with respect to that Covered Tax Agreement.
d) Each Party shall notify the Depositary of:
   i) the list of its Covered Tax Agreements which do not contain a provision described in clause i) of subparagraph c) of paragraph 4; the first sentence of paragraph 3 shall apply to a Covered Tax Agreement only where all Contracting Jurisdictions have made such a notification with respect to that Covered Tax Agreement;
   ii) the list of its Covered Tax Agreements which do not contain a provision described in clause ii) of subparagraph c) of paragraph 4; the second sentence of paragraph 3 shall apply to a Covered Tax Agreement only where all Contracting Jurisdictions have made such a notification with respect to that Covered Tax Agreement.

Article 17
Corresponding Adjustments

1. Where a Contracting Jurisdiction includes in the profits of an enterprise of that Contracting Jurisdiction — and taxes accordingly — profits on which an enterprise of the other Contracting Jurisdiction has been charged to tax in that other Contracting Jurisdiction

and the profits so included are profits which would have accrued to the enterprise of the first-mentioned Contracting Jurisdiction if the conditions made between the two enterprises had been those which would have been made between independent enterprises, then that other Contracting Jurisdiction shall make an appropriate adjustment to the amount of the tax charged therein on those profits. In determining such adjustment, due regard shall be had to the other provisions of the Covered Tax Agreement and the competent authorities of the Contracting Jurisdictions shall if necessary consult each other.

2. Paragraph 1 shall apply in place of or in the absence of a provision that requires a Contracting Jurisdiction to make an appropriate adjustment to the amount of the tax charged therein on the profits of an enterprise of that Contracting Jurisdiction where the other Contracting Jurisdiction includes those profits in the profits of an enterprise of that other Contracting Jurisdiction and taxes those profits accordingly, and the profits so included are profits which would have accrued to the enterprise of that other Contracting Jurisdiction if the conditions made between the two enterprises had been those which would have been made between independent enterprises.

3. A Party may reserve the right:

a) for the entirety of this Article not to apply to its Covered Tax Agreements that already contain a provision described in paragraph 2;
b) for the entirety of this Article not to apply to its Covered Tax Agreements on the basis that in the absence of a provision referred to in paragraph 2 in its Covered Tax Agreement:
   i) it shall make the appropriate adjustment referred to in paragraph 1; or
   ii) its competent authority shall endeavour to resolve the case under the provisions of a Covered Tax Agreement relating to mutual agreement procedure;
c) in the case of a Party that has made a reservation under clause ii) of subparagraph c) of paragraph 5 of Article 16 (Mutual Agreement Procedure), for the entirety of this Article not to apply to its Covered Tax Agreements on the basis that in its bilateral treaty negotiations it shall accept a treaty provision of the type contained in paragraph 1, provided that the Contracting Jurisdictions were able to reach agreement on that provision and on the provisions described in clause ii) of subparagraph c) of paragraph 5 of Article 16 (Mutual Agreement Procedure).

4. Each Party that has not made a reservation described in paragraph 3 shall notify the Depositary of whether each of its Covered Tax Agreements contains a provision described in paragraph 2, and if so, the article and paragraph number of each such provision. Where all Contracting Jurisdictions have made such a notification with respect to a provision of a Covered Tax Agreement, that provision shall be replaced by the provisions of paragraph 1. In other cases, paragraph 1 shall supersede the provisions of the Covered Tax Agreement only to the extent that those provisions are incompatible with paragraph 1.

PART VI.
ARBITRATION

Article 18
Choice to Apply Part VI

A Party may choose to apply this Part with respect to its Covered Tax Agreements and shall notify the Depositary accordingly. This Part shall apply in relation to two Contracting Jurisdictions with respect to a Covered Tax Agreement only where both Contracting Jurisdictions have made such a notification.

Article 19
Mandatory Binding Arbitration

1. Where:

a) under a provision of a Covered Tax Agreement (as it may be modified by paragraph 1 of Article 16 (Mutual Agreement Procedure)) that provides that a person may present a case to a competent authority of a Contracting Jurisdiction where that person considers that the actions of one or both of the Contracting Jurisdictions result or will result for that person in taxation not in accordance with the provisions of the Covered Tax Agreement (as it may be modified by the Convention), a person has presented a case to the competent authority of a Contracting Jurisdiction on the basis that the actions of one or both of the Contracting Jurisdictions have resulted for that person in taxation not in accordance with the provisions of the Covered Tax Agreement (as it may be modified by the Convention); and

b) the competent authorities are unable to reach an agreement to resolve that case pursuant to a provision of a Covered Tax Agreement (as it may be modified by paragraph 2 of Article 16 (Mutual Agreement Procedure)) that provides that the competent authority shall endeavour to resolve the case by mutual agreement with the competent authority of the other Contracting Jurisdiction, within a period of two years beginning on the start date referred to in paragraph 8 or 9, as the case may be (unless, prior to the expiration of that period the competent authorities of the Contracting Jurisdictions have agreed to a different time period with respect to that case and have notified the person who presented the case of such agreement),

any unresolved issues arising from the case shall, if the person so requests in writing, be submitted to arbitration in the manner described in this Part, according to any rules or procedures agreed upon by the competent authorities of the Contracting Jurisdictions pursuant to the provisions of paragraph 10.

2. Where a competent authority has suspended the mutual agreement procedure referred to in paragraph 1 because a case with respect to one or more of the same issues is pending before court or administrative tribunal, the period provided in subparagraph b) of paragraph 1 will stop running until either a final decision has been rendered by the court or administrative tribunal or the case has been suspended or withdrawn. In addition, where a person who presented a case and a competent authority have agreed to suspend the mutual agreement procedure, the period provided in subparagraph b) of paragraph 1 will stop running until the suspension has been lifted.

3. Where both competent authorities agree that a person directly affected by the case has failed to provide in a timely manner any additional material information requested by either competent authority after the start of the period provided in subparagraph b) of paragraph 1, the period provided in subparagraph b) of paragraph 1 shall be extended for an amount of time equal to the period beginning on the date by which the information was requested and ending on the date on which that information was provided.

4.

a) The arbitration decision with respect to the issues submitted to arbitration shall be implemented through the mutual agreement concerning the case referred to in paragraph 1. The arbitration decision shall be final.
b) The arbitration decision shall be binding on both Contracting Jurisdictions except in the following cases:
   i) if a person directly affected by the case does not accept the mutual agreement that implements the arbitration decision. In such a case, the case shall not be eligible for any further consideration by the competent authorities. The mutual agreement that implements the arbitration decision on the case shall be considered not to be accepted by a person directly affected by the case if any person directly affected by the case does not, within 60 days after the date on which notification of the mutual agreement is sent to the person, withdraw all issues resolved in the mutual agreement implementing the arbitration decision from consideration by any court or administrative tribunal or otherwise terminate any pending court or administrative proceedings with respect to such issues in a manner consistent with that mutual agreement.
   ii) if a final decision of the courts of one of the Contracting Jurisdictions holds that the arbitration decision is invalid. In such a case, the request for arbitration under paragraph 1 shall be considered not to have been made, and the arbitration process shall be considered not to have taken place (except for the purposes of Articles 21 (Confidentiality of Arbitration Proceedings) and 25 (Costs of Arbitration Proceedings)). In such a case, a new request for arbitration may be made unless the competent authorities agree that such a new request should not be permitted.
   iii) if a person directly affected by the case pursues litigation on the issues which were resolved in the mutual agreement implementing the arbitration decision in any court or administrative tribunal.

5. The competent authority that received the initial request for a mutual agreement procedure as described in subparagraph a) of paragraph 1 shall, within two calendar months of receiving the request:

a) send a notification to the person who presented the case that it has received the request; and
b) send a notification of that request, along with a copy of the request, to the competent authority of the other Contracting Jurisdiction.

6. Within three calendar months after a competent authority receives the request for a mutual agreement procedure (or a copy thereof from the competent authority of the other Contracting Jurisdiction) it shall either:

a) notify the person who has presented the case and the other competent authority that it has received the information necessary to undertake substantive consideration of the case; or
b) request additional information from that person for that purpose.

7. Where pursuant to subparagraph b) of paragraph 6, one or both of the competent authorities have requested from the person who presented the case additional information necessary

to undertake substantive consideration of the case, the competent authority that requested the additional information shall, within three calendar months of receiving the additional information from that person, notify that person and the other competent authority either:

a) that it has received the requested information; or
b) that some of the requested information is still missing.

8. Where neither competent authority has requested additional information pursuant to subparagraph b) of paragraph 6, the start date referred to in paragraph 1 shall be the earlier of:

a) the date on which both competent authorities have notified the person who presented the case pursuant to subparagraph a) of paragraph 6; and
b) the date that is three calendar months after the notification to the competent authority of the other Contracting Jurisdiction pursuant to subparagraph b) of paragraph 5.

9. Where additional information has been requested pursuant to subparagraph b) of paragraph 6, the start date referred to in paragraph 1 shall be the earlier of:

a) the latest date on which the competent authorities that requested additional information have notified the person who presented the case and the other competent authority pursuant to subparagraph a) of paragraph 7; and
b) the date that is three calendar months after both competent authorities have received all information requested by either competent authority from the person who presented the case.

If, however, one or both of the competent authorities send the notification referred to in subparagraph b) of paragraph 7, such notification shall be treated as a request for additional information under subparagraph b) of paragraph 6.

10. The competent authorities of the Contracting Jurisdictions shall by mutual agreement (pursuant to the article of the relevant Covered Tax Agreement regarding procedures for mutual agreement) settle the mode of application of the provisions contained in this Part, including the minimum information necessary for each competent authority to undertake substantive consideration of the case. Such an agreement shall be concluded before the date on which unresolved issues in a case are first eligible to be submitted to arbitration and may be modified from time to time thereafter.

11. For purposes of applying this Article to its Covered Tax Agreements, a Party may reserve the right to replace the two-year period set forth in subparagraph b) of paragraph 1 with a three-year period.

12. A Party may reserve the right for the following rules to apply with respect to its Covered Tax Agreements notwithstanding the other provisions of this Article:

a) any unresolved issue arising from a mutual agreement procedure case otherwise within the scope of the arbitration process provided for by this Convention shall not be submitted to arbitration, if a decision on this issue has already been rendered by a court or administrative tribunal of either Contracting Jurisdiction;
b) if, at any time after a request for arbitration has been made and before the arbitration panel has delivered its decision to the competent authorities of the Contracting Jurisdictions, a decision concerning the issue is rendered by a court or administrative tribunal of one of the Contracting Jurisdictions, the arbitration process shall terminate.

Article 20
Appointment of Arbitrators

1. Except to the extent that the competent authorities of the Contracting Jurisdictions mutually agree on different rules, paragraphs 2 through 4 shall apply for the purposes of this Part.

2. The following rules shall govern the appointment of the members of an arbitration panel:

a) The arbitration panel shall consist of three individual members with expertise or experience in international tax matters.
b) Each competent authority shall appoint one panel member within 60 days of the date of the request for arbitration under paragraph 1 of Article 19 (Mandatory Binding Arbitration). The two panel members so appointed shall, within 60 days of the latter of their appointments, appoint a third member who shall serve as Chair of the arbitration panel. The Chair shall not be a national or resident of either Contracting Jurisdiction.
c) Each member appointed to the arbitration panel must be impartial and independent of the competent authorities, tax administrations, and ministries of finance of the Contracting Jurisdictions and of all persons directly affected by the case (as well as their advisors) at the time of accepting an appointment, maintain his or her impartiality and independence throughout the proceedings, and avoid any conduct for a reasonable period of time thereafter which may damage the appearance of impartiality and independence of the arbitrators with respect to the proceedings.

3. In the event that the competent authority of a Contracting Jurisdiction fails to appoint a member of the arbitration panel in the manner and within the time periods specified in paragraph 2 or agreed to by the competent authorities of the Contracting Jurisdictions, a member shall be appointed on behalf of that competent authority by the highest ranking official of the Centre for Tax Policy and Administration of the Organisation for Economic Co-operation and Development that is not a national of either Contracting Jurisdiction.

4. If the two initial members of the arbitration panel fail to appoint the Chair in the manner and within the time periods specified in paragraph 2 or agreed to by the competent authorities of the Contracting Jurisdictions, the Chair shall be appointed by the highest ranking official of the Centre for Tax Policy and Administration of the Organisation for Economic Co-operation and Development that is not a national of either Contracting Jurisdiction.

Article 21
Confidentiality of Arbitration Proceedings

1. Solely for the purposes of the application of the provisions of this Part and of the provisions of the relevant Covered Tax Agreement and of the domestic laws of the Contracting Jurisdictions related to the exchange of information, confidentiality, and administrative assistance, members of the arbitration panel and a maximum of three staff per member (and prospective arbitrators solely to the extent necessary to verify their ability to fulfil the requirements of arbitrators) shall be considered to be persons or authorities to whom information may be disclosed. Information received by the arbitration panel or prospective arbitrators and information that the competent authorities receive from the arbitration panel shall be considered information that is exchanged under the provisions of the Covered Tax Agreement related to the exchange of information and administrative assistance.

2. The competent authorities of the Contracting Jurisdictions shall ensure that members of the arbitration panel and their staff agree in writing, prior to their acting in an arbitration proceeding, to treat any information relating to the arbitration proceeding consistently with the confidentiality and nondisclosure obligations described in the provisions of the Covered Tax Agreement related to exchange of information and administrative assistance and under the applicable laws of the Contracting Jurisdictions.

Article 22
Resolution of a Case Prior to the Conclusion of the Arbitration

For the purposes of this Part and the provisions of the relevant Covered Tax Agreement that provide for resolution of cases through mutual agreement, the mutual agreement procedure, as well as the arbitration proceeding, with respect to a case shall terminate if, at any time after a request for arbitration has been made and before the arbitration panel has delivered its decision to the competent authorities of the Contracting Jurisdictions:

a) the competent authorities of the Contracting Jurisdictions reach a mutual agreement to resolve the case; or
b) the person who presented the case withdraws the request for arbitration or the request for a mutual agreement procedure.

Article 23
Type of Arbitration Process

1. Except to the extent that the competent authorities of the Contracting Jurisdictions mutually agree on different rules, the following rules shall apply with respect to an arbitration proceeding pursuant to this Part:

a) After a case is submitted to arbitration, the competent authority of each Contracting Jurisdiction shall submit to the arbitration panel, by a date set by agreement, a proposed resolution which addresses all unresolved issue(s) in the case (taking into account all agreements previously reached in that case between the competent authorities of the Contracting Jurisdictions). The proposed resolution shall be limited to a disposition of specific monetary amounts (for example, of income or expense) or, where specified, the maximum rate of tax charged pursuant to the Covered Tax Agreement, for each adjustment or similar issue in the case. In a case in which the competent authorities of the Contracting Jurisdictions have been unable to reach agreement on an issue regarding the conditions for application of a provision of the relevant Covered Tax Agreement (hereinafter referred to as a "threshold question"), such as whether an individual is a resident or whether a permanent establishment exists, the competent authorities may submit alternative proposed resolutions with respect to issues the determination of which is contingent on resolution of such threshold questions.
b) The competent authority of each Contracting Jurisdiction may also submit a supporting position paper for consideration by the arbitration panel. Each competent authority that submits a proposed resolution or supporting position paper shall provide a copy to the other competent authority by the date on which the proposed resolution and supporting position paper were due. Each competent authority may also submit to the arbitration panel, by a date set by agreement, a reply submission with respect to the proposed resolution and supporting position paper submitted by the other competent

authority. A copy of any reply submission shall be provided to the other competent authority by the date on which the reply submission was due.

c) The arbitration panel shall select as its decision one of the proposed resolutions for the case submitted by the competent authorities with respect to each issue and any threshold questions, and shall not include a rationale or any other explanation of the decision. The arbitration decision will be adopted by a simple majority of the panel members. The arbitration panel shall deliver its decision in writing to the competent authorities of the Contracting Jurisdictions. The arbitration decision shall have no precedential value.

2. For the purpose of applying this Article with respect to its Covered Tax Agreements, a Party may reserve the right for paragraph 1 not to apply to its Covered Tax Agreements. In such a case, except to the extent that the competent authorities of the Contracting Jurisdictions mutually agree on different rules, the following rules shall apply with respect to an arbitration proceeding:

a) After a case is submitted to arbitration, the competent authority of each Contracting Jurisdiction shall provide any information that may be necessary for the arbitration decision to all panel members without undue delay. Unless the competent authorities of the Contracting Jurisdictions agree otherwise, any information that was not available to both competent authorities before the request for arbitration was received by both of them shall not be taken into account for purposes of the decision.

b) The arbitration panel shall decide the issues submitted to arbitration in accordance with the applicable provisions of the Covered Tax Agreement and, subject to these provisions, of those of the domestic laws of the Contracting Jurisdictions. The panel members shall also consider any other sources which the competent authorities of the Contracting Jurisdictions may by mutual agreement expressly identify.

c) The arbitration decision shall be delivered to the competent authorities of the Contracting Jurisdictions in writing and shall indicate the sources of law relied upon and the reasoning which led to its result. The arbitration decision shall be adopted by a simple majority of the panel members. The arbitration decision shall have no precedential value.

3. A Party that has not made the reservation described in paragraph 2 may reserve the right for the preceding paragraphs of this Article not to apply with respect to its Covered Tax Agreements with Parties that have made such a reservation. In such a case, the competent authorities of the Contracting Jurisdictions of each such Covered Tax Agreement shall endeavour to reach agreement on the type of arbitration process that shall apply with respect to that Covered Tax Agreement. Until such an agreement is reached, Article 19 (Mandatory Binding Arbitration) shall not apply with respect to such a Covered Tax Agreement.

4. A Party may also choose to apply paragraph 5 with respect to its Covered Tax Agreements and shall notify the Depositary accordingly. Paragraph 5 shall apply in relation to two Contracting Jurisdictions with respect to a Covered Tax Agreement where either of the Contracting Jurisdictions has made such a notification.

5. Prior to the beginning of arbitration proceedings, the competent authorities of the Contracting Jurisdictions to a Covered Tax Agreement shall ensure that each person that presented the case and their advisors agree in writing not to disclose to any other person any information received during the course of the arbitration proceedings from either competent authority or the arbitration panel. The mutual agreement procedure under the

Covered Tax Agreement, as well as the arbitration proceeding under this Part, with respect to the case shall terminate if, at any time after a request for arbitration has been made and before the arbitration panel has delivered its decision to the competent authorities of the Contracting Jurisdictions, a person that presented the case or one of that person's advisors materially breaches that agreement.

6. Notwithstanding paragraph 4, a Party that does not choose to apply paragraph 5 may reserve the right for paragraph 5 not to apply with respect to one or more identified Covered Tax Agreements or with respect to all of its Covered Tax Agreements.

7. A Party that chooses to apply paragraph 5 may reserve the right for this Part not to apply with respect to all Covered Tax Agreements for which the other Contracting Jurisdiction makes a reservation pursuant to paragraph 6.

Article 24
Agreement on a Different Resolution

1. For purposes of applying this Part with respect to its Covered Tax Agreements, a Party may choose to apply paragraph 2 and shall notify the Depositary accordingly. Paragraph 2 shall apply in relation to two Contracting Jurisdictions with respect to a Covered Tax Agreement only where both Contracting Jurisdictions have made such a notification.

2. Notwithstanding paragraph 4 of Article 19 (Mandatory Binding Arbitration), an arbitration decision pursuant to this Part shall not be binding on the Contracting Jurisdictions to a Covered Tax Agreement and shall not be implemented if the competent authorities of the Contracting Jurisdictions agree on a different resolution of all unresolved issues within three calendar months after the arbitration decision has been delivered to them.

3. A Party that chooses to apply paragraph 2 may reserve the right for paragraph 2 to apply only with respect to its Covered Tax Agreements for which paragraph 2 of Article 23 (Type of Arbitration Process) applies.

Article 25
Costs of Arbitration Proceedings

In an arbitration proceeding under this Part, the fees and expenses of the members of the arbitration panel, as well as any costs incurred in connection with the arbitration proceedings by the Contracting Jurisdictions, shall be borne by the Contracting Jurisdictions in a manner to be settled by mutual agreement between the competent authorities of the Contracting Jurisdictions. In the absence of such agreement, each Contracting Jurisdiction shall bear its own expenses and those of its appointed panel member. The cost of the chair of the arbitration panel and other expenses associated with the conduct of the arbitration proceedings shall be borne by the Contracting Jurisdictions in equal shares.

Article 26
Compatibility

1. Subject to Article 18 (Choice to Apply Part VI), the provisions of this Part shall apply in place of or in the absence of provisions of a Covered Tax Agreement that provide for arbitration of unresolved issues arising from a mutual agreement procedure case. Each Party that chooses to apply this Part shall notify the Depositary of whether each of its Covered Tax Agreements, other than those that are within the scope of a reservation under paragraph 4, contains such a provision, and if so, the article and paragraph number of each

such provision. Where two Contracting Jurisdictions have made a notification with respect to a provision of a Covered Tax Agreement, that provision shall be replaced by the provisions of this Part as between those Contracting Jurisdictions.

2. Any unresolved issue arising from a mutual agreement procedure case otherwise within the scope of the arbitration process provided for in this Part shall not be submitted to arbitration if the issue falls within the scope of a case with respect to which an arbitration panel or similar body has previously been set up in accordance with a bilateral or multilateral convention that provides for mandatory binding arbitration of unresolved issues arising from a mutual agreement procedure case.

3. Subject to paragraph 1, nothing in this Part shall affect the fulfilment of wider obligations with respect to the arbitration of unresolved issues arising in the context of a mutual agreement procedure resulting from other conventions to which the Contracting Jurisdictions are or will become parties.

4. A Party may reserve the right for this Part not to apply with respect to one or more identified Covered Tax Agreements (or to all of its Covered Tax Agreements) that already provide for mandatory binding arbitration of unresolved issues arising from a mutual agreement procedure case.

PART VII.
FINAL PROVISIONS

Article 27
Signature and Ratification, Acceptance or Approval

1. As of 31 December 2016, this Convention shall be open for signature by:

a) all States;
b) Guernsey (the United Kingdom of Great Britain and Northern Ireland); Isle of Man (the United Kingdom of Great Britain and Northern Ireland); Jersey (the United Kingdom of Great Britain and Northern Ireland); and
c) any other jurisdiction authorised to become a Party by means of a decision by consensus of the Parties and Signatories.

2. This Convention is subject to ratification, acceptance or approval.

Article 28
Reservations

1. Subject to paragraph 2, no reservations may be made to this Convention except those expressly permitted by:

a) Paragraph 5 of Article 3 (Transparent Entities);
b) Paragraph 3 of Article 4 (Dual Resident Entities);
c) Paragraphs 8 and 9 of Article 5 (Application of Methods for Elimination of Double Taxation);
d) Paragraph 4 of Article 6 (Purpose of a Covered Tax Agreement);
e) Paragraphs 15 and 16 of Article 7 (Prevention of Treaty Abuse);
f) Paragraph 3 of Article 8 (Dividend Transfer Transactions);
g) Paragraph 6 of Article 9 (Capital Gains from Alienation of Shares or Interests of Entities Deriving their Value Principally from Immovable Property);

h) Paragraph 5 of Article 10 (Anti-abuse Rule for Permanent Establishments Situated in Third Jurisdictions);
i) Paragraph 3 of Article 11 (Application of Tax Agreements to Restrict a Party's Right to Tax its Own Residents);
j) Paragraph 4 of Article 12 (Artificial Avoidance of Permanent Establishment Status through Commissionnaire Arrangements and Similar Strategies);
k) Paragraph 6 of Article 13 (Artificial Avoidance of Permanent Establishment Status through the Specific Activity Exemptions);
l) Paragraph 3 of Article 14 (Splitting-up of Contracts);
m) Paragraph 2 of Article 15 (Definition of a Person Closely Related to an Enterprise);
n) Paragraph 5 of Article 16 (Mutual Agreement Procedure);
o) Paragraph 3 of Article 17 (Corresponding Adjustments);
p) Paragraphs 11 and 12 of Article 19 (Mandatory Binding Arbitration);
q) Paragraphs 2, 3, 6, and 7 of Article 23 (Type of Arbitration Process);
r) Paragraph 3 of Article 24 (Agreement on a Different Resolution);
s) Paragraph 4 of Article 26 (Compatibility);
t) Paragraphs 6 and 7 of Article 35 (Entry into Effect); and
u) Paragraph 2 of Article 36 (Entry into Effect of Part VI).

2.

a) Notwithstanding paragraph 1, a Party that chooses under Article 18 (Choice to Apply Part VI) to apply Part VI (Arbitration) may formulate one or more reservations with respect to the scope of cases that shall be eligible for arbitration under the provisions of Part VI (Arbitration). For a Party which chooses under Article 18 (Choice to Apply Part VI) to apply Part VI (Arbitration) after it has become a Party to this Convention, reservations pursuant to this subparagraph shall be made at the same time as that Party's notification to the Depositary pursuant to Article 18 (Choice to Apply Part VI).
b) Reservations made under subparagraph a) are subject to acceptance. A reservation made under subparagraph a) shall be considered to have been accepted by a Party if it has not notified the Depositary that it objects to the reservation by the end of a period of twelve calendar months beginning on the date of notification of the reservation by the Depositary or by the date on which it deposits its instrument of ratification, acceptance, or approval, whichever is later. For a Party which chooses under Article 18 (Choice to Apply Part VI) to apply Part VI (Arbitration) after it has become a Party to this Convention, objections to prior reservations made by other Parties pursuant to subparagraph a) can be made at the time of the first- mentioned Party's notification to the Depositary pursuant to Article 18 (Choice to Apply Part VI). Where a Party raises an objection to a reservation made under subparagraph a), the entirety of Part VI (Arbitration) shall not apply as between the objecting Party and the reserving Party.

3. Unless explicitly provided otherwise in the relevant provisions of this Convention, a reservation made in accordance with paragraph 1 or 2 shall:

a) modify for the reserving Party in its relations with another Party the provisions of this Convention to which the reservation relates to the extent of the reservation; and
b) modify those provisions to the same extent for the other Party in its relations with the reserving Party.

4. Reservations applicable to Covered Tax Agreements entered into by or on behalf of a jurisdiction or territory for whose international relations a Party is responsible, where that jurisdiction or territory is not a Party to the Convention pursuant to subparagraph b) or c) of paragraph 1 of Article 27 (Signature and Ratification, Acceptance or Approval), shall be made by the responsible Party and can be different from the reservations made by that Party for its own Covered Tax Agreements.

5. Reservations shall be made at the time of signature or when depositing the instrument of ratification, acceptance or approval, subject to the provisions of paragraphs 2, 6 and 9 of this Article, and paragraph 5 of Article 29 (Notifications). However, for a Party which chooses under Article 18 (Choice to Apply Part VI) to apply Part VI (Arbitration) after it has become a Party to this Convention, reservations described in subparagraphs p), q), r) and s) of paragraph 1 of this Article shall be made at the same time as that Party's notification to the Depositary pursuant to Article 18 (Choice to Apply Part VI).

6. If reservations are made at the time of signature, they shall be confirmed upon deposit of the instrument of ratification, acceptance or approval, unless the document containing the reservations explicitly specifies that it is to be considered definitive, subject to the provisions of paragraphs 2, 5 and 9 of this Article, and paragraph 5 of Article 29 (Notifications).

7. If reservations are not made at the time of signature, a provisional list of expected reservations shall be provided to the Depositary at that time.

8. For reservations made pursuant to each of the following provisions, a list of agreements notified pursuant to clause ii) of subparagraph a) of paragraph 1 of Article 2 (Interpretation of Terms) that are within the scope of the reservation as defined in the relevant provision (and, in the case of a reservation under any of the following provisions other than those listed in subparagraphs c), d) and n), the article and paragraph number of each relevant provision) must be provided when such reservations are made:

a) Subparagraphs b), c), d), e) and g) of paragraph 5 of Article 3 (Transparent Entities);
b) Subparagraphs b), c) and d) of paragraph 3 of Article 4 (Dual Resident Entities);
c) Paragraphs 8 and 9 of Article 5 (Application of Methods for Elimination of Double Taxation);
d) Paragraph 4 of Article 6 (Purpose of a Covered Tax Agreement);
e) Subparagraphs b) and c) of paragraph 15 of Article 7 (Prevention of Treaty Abuse);
f) Clauses i), ii), and iii) of subparagraph b) of paragraph 3 of Article 8 (Dividend Transfer Transactions);
g) Subparagraphs d), e) and f) of paragraph 6 of Article 9 (Capital Gains from Alienation of Shares or Interests of Entities Deriving their Value Principally from Immovable Property);
h) Subparagraphs b) and c) of paragraph 5 of Article 10 (Anti-abuse Rule for Permanent Establishments Situated in Third Jurisdictions);
i) Subparagraph b) of paragraph 3 of Article 11 (Application of Tax Agreements to Restrict a Party's Right to Tax its Own Residents);
j) Subparagraph b) of paragraph 6 of Article 13 (Artificial Avoidance of Permanent Establishment Status through the Specific Activity Exemptions);
k) Subparagraph b) of paragraph 3 of Article 14 (Splitting-up of Contracts);
l) Subparagraph b) of paragraph 5 of Article 16 (Mutual Agreement Procedure);

m) Subparagraph a) of paragraph 3 of Article 17 (Corresponding Adjustments);
n) Paragraph 6 of Article 23 (Type of Arbitration Process); and
o) Paragraph 4 of Article 26 (Compatibility).

The reservations described in subparagraphs a) through o) above shall not apply to any Covered Tax Agreement that is not included on the list described in this paragraph.

9. Any Party which has made a reservation in accordance with paragraph 1 or 2 may at any time withdraw it or replace it with a more limited reservation by means of a notification addressed to the Depositary. Such Party shall make any additional notifications pursuant to paragraph 6 of Article 29 (Notifications) which may be required as a result of the withdrawal or replacement of the reservation. Subject to paragraph 7 of Article 35 (Entry into Effect), the withdrawal or replacement shall take effect:

a) with respect to a Covered Tax Agreement solely with States or jurisdictions that are Parties to the Convention when the notification of withdrawal or replacement of the reservation is received by the Depositary:
   i) for reservations in respect of provisions relating to taxes withheld at source, where the event giving rise to such taxes occurs on or after 1 January of the year next following the expiration of a period of six calendar months beginning on the date of the communication by the Depositary of the notification of withdrawal or replacement of the reservation; and
   ii) for reservations in respect of all other provisions, for taxes levied with respect to taxable periods beginning on or after 1 January of the year next following the expiration of a period of six calendar months beginning on the date of the communication by the Depositary of the notification of withdrawal or replacement of the reservation; and
b) with respect to a Covered Tax Agreement for which one or more Contracting Jurisdictions becomes a Party to this Convention after the date of receipt by the Depositary of the notification of withdrawal or replacement: on the latest of the dates on which the Convention enters into force for those Contracting Jurisdictions.

Article 29
Notifications

1. Subject to paragraphs 5 and 6 of this Article, and paragraph 7 of Article 35 (Entry into Effect), notifications pursuant to the following provisions shall be made at the time of signature or when depositing the instrument of ratification, acceptance or approval:

a) Clause ii) of subparagraph a) of paragraph 1 of Article 2 (Interpretation of Terms);
b) Paragraph 6 of Article 3 (Transparent Entities);
c) Paragraph 4 of Article 4 (Dual Resident Entities);
d) Paragraph 10 of Article 5 (Application of Methods for Elimination of Double Taxation);
e) Paragraphs 5 and 6 of Article 6 (Purpose of a Covered Tax Agreement);
f) Paragraph 17 of Article 7 (Prevention of Treaty Abuse);
g) Paragraph 4 of Article 8 (Dividend Transfer Transactions);
h) Paragraphs 7 and 8 of Article 9 (Capital Gains from Alienation of Shares or Interests of Entities Deriving their Value Principally from Immovable Property);
i) Paragraph 6 of Article 10 (Anti-abuse Rule for Permanent Establishments Situated in Third Jurisdictions);

j) Paragraph 4 of Article 11 (Application of Tax Agreements to Restrict a Party's Right to Tax its Own Residents);
k) Paragraphs 5 and 6 of Article 12 (Artificial Avoidance of Permanent Establishment Status through Commissionnaire Arrangements and Similar Strategies);
l) Paragraphs 7 and 8 of Article 13 (Artificial Avoidance of Permanent Establishment Status through the Specific Activity Exemptions);
m) Paragraph 4 of Article 14 (Splitting-up of Contracts);
n) Paragraph 6 of Article 16 (Mutual Agreement Procedure);
o) Paragraph 4 of Article 17 (Corresponding Adjustments);
p) Article 18 (Choice to Apply Part VI);
q) Paragraph 4 of Article 23 (Type of Arbitration Process);
r) Paragraph 1 of Article 24 (Agreement on a Different Resolution);
s) Paragraph 1 of Article 26 (Compatibility); and
t) Paragraphs 1, 2, 3, 5 and 7 of Article 35 (Entry into Effect).

2. Notifications in respect of Covered Tax Agreements entered into by or on behalf of a jurisdiction or territory for whose international relations a Party is responsible, where that jurisdiction or territory is not a Party to the Convention pursuant to subparagraph b) or c) of paragraph 1 of Article 27 (Signature and Ratification, Acceptance or Approval), shall be made by the responsible Party and can be different from the notifications made by that Party for its own Covered Tax Agreements.

3. If notifications are made at the time of signature, they shall be confirmed upon deposit of the instrument of ratification, acceptance or approval, unless the document containing the notifications explicitly specifies that it is to be considered definitive, subject to the provisions of paragraphs 5 and 6 of this Article, and paragraph 7 of Article 35 (Entry into Effect).

4. If notifications are not made at the time of signature, a provisional list of expected notifications shall be provided at that time.

5. A Party may extend at any time the list of agreements notified under clause ii) of subparagraph a) of paragraph 1 of Article 2 (Interpretation of Terms) by means of a notification addressed to the Depositary. The Party shall specify in this notification whether the agreement falls within the scope of any of the reservations made by the Party which are listed in paragraph 8 of Article 28 (Reservations). The Party may also make a new reservation described in paragraph 8 of Article 28 (Reservations) if the additional agreement would be the first to fall within the scope of such a reservation. The Party shall also specify any additional notifications that may be required under subparagraphs b) through s) of paragraph 1 to reflect the inclusion of the additional agreements. In addition, if the extension results for the first time in the inclusion of a tax agreement entered into by or on behalf of a jurisdiction or territory for whose international relations a Party is responsible, the Party shall specify any reservations (pursuant to paragraph 4 of Article 28 (Reservations)) or notifications (pursuant to paragraph 2 of this Article) applicable to Covered Tax Agreements entered into by or on behalf of that jurisdiction or territory. On the date on which the added agreement(s) notified under clause ii) of subparagraph a) of paragraph 1 of Article 2 (Interpretation of Terms) become Covered Tax Agreements, the provisions of Article 35 (Entry into Effect) shall govern the date on which the modifications to the Covered Tax Agreement shall have effect.

6. A Party may make additional notifications pursuant to subparagraphs b) through s) of paragraph 1 by means of a notification addressed to the Depositary. These notifications shall take effect:

a) with respect to Covered Tax Agreements solely with States or jurisdictions that are Parties to the Convention when the additional notification is received by the Depositary:
   i) for notifications in respect of provisions relating to taxes withheld at source, where the event giving rise to such taxes occurs on or after 1 January of the year next following the expiration of a period of six calendar months beginning on the date of the communication by the Depositary of the additional notification; and
   ii) for notifications in respect of all other provisions, for taxes levied with respect to taxable periods beginning on or after 1 January of the year next following the expiration of a period of six calendar months beginning on the date of the communication by the Depositary of the additional notification; and
b) with respect to a Covered Tax Agreement for which one or more Contracting Jurisdictions becomes a Party to this Convention after the date of receipt by the Depositary of the additional notification: on the latest of the dates on which the Convention enters into force for those Contracting Jurisdictions.

Article 30
Subsequent Modifications of Covered Tax Agreements

The provisions in this Convention are without prejudice to subsequent modifications to a Covered Tax Agreement which may be agreed between the Contracting Jurisdictions of the Covered Tax Agreement.

Article 31
Conference of the Parties

1. The Parties may convene a Conference of the Parties for the purposes of taking any decisions or exercising any functions as may be required or appropriate under the provisions of this Convention.

2. The Conference of the Parties shall be served by the Depositary.

3. Any Party may request a Conference of the Parties by communicating a request to the Depositary. The Depositary shall inform all Parties of any request. Thereafter, the Depositary shall convene a Conference of the Parties, provided that the request is supported by one-third of the Parties within six calendar months of the communication by the Depositary of the request.

Article 32
Interpretation and Implementation

1. Any question arising as to the interpretation or implementation of provisions of a Covered Tax Agreement as they are modified by this Convention shall be determined in accordance with the provision(s) of the Covered Tax Agreement relating to the resolution by mutual agreement of questions of interpretation or application of the Covered Tax Agreement (as those provisions may be modified by this Convention).

2. Any question arising as to the interpretation or implementation of this Convention may be addressed by a Conference of the Parties convened in accordance with paragraph 3 of Article 31 (Conference of the Parties).

Article 33
Amendment

1. Any Party may propose an amendment to this Convention by submitting the proposed amendment to the Depositary.

2. A Conference of the Parties may be convened to consider the proposed amendment in accordance with paragraph 3 of Article 31 (Conference of the Parties).

Article 34
Entry into Force

1. This Convention shall enter into force on the first day of the month following the expiration of a period of three calendar months beginning on the date of deposit of the fifth instrument of ratification, acceptance or approval.

2. For each Signatory ratifying, accepting, or approving this Convention after the deposit of the fifth instrument of ratification, acceptance or approval, the Convention shall enter into force on the first day of the month following the expiration of a period of three calendar months beginning on the date of the deposit by such Signatory of its instrument of ratification, acceptance or approval.

Article 35
Entry into Effect

1. The provisions of this Convention shall have effect in each Contracting Jurisdiction with respect to a Covered Tax Agreement:

a) with respect to taxes withheld at source on amounts paid or credited to non-residents, where the event giving rise to such taxes occurs on or after the first day of the next calendar year that begins on or after the latest of the dates on which this Convention enters into force for each of the Contracting Jurisdictions to the Covered Tax Agreement; and
b) with respect to all other taxes levied by that Contracting Jurisdiction, for taxes levied with respect to taxable periods beginning on or after the expiration of a period of six calendar months (or a shorter period, if all Contracting Jurisdictions notify the Depositary that they intend to apply such shorter period) from the latest of the dates on which this Convention enters into force for each of the Contracting Jurisdictions to the Covered Tax Agreement.

2. Solely for the purpose of its own application of subparagraph a) of paragraph 1 and subparagraph a) of paragraph 5, a Party may choose to substitute "taxable period" for "calendar year", and shall notify the Depositary accordingly.

3. Solely for the purpose of its own application of subparagraph b) of paragraph 1 and subparagraph b) of paragraph 5, a Party may choose to replace the reference to "taxable periods beginning on or after the expiration of a period" with a reference to "taxable periods beginning on or after 1 January of the next year beginning on or after the expiration of a period", and shall notify the Depositary accordingly.

4. Notwithstanding the preceding provisions of this Article, Article 16 (Mutual Agreement Procedure) shall have effect with respect to a Covered Tax Agreement for a case presented to the competent authority of a Contracting Jurisdiction on or after the latest of the dates

on which this Convention enters into force for each of the Contracting Jurisdictions to the Covered Tax Agreement, except for cases that were not eligible to be presented as of that date under the Covered Tax Agreement prior to its modification by the Convention, without regard to the taxable period to which the case relates.

5. For a new Covered Tax Agreement resulting from an extension pursuant to paragraph 5 of Article 29 (Notifications) of the list of agreements notified under clause ii) of subparagraph a) of paragraph 1 of Article 2 (Interpretation of Terms), the provisions of this Convention shall have effect in each Contracting Jurisdiction:

a) with respect to taxes withheld at source on amounts paid or credited to non-residents, where the event giving rise to such taxes occurs on or after the first day of the next calendar year that begins on or after 30 days after the date of the communication by the Depositary of the notification of the extension of the list of agreements; and
b) with respect to all other taxes levied by that Contracting Jurisdiction, for taxes levied with respect to taxable periods beginning on or after the expiration of a period of nine calendar months (or a shorter period, if all Contracting Jurisdictions notify the Depositary that they intend to apply such shorter period) from the date of the communication by the Depositary of the notification of the extension of the list of agreements.

6. A Party may reserve the right for paragraph 4 not to apply with respect to its Covered Tax Agreements.

7.

a) A Party may reserve the right to replace:
   i) the references in paragraphs 1 and 4 to "the latest of the dates on which this Convention enters into force for each of the Contracting Jurisdictions to the Covered Tax Agreement"; and
   ii) the references in paragraph 5 to "the date of the communication by the Depositary of the notification of the extension of the list of agreements";
   with references to "30 days after the date of receipt by the Depositary of the latest notification by each Contracting Jurisdiction making the reservation described in paragraph 7 of Article 35 (Entry into Effect) that it has completed its internal procedures for the entry into effect of the provisions of this Convention with respect to that specific Covered Tax Agreement";
   iii) the references in subparagraph a) of paragraph 9 of Article 28 (Reservations) to "on the date of the communication by the Depositary of the notification of withdrawal or replacement of the reservation"; and
   iv) the reference in subparagraph b) of paragraph 9 of Article 28 (Reservations) to "on the latest of the dates on which the Convention enters into force for those Contracting Jurisdictions";
   with references to "30 days after the date of receipt by the Depositary of the latest notification by each Contracting Jurisdiction making the reservation described in paragraph 7 of Article 35 (Entry into Effect) that it has completed its internal procedures for the entry into effect of the withdrawal or replacement of the reservation with respect to that specific Covered Tax Agreement";
   v) the references in subparagraph a) of paragraph 6 of Article 29 (Notifications) to "on the date of the communication by the Depositary of the additional notification"; and

vi) the reference in subparagraph b) of paragraph 6 of Article 29 (Notifications) to "on the latest of the dates on which the Convention enters into force for those Contracting Jurisdictions";
with references to "30 days after the date of receipt by the Depositary of the latest notification by each Contracting Jurisdiction making the reservation described in paragraph 7 of Article 35 (Entry into Effect) that it has completed its internal procedures for the entry into effect of the additional notification with respect to that specific Covered Tax Agreement";

vii) the references in paragraphs 1 and 2 of Article 36 (Entry into Effect of Part VI) to "the later of the dates on which this Convention enters into force for each of the Contracting Jurisdictions to the Covered Tax Agreement";
with references to "30 days after the date of receipt by the Depositary of the latest notification by each Contracting Jurisdiction making the reservation described in paragraph 7 of Article 35 (Entry into Effect) that it has completed its internal procedures for the entry into effect of the provisions of this Convention with respect to that specific Covered Tax Agreement"; and

viii) the reference in paragraph 3 of Article 36 (Entry into Effect of Part VI) to "the date of the communication by the Depositary of the notification of the extension of the list of agreements";

ix) the references in paragraph 4 of Article 36 (Entry into Effect of Part VI) to "the date of the communication by the Depositary of the notification of withdrawal of the reservation", "the date of the communication by the Depositary of the notification of replacement of the reservation" and "the date of the communication by the Depositary of the notification of withdrawal of the objection to the reservation"; and

x) the reference in paragraph 5 of Article 36 (Entry into Effect of Part VI) to "the date of the communication by the Depositary of the additional notification";
with references to "30 days after the date of receipt by the Depositary of the latest notification by each Contracting Jurisdiction making the reservation described in paragraph 7 of Article 35 (Entry into Effect) that it has completed its internal procedures for the entry into effect of the provisions of Part VI (Arbitration) with respect to that specific Covered Tax Agreement".

b) A Party making a reservation in accordance with subparagraph a) shall notify the confirmation of the completion of its internal procedures simultaneously to the Depositary and the other Contracting Jurisdiction(s).

c) If one or more Contracting Jurisdictions to a Covered Tax Agreement makes a reservation under this paragraph, the date of entry into effect of the provisions of the Convention, of the withdrawal or replacement of a reservation, of an additional notification with respect to that Covered Tax Agreement, or of Part VI (Arbitration) shall be governed by this paragraph for all Contracting Jurisdictions to the Covered Tax Agreement.

Article 36
Entry into Effect of Part VI

1. Notwithstanding paragraph 9 of Article 28 (Reservations), paragraph 6 of Article 29 (Notifications), and paragraphs 1 through 6 of Article 35 (Entry into Effect), with respect

to two Contracting Jurisdictions to a Covered Tax Agreement, the provisions of Part VI (Arbitration) shall have effect:

a) with respect to cases presented to the competent authority of a Contracting Jurisdiction (as described in subparagraph a) of paragraph 1 of Article 19 (Mandatory Binding Arbitration)), on or after the later of the dates on which this Convention enters into force for each of the Contracting Jurisdictions to the Covered Tax Agreement; and
b) with respect to cases presented to the competent authority of a Contracting Jurisdiction prior to the later of the dates on which this Convention enters into force for each of the Contracting Jurisdictions to the Covered Tax Agreement, on the date when both Contracting Jurisdictions have notified the Depositary that they have reached mutual agreement pursuant to paragraph 10 of Article 19 (Mandatory Binding Arbitration), along with information regarding the date or dates on which such cases shall be considered to have been presented to the competent authority of a Contracting Jurisdiction (as described in subparagraph a) of paragraph 1 of Article 19 (Mandatory Binding Arbitration)) according to the terms of that mutual agreement.

2. A Party may reserve the right for Part VI (Arbitration) to apply to a case presented to the competent authority of a Contracting Jurisdiction prior to the later of the dates on which this Convention enters into force for each of the Contracting Jurisdictions to the Covered Tax Agreement only to the extent that the competent authorities of both Contracting Jurisdictions agree that it will apply to that specific case.

3. In the case of a new Covered Tax Agreement resulting from an extension pursuant to paragraph 5 of Article 29 (Notifications) of the list of agreements notified under clause ii) of subparagraph a) of paragraph 1 of Article 2 (Interpretation of Terms), the references in paragraphs 1 and 2 of this Article to "the later of the dates on which this Convention enters into force for each of the Contracting Jurisdictions to the Covered Tax Agreement" shall be replaced with references to "the date of the communication by the Depositary of the notification of the extension of the list of agreements".

4. A withdrawal or replacement of a reservation made under paragraph 4 of Article 26 (Compatibility) pursuant to paragraph 9 of Article 28 (Reservations), or the withdrawal of an objection to a reservation made under paragraph 2 of Article 28 (Reservations) which results in the application of Part VI (Arbitration) between two Contracting Jurisdictions to a Covered Tax Agreement, shall have effect according to subparagraphs a) and b) of paragraph 1 of this Article, except that the references to "the later of the dates on which this Convention enters into force for each of the Contracting Jurisdictions to the Covered Tax Agreement" shall be replaced with references to "the date of the communication by the Depositary of the notification of withdrawal of the reservation", "the date of the communication by the Depositary of the notification of replacement of the reservation" or "the date of the communication by the Depositary of the notification of withdrawal of the objection to the reservation", respectively.

5. An additional notification made pursuant to subparagraph p) of paragraph 1 of Article 29 (Notifications) shall have effect according to subparagraphs a) and b) of paragraph 1, except that the references in paragraphs 1 and 2 of this Article to "the later of the dates on which this Convention enters into force for each of the Contracting Jurisdictions to the Covered Tax Agreement" shall be replaced with references to "the date of the communication by the Depositary of the additional notification".

Article 37
Withdrawal

1. Any Party may, at any time, withdraw from this Convention by means of a notification addressed to the Depositary.

2. Withdrawal pursuant to paragraph 1 shall become effective on the date of receipt of the notification by the Depositary. In cases where this Convention has entered into force with respect to all Contracting Jurisdictions to a Covered Tax Agreement before the date on which a Party's withdrawal becomes effective, that Covered Tax Agreement shall remain as modified by this Convention.

Article 38
Relation with Protocols

1. This Convention may be supplemented by one or more protocols.

2. In order to become a party to a protocol, a State or jurisdiction must also be a Party to this Convention.

3. A Party to this Convention is not bound by a protocol unless it becomes a party to the protocol in accordance with its provisions.

Article 39
Depositary

1. The Secretary-General of the Organisation for Economic Co-operation and Development shall be the Depositary of this Convention and any protocols pursuant to Article 38 (Relation with Protocols).

2. The Depositary shall notify the Parties and Signatories within one calendar month of:

a) any signature pursuant to Article 27 (Signature and Ratification, Acceptance or Approval);
b) the deposit of any instrument of ratification, acceptance or approval pursuant to Article 27 (Signature and Ratification, Acceptance or Approval);
c) any reservation or withdrawal or replacement of a reservation pursuant to Article 28 (Reservations);
d) any notification or additional notification pursuant to Article 29 (Notifications);
e) any proposed amendment to this Convention pursuant to Article 33 (Amendment);
f) any withdrawal from this Convention pursuant to Article 37 (Withdrawal); and
g) any other communication related to this Convention.

3. The Depositary shall maintain publicly available lists of:

a) Covered Tax Agreements;
b) reservations made by the Parties; and
c) notifications made by the Parties.

In witness whereof the undersigned, being duly authorised thereto, have signed this Convention.

Done at Paris, the 24th day of November 2016, in English and French, both texts being equally authentic, in a single copy which shall be deposited in the archives of the Organisation for Economic Co-operation and Development.

Index